THE ILLUSTRATED GUIDE TO THE

VALLEY of the KINGS and the Theban Necropolises and Temples

Alberto Siliotti

THE AMERICAN UNIVERSITY IN CAIRO PRESS

VALLEY of the KINGS and the Theban Necropolises and Temples

Texts and photographs
Alberto Siliotti

Editorial coordination
Laura Accomazzo

Graphic design
Patrizia Balocco Lovisetti

Maps
Oxford Cartographers

Translation by
Hever, Tel Aviv (Israel)
Ann Ghiringhelli

First published in Egypt in 2004 by
The American University in Cairo Press
113 Sharia Kasr el Aini, Cairo, Egypt
www.aucpress.com

Via Candido Sassone, 22/24
13100 Vercelli, Italy
www.whitestar.it

Dar el Kutub No. 21350/03
ISBN 977 424 854 6

Printed in China
Color separation by Fotomec, Turin

1 This little gilded wooden statue of the goddess Selkis was found in the tomb of Tutankhamun (KV no. 62) near the large shrine of gilded wood containing the canopic vases with the king's entrails.
(Cairo Museum)

2-3 The gold mask of Tutankhamun is one of the masterpieces of world art and is undoubtedly the most admired exhibit of the Cairo Museum.
The solid gold mask, weighing about ten kilos, was fitted directly over the king's mummy.
(Cairo Museum)

4 Gold amulet of a female-headed winged uraeus *discovered on the mummy in the tomb of Tutankhamun (KV no. 62). The* uraeus *was the sacred cobra, protector of royalty, and it appeared among the numerous amulets arranged on the pharaoh's mortal remains so as to ensure him a magical protection.*
(Cairo Museum)

5 In the vestibule of her tomb (QV no. 66), Nefertari Meri-en-Mut, Ramesses II's "Great Royal Bride", whose name means "the Most Beautiful, Beloved of Mut", is introduced to different deities.
In the image shown here, from the southern side of the vestibule, the queen is led hand in hand by the falcon-headed god Harsiesis.

PRESENTATION

The Valley of the Kings and the tombs of the nobles are, together with the pyramids of Giza, the most visited and best-known archaeological sites of all Egypt and constitute a never-failing attraction to the tourists coming to visit Luxor, the ancient Thebes, even for a single day during their stay at Hurghada on the shores of the Red Sea or at Sharm el-Sheikh in Sinai. However, unlike the Giza pyramids, the tombs of Thebes, which represent one of the masterpieces of world art for the quality of their pictorial decorations, so much so that they were included by UNESCO among the sites classified as "World Heritage", are extremely heterogeneous and their topography is complex and hardly understandable for the hasty tourist who finds himself being literally "carried" from one monument and from one tomb to the other, often receiving fanciful or very scanty explanations. Incredibly, notwithstanding the very high number of visitors, a complete guide of the Theban necropolis has never been published. Now, this gap is being filled by this "Guide to the Valley of the Kings and to the Theban Necropolises and Temples" that presents, for the first time, in its globality and completeness, the whole archaeological area under consideration, making use of topographical maps and reliefs prepared especially for this work, and sets out updated and scientifically accurate data, until today jealously hidden in obscure specialised journals, utterly out of the reach of a non-Egyptologist. For the first time, each tomb is described in a concise, yet complete manner, with a plan in which the most important or interesting mural paintings are located and shown. The Theban temples are also explained point by point in their architectural structures and decorations with the assistance of numerous topographical plans. The guide is completed by a chapter on walking itineraries in the Theban mountain, with a map of all the routes, allowing the visitor not only to see Thebes' monuments from unusual points of view, but also to explore new and surprising spots: prehistorical sites, rocky temples, graffiti of the Pharaonic era, huts and villages where the ancient craftsmen used to live, rock quarries from which the colors used for the decoration of the tombs were extracted. A glossary setting out technical terms and names of divinities, concisely presented for the purpose of rendering the text more "reader-friendly", closes this unique guide, the fruit of five years of work and field surveys.

6 top left This small solid gold statue was discovered in the tomb of Tutankhamun (KV no. 62) inside a miniaturized sarcophagus on which the name of Queen Tiy, wife of Amenophis III, Tutankhamun's grandfather, was engraved. The jewel may represent Amenophis III but more probably it is Tutankhamun himself. (Cairo Museum)

6 top right Gilded wood statuette from the tomb of Tutankhamun, portraying the god Ptah-Sokari-Osiris. (Cairo Museum)

6-7 The vaulted ceiling of the sepulchral chamber in the tomb of Sennedjem (TT no. 1) "Servant in the Place of Truth" who lived in the age of the Nineteenth Dynasty at Deir el-Medina, is decorated with eight large scenes: here the deceased with his wife Iyneferti worships five stellar deities.

7 bottom left This photograph shows the Deir el-Bahri site with the temple of Hatshepsut and, on the left, the temples of Tuthmosis III and Nebhepetre-Mentuhotep.

7 bottom right The first pylon of Ramesses III's great memorial temple at Medinet Habu. On the left there is the chapel of the Divine Worshippers of Amun who enjoyed a very great power and prestige in the age of the Twenty-Fifth and Twenty-Sixth Dynasty. The temple of Ramesses III is the best preserved among all the royal cult temples built on the western bank of the Nile.

INTRODUCTION

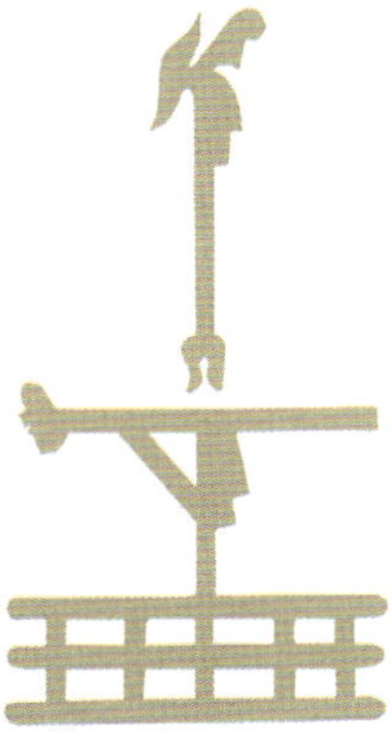

Thebes, the great capital of Egypt during the New Kingdom, was a crowded city stretching along the Nile's eastern bank, in the area extending between the present little town of Luxor and its suburb Karnak, about 500 kilometers south of Cairo. The ancient Egyptians called the city *Waset* "the city of the sceptre" capital of Egypt's IV nome. It was the Greeks, many centuries later, who called it *Thebes*, a name already used by Homer who speaks of "Thebes of the Hundred Gates" referring not so much to the city's "gates", but to the impressive pillars of *Ipet-isut* "the most privileged of seats", as the nearby temple of Karnak, Egypt's largest temple built to the glory of Amun "the Unknowable, the king of gods", was called. If Thebes, the city of the living built on the Nile's eastern bank, was the kingdom of Amun, whose earthly son was the pharaoh, on the opposite bank of the Nile, at the feet of the Theban mountain, the sacred mountain, where the sun sets, stretched the capital's huge royal and civilian necropolis: it was the kingdom of Osiris, "Lord of Afterlife", called by the Egptians *imentit en waset*, "the West of Thebes", *ta geser* "the sacred land". The west bank did not, however, include only the tombs of the kings of Egypt, of their families and of the leading dignitaries, whose paintings are among the highest expressions of the art of all times. It was also the place where the worship of the deified living king, besides that of the dead kings, was conducted in the so-called temples "of the millions of years", masterpieces of ancient architecture. The royal necropolises, referred to as "Valley of the Kings" and "Valley of the Queens", the private necropolises, best known by the name of "tombs of the nobles", and the great memorial temples such as Deir el-Bahri, the Ramesseum or Medinet Habu, have nowadays become touristic attractions visited every year by millions of tourists wishing to admire the works of art enclosed in the ancient kingdom of Osiris.

CHRONOLOGICAL TABLE

8 left The emblem of the Fourth nome, called waset "the Sceptre", which included the Theban area, was at the same time Thebes' old toponym. The nomes were Egypt's administrative subdivisions. During the New Kingdom, there were forty-two of them.

8 right Amun was the main deity in the Theban pantheon. Together with his spouse Mut and his son Khonsu, they formed the so-called "Theban Triad". Amun, a name that means "the Unknowable", was the king of the gods and used to be represented in human shape with his head decorated with two tall plumes, while his flesh was painted in blue, color of the air and of the sky.
(Ippolito Rosellini, Monumenti Storici)

8-9 The tomb of Ramose (TT no. 55) in the necropolis of Sheikh Abd el-Qurna, is decorated with bas reliefs of supreme stylistic perfection like these, showing several guests attending the funeral banquet. Ramose was a very high-ranking personality who bore the title of "Governor of the Town and Vizier" and lived in the time of Amenophis IV.

OLD KINGDOM 2658-2150 BC
FIRST INTERMEDIATE PERIOD 2150-2100 BC
MIDDLE KINGDOM 2100-1750 BC
SECOND INTERMEDIATE PERIOD 1750-1550 BC

NEW KINGDOM 1550-1076 BC

Eighteenth Dynasty 1550-1295 BC

Ahmosis	1550-1525
Amenophis I	1525-1504
Thutmosis I	1504-1492
Thutmosis II	1492-1479
Hatshepsut	1479-1457
Thutmosis III	1479-1425
Amenophis II	1427-1397
Thutmosis IV	1397-1387
Amenophis III	1387-1349
Amenophis IV-Akhenaten	1349-1333
Smenkhkare	1335-1333
Tutankhamun	1333-1324
Ay	1324-1321
Horemheb	1321-1295

Nineteenth Dynasty 1295-1188 BC

Ramesses I	1295-1294
Sethos I	1294-1279
Ramesses II	1279-1213
Merneptah	1213-1204
Amenemesses	1204-1201
Sethos II	1201-1195
Siptah	1195-1190
Twosret	1190-1188

Twentieth Dynasty 1188-1076 BC

Setenakhte	1188-1186
Ramesses III	1186-1154
Ramesses IV	1154-1148
Ramesses V	1148-1144
Ramesses VI	1144-1136
Ramesses VII	1136-1128
Ramesses VIII	1128-1125
Ramesses IX	1125-1107
Ramesses X	1107-1098
Ramesses XI	1098-1076

THIRD INTERMEDIATE PERIOD 1076-712 BC
LATE PERIOD 712-332 BC
GRAECO-ROMAN PERIOD 332 BC - 395 AD

WESTERN THEBES
Western Valley
WV no. 22
Amenophis III
WV no. 23
Ay
KV no. 62
Tutankhamun
Valley of the King
Deir el-Bahri
Temple of Hatschepsut
Temple of Mentuhotep
El-Qurn
Sheikh Abd el-Qurna
Upper Enclosure
Lowe
Enclosu
Deir el-Medina
Ptolemaic Temple
Ramesseum
Valley of the Queens
Temple of Thutmosis IV
Temple of Merneptah
Temple of Amenophis III
Medinet Habu
E.A.O. Office (Egyptian Antiquities Organization)
Temple of Ramesses III
Colossi of Memnon
Temple of the Tuthmosids
Malqatta Royal Palace of Amenophis III

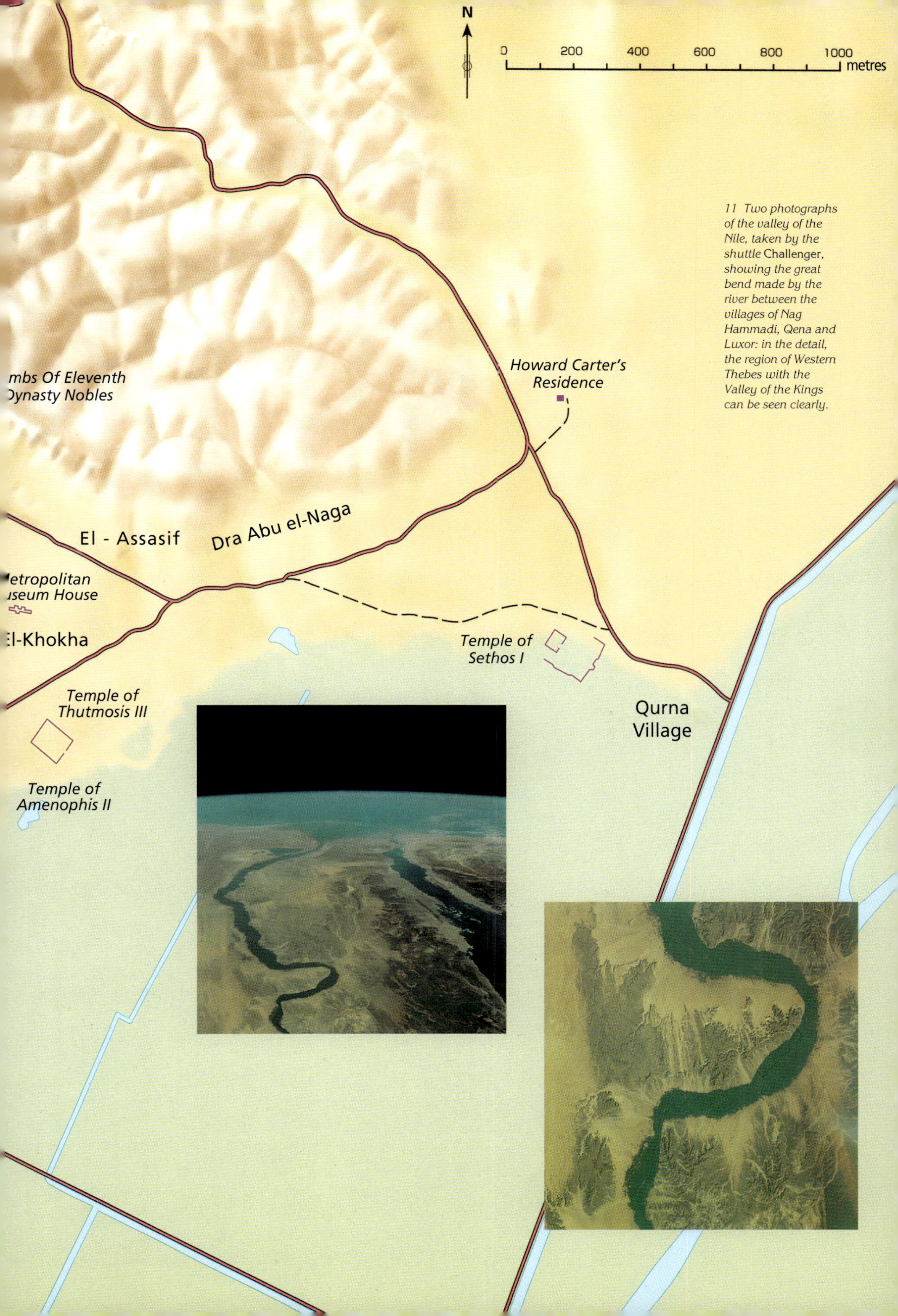

11 Two photographs of the valley of the Nile, taken by the shuttle Challenger, *showing the great bend made by the river between the villages of Nag Hammadi, Qena and Luxor: in the detail, the region of Western Thebes with the Valley of the Kings can be seen clearly.*

THE ROYAL NECROPOLISES
THE VALLEY OF THE KINGS

12-13 The Valley of the Kings, the name by which Champollion first called this site, was the royal necropolis of the Theban pharaohs of the New Kingdom. The Egyptians in fact called this site by the official name "the Great and Majestic Necropolis of the Millions of Years of the Pharaoh, Life, Strength, Health in the Occident of Thebes", or more simply as Ta-sekhet-aat *"Great Field". The Valley of the Kings is a deep wadi, hollowed in the rocks of the Theban mountain, which splits into two arms: the main one forming the Valley of the Kings proper and the Western Valley where only four tombs are found, among which are those of the pharaohs Ay (WV no. 23), Tutankhamun's successor, and of Amenophis III (WV no. 22).*

The Valley of the Kings, called by the Arabs *Biban el-Muluk* (that is "the gates of the kings") because of the entrances of several tombs opening in the valley's rocky walls, is a deep erosion dug out in the limestones of the Libyan range and directed mainly north-west.
The ancient Egyptians referred to it in different ways such as *Ta sekhet aat* "Great Field" or "the beautiful ladder of the West", but its official name was "the great and majestic necropolis of Pharaoh's millions of years Life Strength Health in the West of Thebes". Today the access to the valley, several kilometers long, is over a wide asphalted road that follows the ancient track used in the pharaonic era and referred to as the "road where Re sets". The valley is successively divided into two branches: the western one is called the Western Valley, as well as the Valley of the Monkeys and it shelters four tombs, two of which are royal and belong to the Pharaohs Amenophis III (WV no. 22) and Ay (WV no. 23), while the main branch, which is found on the extension of the access road, is the one commonly referred to as "Valley of the Kings" and encloses 58 tombs.
The Valley of the Kings is dominated by the Theban Peak, called by the natives el-Qurna "the Horn" from its curious pyramid-like shape, identified in ancient times with the snake-goddess Mertseger "She Who Loves Silence". It was probably the presence of such a geomorphological element, clearly calling to mind the pyramid, a peculiarity of the Old Kingdom's royal burials, that prompted the first pharaohs of the Eighteenth Dynasty to single out this imposing spot, burnt by the desert sun, for the establishment of their eternal dwellings. To this religious and ritual motive a more practical one is certainly to be added: as a result of its position and its geographical conformation, the access to this valley was difficult and in any case it could easily be supervised by the *Medjay*, the special police corps entrusted with the guarding of the necropolises. It is hard to ascertain who really was the first pharaoh who had himself buried in the valley, although apparently Tuthmosis I, occupying KV no. 38, seems to be entitled to the priority. This tomb, however, may have been arranged later, at the time of Tuthmosis III, who may have transferred there the sarcophagus of the first of the Tuthmosides, as is indicated by the objects found in it, which go back to the times of Tuthmosis III.
One of the most ancient tombs, if not the most ancient, is certainly the gigantic and unusual one intended by Hatshepsut for herself and her father Tuthmosis I (KV no. 20). However, the possibility cannot be ruled out that the hypogeum was originally indeed built for Tuthmosis I and that Hatshepsut had extended the original plan.

12 bottom Mount el-Qurna, also called the "Theban Peak" owing to its shape reminiscent of a pyramid, dominates the Theban necropolis and the Valley of the Kings: the presence of this natural element, so highly evocative, was probably one of the reasons that contributed to the choice of the Valley of the Kings as a royal necropolis.

13 top The cobra-goddess Mertseger, "She Who Loves the Silence" was thought of as the incarnation of Mount el-Qurn, the Theban Mountain, and was generally represented in the shape of a cobra-headed woman, occasionally adorned with a Hathoric crown. Mertseger exercised a protective function on the necropolises and on the dead.

13 bottom Pharaoh Tuthmosis I, who reigned between 1504 and 1492 BC, (Queen Hatshepsut's father and the successor of Amenophis I) was probably the first pharaoh to be buried in the Valley of the Kings, but the exact circumstances of his burial and which tomb was his original one still remain a mystery.

THE VALLEY OF THE KINGS

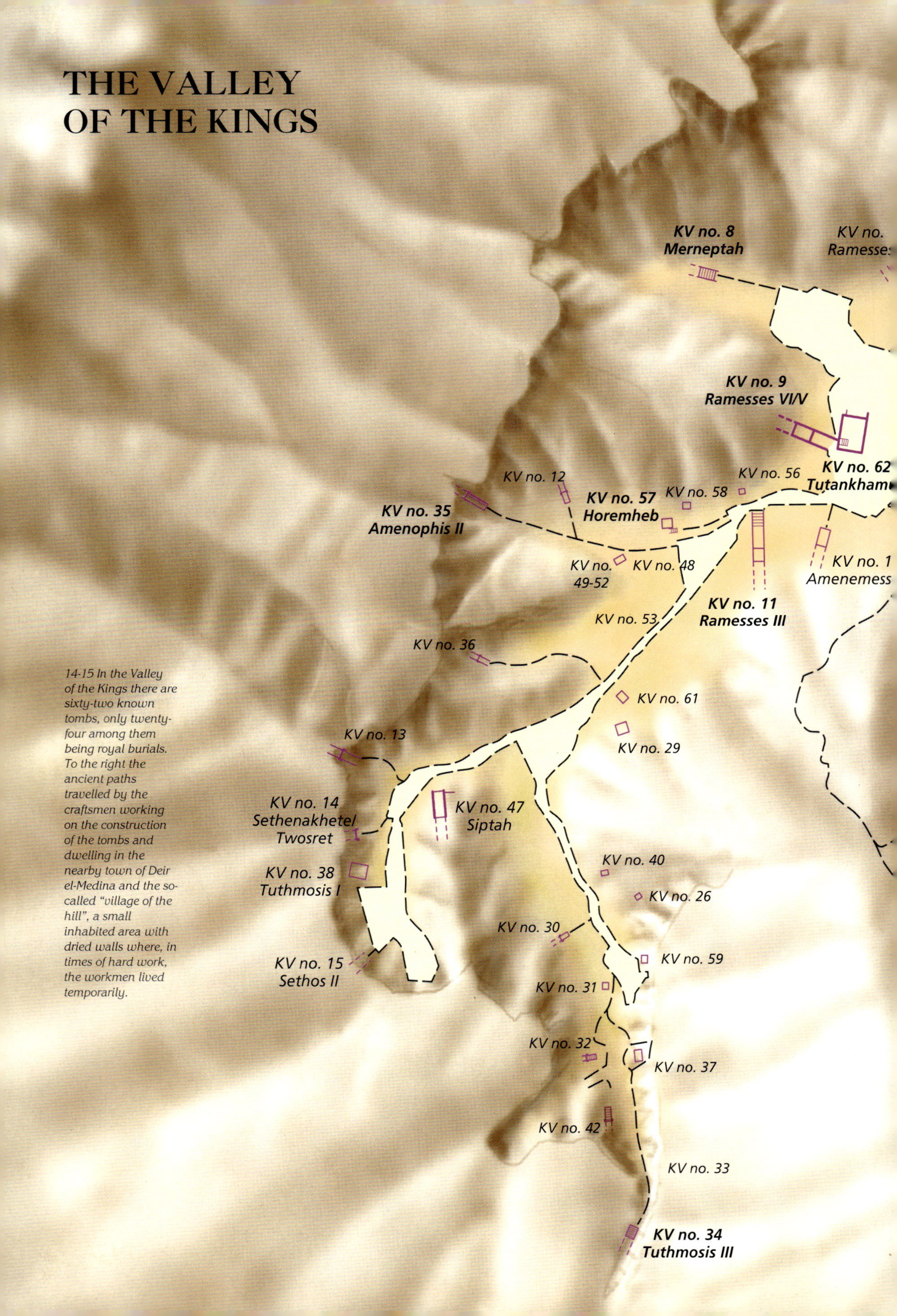

14-15 In the Valley of the Kings there are sixty-two known tombs, only twenty-four among them being royal burials. To the right the ancient paths travelled by the craftsmen working on the construction of the tombs and dwelling in the nearby town of Deir el-Medina and the so-called "village of the hill", a small inhabited area with dried walls where, in times of hard work, the workmen lived temporarily.

Luxor
Toward KV no. 1 (Tomb of Ramesses VII), Western Valley, Car Parking
KV no. 2
Ramesses IV
KV no. 3
KV no. 46
KV no. 4
Ramesses XI
KV no. 5
KV no. 6
Ramesses IX
V no. 55
KV no. 45
KV no. 44
KV no. 16
Ramesses I
KV no. 28
KV no. 27
V no. 17
ethos I
KV no. 18
Ramesses X
KV no. 54
KV no. 21
Path to
Deir el-Bahri
KV no. 60
KV no. 20
Hatshepsut
KV no. 19
Montu-her-khepsef
KV no. 43
Tuthmosis IV
N
0
20
40
60
80
100 metres

In any case, starting from the times of Hatshepsut and Tuthmosis III, the Valley of the Kings became the Theban pharaohs' burial place and continued serving as a royal necropolis until the end of the Twentieth Dynasty, specifically until the times of Ramesses XI, who was the last pharaoh buried in the Valley. Contrary to prevailing belief, the entrances to the royal tombs were not hidden but clearly visible and the necropolis police, besides watching the road leading to the valley, regularly inspected the entrances to the tombs to ascertain that the seals, affixed at the moment of burial, were unbroken. Unfortunately quite early all these precautions turned out to be useless. In fact, during a difficult and insecure period of political and social instability like the one that occurred at the end of Ramesses III's reign and that worsened until the end of the Twentieth Dynasty, the great amount of treasures heaped up in the tombs attracted ever more frequent robberies and pillages. It was therefore decided not to use that site any longer, since by then it was too well-known to the thieves and the pillagers. The priests removed the royal mummies to safer and better concealed places, (such as the Deir el-Bahri cache) in order to save them from profanation. From the papyruses concerning the robberies in the tombs at the time of the Twentieth Dynasty, such as "Papyrus Mayer B", "Papyrus Salt 124" and "Papyrus Abbott", we learn that already at that time many private and royal tombs had been violated: the tomb of Tutankhamun represents a happy exception, having been covered up with the debris from the excavation of the tomb of Ramesses IV, located above its entrance. Silence fell on the Valley for many centuries, until the Ptolemaic era when the first Greek and Roman "tourists" arrived: the historian Diodorus Siculus, who was in Egypt in 57 BC writes: "They say that these are the tombs of the ancient kings: they are magnificent and they do not leave to posterity the possibility of creating anything more beautiful" and on the walls of the tomb of Ramesses IV, for exemple, may be seen numerous graffiti left by the tourists of the Roman period. Then, silence again descended on this sacred site, until the times of the Jesuit Claude Sicard, who was in Egypt between 1708 and 1712 and identified the site of ancient Thebes, rediscovering the tombs in the Valley of the Kings. Afterwards in 1734 the English clergyman Richard Pococke visited the Valley and drew its first plan, in which eighteen tombs appeared, only half of which were accessible. Later on, the Scotsman James Bruce explored the tomb of Ramesses III in 1769 and the scholars following Napoleon's 1798 expedition discovered the tomb of Amenophis III (WV no. 22) in the Western Valley and undertook the first scientific survey of the site.

16 top left James Bruce of Kinnaird, the great Scots traveller, visited Egypt between 1768 and 1769 and was among the first Europeans who went to the Valley of the Kings, where he was struck by a bas-relief decorating the wall of a tomb and representing two harpists. Bruce called this tomb, later referred to also as "Tomb of Bruce", by the name of "Tomb of the Harpists": the tomb was subsequently identified by Champollion with that of pharaoh Ramesses III (KV no. 11).

16 top right Bruce drew the bas-relief of the harpists which fascinated him so much, thus performing the first survey of a scene depicted in a royal tomb.

16 bottom The first drawing of the Valley of the Kings was published by the Reverend Pococke in 1743.

16-17 The Valley of the Kings in a famous lithograph by David Roberts, one of the leading British orientalist painters of the Nineteenth century, who travelled to Egypt and to the Near East in 1838-39.

17 top The two harpists of the tomb of Bruce in a sketch executed by John Gardner Wilkinson, who travelled to Egypt between 1824 and 1836 visiting all the great archaeological sites and publishing numerous books, among which is a monumental work called Manners and Customs of the Ancient Egyptians. To Wilkinson we owe the first numbering of the tombs in the Valley of the Kings.

17 bottom Jean François Champollion and Ippolito Rosellini visited the Valley of the Kings in 1828, identifying for the first time numerous tombs, among them the tomb Bruce had identified as belonging to pharaoh Ramesses III. Champollion was the first to identify the Valley of the Kings as the necropolis of the Theban pharaohs of the New Kingdom.

Several years later, in 1817, Giovanni Battista Belzoni from Padua discovered the tombs of Ramesses I (KV no. 16), of Sethos I (KV no. 17) and of Ay, this last one in the Western Valley (WV no. 23). These exceptional discoveries were followed, three years later, by those of the Englishman James Burton who discovered two uninscribed tombs and a third one (KV no. 5) assigned to prince Meriatum "He who is loved by Atum, son of Ramesses II". Between 1824 and 1830, in the years following the decipherment of hieroglyphic writing, John Gardiner Wilkinson tenaciously worked in the Valley of the Kings identifying and assigning for the first time to the tombs a numeration still in use in our own days. In the years between 1828 and 1850 the Valley was the goal of scientists, travelers and artists among whom were Champollion and Rossellini, Robert Hay, and Richard Lepsius, but new discoveries were not registered until 1898, when the Frenchman Victor Loret discovered two new tombs belonging to Tuthmosis III (KV no. 34) and Amenophis II (KV no. 35) and in the next year the tomb, by far smaller and more modest, of Tuthmosis I (KV no. 38). Finally, in 1903, Howard Carter discovered the tomb of Tuthmosis IV (KV no. 43) and, in 1905 Theodore Davis discovered the untouched tomb of Yuya and Tuyu (KV no. 46), the parents of Queen Tiy, Amenophis III's wife. In that same period Edward Ayrton discovered the tombs of pharaoh Siptah (KV no. 47) and of Horemheb (KV no. 57), the last ruler of the Eighteenth Dynasty.

18 top Giovanni Battista Belzoni, born in Padua in 1778, was one of the greatest travelers and explorers of Egypt in the period preceding the decipherment of the hieroglyphs. Belzoni reached Egypt in 1815 and remained there until 1819, linking his name to exceptional undertakings such as the opening of the temple of Abu Simbel and of the pyramid of Chephren.

18 bottom The plan of the Valley of the Kings drawn by Belzoni, emphasizing in black the tombs he discovered; to Belzoni, who operated in the Valley of the Kings in 1817, we owe, among other things, the discovery of the tomb of Ramesses I (KV no. 16), the tomb of Sethos I (KV no. 17), subsequently called "Belzoni Tomb" and of the tomb of Ay (WV no. 23) in the Western Valley.

19 top left
The cartouche with the praenomen of Sethos I, Menmaatre Sethos.

19 top right Survey of the famous astronomic ceiling of the sarcophagus hall in the tomb of Sethos I, published in London in 1820 in a large album containing 44 watercolors for the illustration of the book written by Belzoni Narrative of the Operations and Recent Discoveries... *in which the traveler drew up the report of his extraordinary adventure in Egypt.*

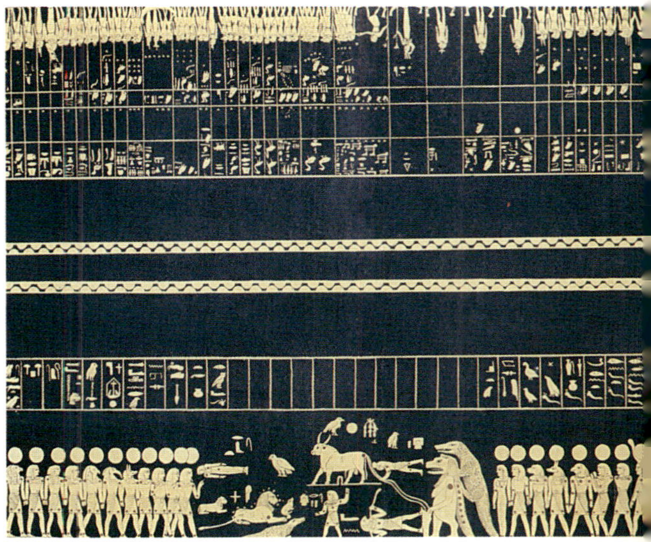

19 bottom left
Study executed by Alessandro Ricci, of one of the pillars of what Belzoni called "Hall of Beauties" in the tomb of Sethos I, showing the king in the presence of the goddess Hathor.

Alessandro Ricci from Siena, a physician and a great draftsman, worked in Egypt at the side of Belzoni greatly contributing to the execution of the surveys of Sethos I's huge tomb.

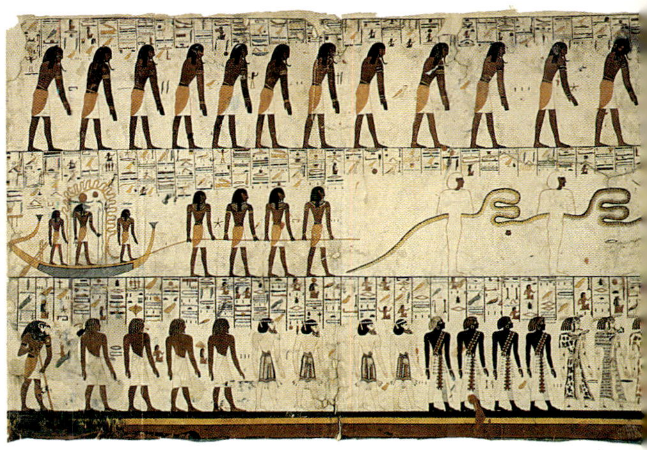

19 bottom right
An original, unedited survey by Belzoni and Ricci executed in the tomb of Sethos I: Belzoni was the first to carry out a complete survey of the wall paintings in a tomb of the Valley of the Kings. The fruit of this huge work was shown to the public in an enormously successful exhibition opened in London in 1821 and repeated later in Paris, in which the two most beautiful halls of Sethos I's tomb were reconstructed.

A few years later, in 1922, Carter discovered the last royal tomb of the Valley, the only royal burial site that had remained practically untouched: the very famous one of Tutankhamun (KV no. 62). Chronologically, the last discovery occurred in February 1995, when Kent Weeks of the American University in Cairo found a series of new rooms arranged for the sons of Ramesses II in the tomb located opposite that of Ramesses II (KV no. 5) already visited by Burton in 1820,

20 top left George Edward Stanhope Molyneux Herbert, fifth Earl of Carnarvon, the English aristocratic patron of the arts who agreed to finance the researches of an unemployed and practically unknown archaeologist by the name of Howard Carter. Carnarvon obtained the concession for the Valley of the Kings in 1914 but the excavations started only in 1917 owing to the outbreak of World War I. On April 5, 1923 Lord Carnarvon died under mysterious and dramatic circumstances that gave birth to the legend of the "curse of the pharaohs".

20 bottom left Photograph of the tomb of Tutankhamun (KV no. 62) taken shortly after the discovery that took place on November 4, 1922. The tomb was located right below the tomb of Ramesses VI (at the center of the photo) and its entrance had been providentially concealed by the huge bulk of the debris produced by the digging of this last-mentioned burial site.

20 bottom right A train of workmen carries baskets of rubble away from a trench excavation of the tomb of Tutankhamun. The tomb included over 3,500 articles, and the emptying of the antechamber alone took some fifty days and the last objects were removed from the tomb only in 1930.

20-21 The doors of the second of the four huge shrines of gilded wood that contained the royal sarcophagi still carried the necropolis seal, unequivocal sign that the pharaoh's mummy was still intact while the outmost shrine had been opened.

21 bottom left
On February 17, 1923 Carter (at the center) officially started the work for the opening of the burial chamber.

21 top right Carter with his trusted associate Arthur Callender and two workmen removing the walled structure that separated the antechamber from the burial chamber so as to be able to take out the wooden shrines containing the sarcophagi.

21 centre right
One of the two statues posted to watch the sepulchral hall is being carefully wrapped up before being carried outside the tomb. The wooden statues, painted with a black resin, were provided with a gold lamina covering the headdress and the triangular tunic, on which were found the pharaoh's cartouches, and they probably represented the royal ka.

21 bottom right
The northern wall of the antechamber partially demolished in order to allow access to the burial chamber, inside which the outer shrine of gilded wood containing the sarcophagi can be seen. On both sides of the wall, next to the door jambs, were found two life-sized wooden statues meant to protect the king's eternal rest.

22 top Numerous models of boats were found in the small room annexed to the burial chamber and called by Carter "the Treasury", in which there also was the shrine of the canopic vases. In the foreground can be seen the model of a sailing boat resting on a wooden model of a granary.

22 centre left An image of the goddess Hathor, represented with a cow's head and with a linen cloth around her neck, was found in the "Treasury" in front of the shrine of the canopic vases and behind a wooden statue of Anubis, already removed when this photograph was taken. On the left side several small boxes of painted wood can be seen, which contained jewels and other objects of funerary furniture.

22 centre right In the antechamber we can see the pharaoh's four dismantled chariots and two of the three large ritual couches of gilded wood intended for the rest of the king's soul, over which were found several caskets of painted wood. Under the second couch can be distinguished several oval containers covered with white stucco, inside which were found food offerings for the feeding of the deceased pharaoh.

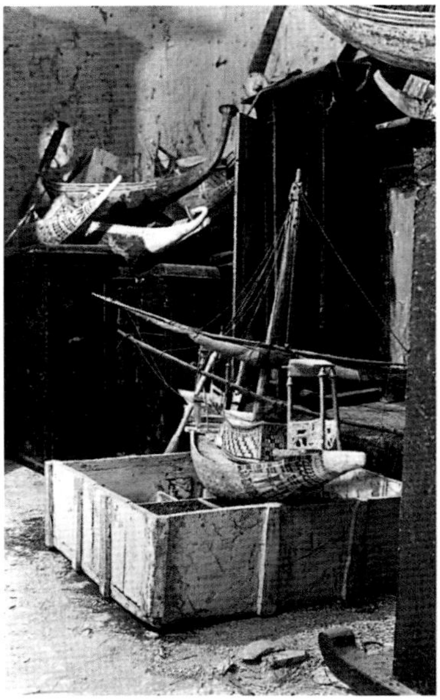

of which practically every trace had since been lost. This new section of the tomb, prepared for the sons of Ramesses II, basically changes our knowledge of Ramesside tomb architecture and makes this strange tomb with a "T" plan and a series of 67 rooms found until now (which may increase following the exploration of a lower floor) the largest of all the Valley's tombs.

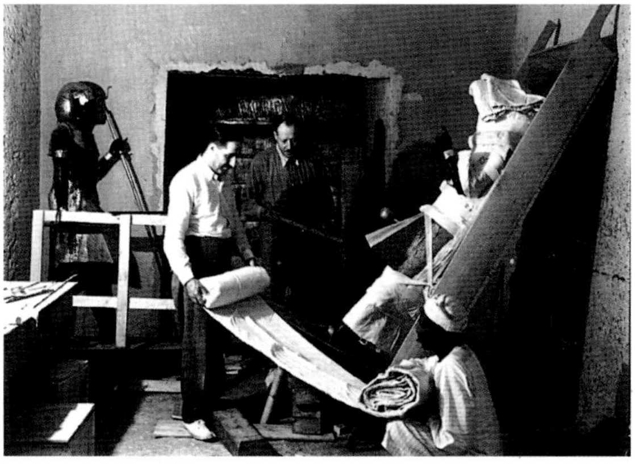

22-23 After opening the second anthropoid coffin of gilded wood, by lifting its cover with the help of a complicated system of pulleys, the third solid gold coffin appeared, containing the pharaoh's mummy. The third coffin was covered, like the preceding one, with a linen shroud on which a wreath of flowers, leaves and fruits had been placed, but the whole was impregnated with a blackish solidified ointment.

23 top Carter cleans up the second coffin of gilded wood inlaid with colored glass, after having gently removed the very thin linen cloth that covered it and on which were laid down festoons of flowers and of olive leaves.

22 bottom Howard Carter, in the foreground, is busy carefully wrapping up one of the two sentry statues posted on the northern wall of the antechamber, before their transfer to the nearby warehouse-laboratory. Contrary to the practice of many archaeologists of the time, Carter documented with great accuracy each stage of the emptying of the tomb, which therefore proceeded rather slowly.

23 bottom left A little wooden chapel found in the "Treasury" contained three small ritual gilded wooden statues of the king and covered with linen shrouds. The first small statue figures Tutankhamun in the act of walking, while the two other inner statues portray him on a papyrus boat in the act of hunting Seth's hippopotamus with a harpoon, evoking the myth of the fight that set Horus against Seth.

23 bottom right Carter and Callender open the doors of the four shrines of gilded wood containing the royal coffins. The doors of the first shrine did not carry seals, having perhaps been tampered with by the thieves who broke into the tomb in antiquity, without however succeeding in plundering it, but the doors of the second and the third shrines were left intact.

THE BUILDING OF A ROYAL TOMB

The building of his own tomb, the place where the transformation and the regeneration of the deceased king occurred, was one of the living pharaoh's deepest concerns: generally, already during his first year of reign the spot of the future tomb was chosen and a plan was worked out in which not only the architectural peculiarities were specified, but also the decorations, the paintings and the texts to be represented on the walls. Subsequently, they immediately proceeded to the implementation stage, entrusted to the architect and to the craftsmen who lived in the village of Deir el-Medina and went to work following a trail over the mountain's crest that can still be easily crossed today (See itinerary no. 2). The working days were of variable length, according to the tomb's dimensions which, in their turn, were proportionate at least within certain limits, to the duration of the reign. The working day started at dawn and lasted eight hours with a break for lunch after the first four hours of work. The working pace was therefore

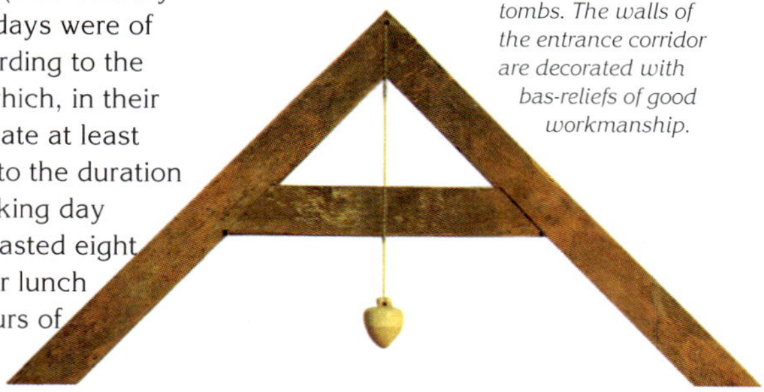

24 top The master-builders used sophisticated instruments, such as this wooden set square to make sure of the verticality of the walls. (Cairo Museum)

24-25 The tomb of Sethos II (KV no. 15), who reigned towards the end of the Nineteenth Dynasty, already presents the linear and simplified plan characteristic of the tombs of the Twentieth Dynasty. From this elongated structure originates the word "syringe", used by the Greeks to indicate the Egyptian tombs. The walls of the entrance corridor are decorated with bas-reliefs of good workmanship.

25 top left
The instruments used for the digging of a tomb and the modelling of its walls consisted mainly of a small wooden hammer and a metallic chisel. (Egyptian Museum, Turin)

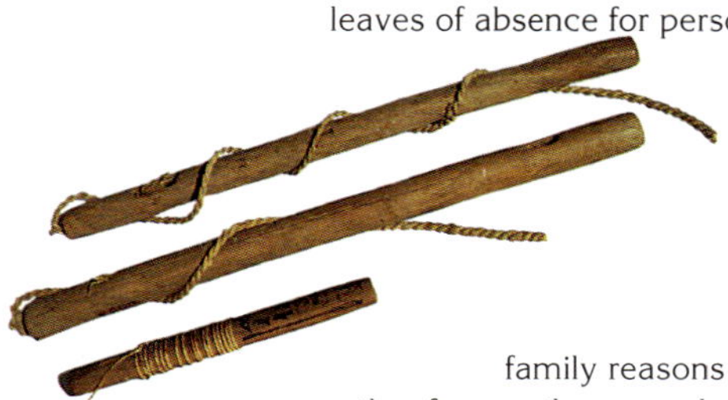

25 top right *On this little ostracon, preserved at the Fitzwilliam Museum in Cambridge, a workman can be seen using ordinary instruments.*

25 center *This large brush was probably used to spread the tomb walls with a thin plaster made of clay and limestone, with the final coating made up of a mixture of chalk and water. (Egyptian Museum, Turin)*

25 bottom *To draw straight lines the ancients made use of small wooden sticks to which were attached fine cords, whose imprint in some cases can still be seen nowadays. (Egyptian Museum, Turin)*

not exhausting and during the working week, lasting ten days, there were two rest days. To these weekly holidays many others were added on the occasion of the numerous religious festivities, and leaves of absence for personal or family reasons, occurring rather frequently, were also granted. The craftsmen were organised in teams working under the supervision of an architect. The team was divided into two groups, the right and the left, working simultaneously under the orders of two foremen in the respective parts of the tomb. The head of the team, originally appointed by the pharaoh himself or by the vizier (a dignitary acting as a prime minister), was directly responsible for the work, checked the reasons for the absences of the workmen and had dealings with the vizier himself through a scribe specifically entrusted with this duty. The scribes, who fulfilled a highly important and prestigious task in Egyptian society, were also charged with the withdrawal from the pharaoh's warehouses of the food distributed as wages to the workmen, with the settling of quarrels and with the administration of justice in the village of Deir el-Medina. The foremen, on the other hand, had to inspect the distribution of the material kept in the warehouses and draw up the list of presences and absences.

The groups did not have a fixed number of members, but the average strength numbered between thirty and sixty persons: this figure, however, could increase if need be, up to one hundred and twenty persons. The workmen's duties were specialised and complementary: stone-cutters, plasterers, sculptors, draftsmen and decorators worked side by side and simultaneously in a sort of assembly line. The quarrymen came into operation first and, while the digging went on, penetrating always deeper inside the mountain, the plasterers smoothed the walls of the parts not too far from the surface, affixing a layer of *muna*, a kind of plaster obtained from a mixture of clay and quartz, limestone and crushed straw, over which were laid a thinner plaster made of clay and limestone, successively whitened with a layer of gypsum dissolved in water.

The execution of the decorative program, chosen by the high priests in agreement with the pharaoh, was entrusted to the draftsmen.

These worked using a red ochre after having subdivided the surface to paint into numerous squares, by means of a string fastened to a stick, in order to be able to place correctly the figures and the texts and make sure that proportions were respected according to very precise rules. The draftsmen were under the supervision of a chief draftsman who made necessary corrections using black charcoal.

Then the sculptors stepped in and started carving the rock to obtain a bas relief, to be colored later by the painters, who used six basic colors with precise symbolic and ritual meanings.

ARCHITECTURE AND DECORATION OF THE TOMBS

26 top The painters, proceeding to the final stage of the decoration, used small palettes, similar to those preserved in the Cairo Museum.

The plan of the royal tombs is complex and each one has a peculiar physiognomy of its own, even though there generally are constant elements such as the ladder, the descending corridor onto which halls open, and the burial chamber designed to contain the pharaoh's sarcophagus.
An important architectural peculiarity distinguishes (even though some exceptions are known) the tombs of the Eighteenth Dynasty from those of the Nineteenth: in the first the descending corridor generally forms a 90° bend before penetrating into the sarcophagus hall, while in the second it proceeds in a straight line. This tendency to a linear development along the major axis becomes ever more evident in the tombs of the Twentieth Dinasty and was probably related to a change in religious conceptions, according to which the tomb's structure itself had to reflect somehow the trajectory of the solar star.
As to the wall decorations, the scenes represented never dealt with aspects of everyday life, or with historical-biographical elements, but only and absolutely with after-life and the trip the pharaoh had to undertake overcoming numerous trials in order to reach the kingdom of Osiris. The style of the decorations varies from imitations of papyrus to elaborate and painted bas reliefs, but the subjects remain overall the same: the texts painted on the walls, taken from the great magical-religious anthologies of the time, such as the *Book of the Dead*, the *Book of Amduat*, the *Book of the Gates*, the *Book of the Caverns*, the *Book of Earth*, and *Litanies of Re*, and generally illustrated with scenes related to them, assured the deceased of the requisite knowledge of the magic formulas needed to overcome the hardships he would face. In fact, for the ancient Egyptians, the tomb had a totally different meaning than it has nowadays, it had a "sacred architecture" and a sacred orientation of its own, which did not coincide at all with the geographical and terrestrial one: in it the deceased accomplishes a ritual journey. The deceased descends to the kingdom of the dead, symbolized by the tomb, overcomes the numerous obstacles standing in his way thanks to the appropriate use of the magic formulas prescribed in the *Book of the Dead* and is introduced by kindly divinities into the kingdom of Osiris, Lord of the Afterlife, symbolized by the hall of the sarcophagus.
This hall, called by the Egyptians the "golden hall", referring to the gold that represents the incorruptible flesh of the gods, was the spot where was supposed to take place the pharaoh's transformation into a divine entity, whose soul "came out to the light", that is climbed to the sky to be reunited with the sun god Re, his godly father.

26 centre The decorative plan of the royal tombs was established in detail by the priests and it concerned exclusively the world of the Afterlife, the journey the deceased pharaoh had to accomplish in order to reach the kingdom of Osiris, with texts taken from the great magical-religious anthologies of the time. The photograph shows a detail of the decoration of the western wall of the burial chamber of Tutankhamun's tomb (KV no. 62), illustrating a passage of the Book of Amduat.

26 bottom After the sculptors had modelled the tomb's wall by incising the rock with metal points, generally using the bas-relief technique, the surfaces were further smoothed and colored by decorator-painters.

27 top The tomb had its precise geographical and ritual orientations, related to the decorative plan and sometimes on the walls of the tomb under construction the workmen drew the symbols of the cardinal points, as can be noticed in the burial chamber of Horemheb's tomb (KV no. 57). The photograph shows the symbol of the West.

27 centre Horemheb's tomb (KV no. 57) and that of Sat-re (QV. no. 38) have been instrumental in helping us understand the decorative techniques used by the artists of that age, in that we have incomplete walls left in different working stages. It is thus possible to see how the primitive red ochre sketch was being corrected with a black charcoal. At this stage the sculptors stepped in, carving the surface of the rock and then whitewashing it with water and chalk before handing over to the painters.

The pigments used in the tombs

While the digging went on in the deepest parts of the tomb, the external parts were practically finished. This rational organization allowed work to proceed at an incredible speed and, even though the tombs were dug with rather rudimentary tools, a royal tomb could be completed within a few months and, in the case of the larger and more complex tombs, a variable period of only six to ten years was required. The sons of the craftsmen were also employed in the work, being entrusted with simple and not very wearisome tasks.

These boys used to work hoping to become in their turn "servants in the Seat of Truth", as Deir el-Medina craftsmen were referred to at the time. Side by side with all these persons were also the serfs, simple labourers provided to the craftsmen's community by the pharaoh and entrusted with the humblest and the more tiresome labours, yet necessary to the functioning of the groups of specialised workmen, such as, for instance, the carrying of water, the preparing of plaster, the preparing of torches for lighting. The torches were made of baked clay containers filled with oil of sesame and salt or with animal fat and salt, inside which floated a twisted linen taper.

It seems that salt was used to prevent the combustion releasing smoke, which would have harmed the paintings.

THE PIGMENTS USED IN THE TOMBS

COLOR	PIGMENT	SYMBOLIC MEANING	NOTES
white	gypsum - huntite	represents silver	used also as background
blue	cuprorivaite or Egyptian blue	symbolizes the sky and the body of the celestial divinities	obtained artificially by synthesis
yellow	yellow ochre - orpiment	represents gold, gods' flesh. Expresses the idea of preciousness	used also as background. Orpiment was imported from Asia
black	coal	death and eternal preservation	
red	red ochre	symbolizes fire and blood	easily found in the clayey formations of the Theban mountain
green	copper wollastonite	regeneration	artificially obtained by synthesis

27 bottom Red and blue were colors widely employed in the decoration of the tombs but their origins were quite different. The red color was generally obtained by grinding red ochres containing iron oxide, while the blue was a synthetic color, the first synthetic color in history, produced by heating at over 700° C a mixture of copper salts, calcium and sand mixed with a flux (sodium salts).

THE BURIAL OF THE PHARAOH

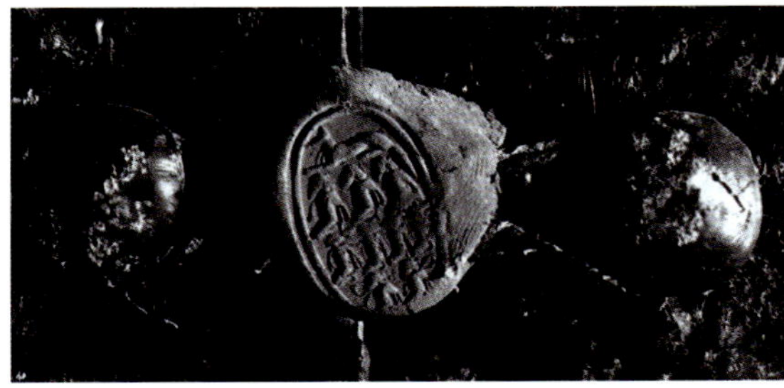

The news of the pharaoh's death was generally received with a degree of joy by the Deir el-Medina craftsmen, not just because the enthroning of a new king meant new work, but also because it was necessary to quickly put the final touches to the tomb and to the very numerous funerary furnishings that had to accompany the king in his last dwelling, operations that all offered increased opportunities for additional income. Generally a three-month period intervened between the king's death and his burial: the time needed for the complex ritual of the embalming and preparation of the king's corpse, which, after having been immersed for seventy days in natron, was wrapped in a first layer of very thin linen bandages on which were laid, in well-determined spots, numerous amulets, later covered with a second layer of broader bandages soaked in resin and aromatic essential oils.
The procession, setting out from the royal palace, reached the West of Thebes and entered "the road where Re sets" heading for "the great and majestic necropolis of the Pharaoh's millions of years Life Strenght Health in the West of Thebes". The royal mummy in its wooden sarcophagus was followed by parties of women screaming and crying, while the bald-headed priests burnt incense, shaking their sistrums. As it reached the tomb and faced it, the coffin was stood upright and the high priest or, sometimes, the new pharaoh accomplished the ritual "of the opening of the mouth", thanks to which the deceased magically reacquired the use of his mouth and was able, in such a way, to speak again, to drink and to eat.
Then, the mortal remains were carried to the burial chamber where a monumental stone sarcophagus had been prepared long since, on which was laid the heavy cover carved in high relief with the king's image. At that time, while family and friends started the funerary banquet, the workmen hermetically closed the entrance to the tomb, on which the necropolis seals were affixed.
The entrance was not always hidden but, mainly starting from the Nineteenth Dynasty, it was left in plain view and the necropolis guards, beside garrisoning the road leading to the valley, regularly inspected the seals in order to verify their integrity, after which they drew up careful reports. Once the tomb was closed and sealed, nobody was permitted to penetrate it any more and the Valley itself was a forbidden spot where nobody, except the craftsmen and the guards, was entitled to go: the worship of the deceased king never required a return to the place of burial and was performed far away, in the plain of the Nile Valley in the "castles of the millions of years" where the king united with eternity in the estates of Amun in the West of Thebes.

28 top right The seals were of two kinds: a first kind was impressed on the plaster of the doors, while a second kind was affixed on a small clay block around the fine cords with which the doors of the shrines containing the sarcophagi or the canopic vases were closed.

28 top left Seals were placed on the necropolis by officials responsibile for the security of the tombs. Different types were used but they generally included the figure of Anubis, who appeared as a crouched jackal; in some cases the royal scroll was depicted at the side and, underneath, a number of prisoners (nine or, less frequently, four) tied with their hands behind their backs and sometimes beheaded.

28-29 This scene depicted on the east wall of the burial chamber of the tomb of Tutankhamun (KV no. 62) shows the coffin of the dead king, placed in a shrine and mounted on a sleigh. It is being pulled along by twelve high dignitaries, among them the viziers of Upper and Lower Egypt, distinguishable from the others by the style of their tunic which leaves their right shoulder bare. As the hieroglyphs tell us, they are chanting in unison: "Oh Nebkheprure, come in peace, oh god protector of the Earth."

28 bottom left The iconographic documentation concerning the royal funerary ritual is rather scanty, while the scenes showing the funerary ritual in private tombs are more numerous. In this wall painting we see the priest performing a cleansing in front of the coffin of the deceased, standing upright at the tomb door before proceeding to the ceremony of the "Opening of the Mouth".

DYNASTIES	KV n. tomb	Date of discovery	Discoverer	Length (meters)
EIGHTEENTH DYNASTY				
Tuthmosis I	38	1899	Loret	25
Tuthmosis II	42 ?	1900	Carter	50
Hatshepsut	20	1903	Carter	200
Tuthmosis III	34	1898	Loret	55
Amenophis II	35	1898	Loret	60
Tuthmosis IV	43	1903	Carter	90
Amenophis III	WV 22	1799	Jollois/Devillier	100
Tutankhamun	62	1922	Carter	40
Ay	WV 23	1816	Belzoni	55
Horemheb	57	1908	Ayrton	114
NINETEENTH DYNASTY				
Ramesses I	16	1817	Belzoni	29
Sethos I	17	1817	Belzoni	100
Ramesses II	7	antiquity		100
Merneptah	8	antiquity		115
Sethos II	15	?		72
Amenemesses	10	1907	Ayrton	75
Siptah	47	1905	Ayrton	90
Twosret	14	antiquity		110
TWENTIETH DYNASTY				
Sethenakhte	14	antiquity		110
Ramesses III	11	antiquity		125
Ramesses IV	2	antiquity		66
Ramesses VI / V	9	antiquity		104
Ramesses VII	1	antiquity		40
Ramesses IX	6	antiquity		86
Ramesses X	18	?		40
Ramesses XI	4	antiquity		93

The tombs of the Valley of the Kings

Out of the sixty-two tombs known to this day in the Valley of the Kings, only about twenty actually sheltered pharaohs: indeed, many were abandoned because the workmen came up against unsuitable rock formations, some were only undecorated corridors with little rooms in the back, while others were used for various members of the royal family. Among the royal tombs, fifteen are generally open to the public, even though several of them may temporarily be closed for restoration works, rendered increasingly necessary both by the influx of a considerable crowd of tourists upsetting by their very presence, even though unintentionally, the sensitive microclimate of these monuments, and by the unstable hydrogeological conditions of the valley itself. Since the complete description of all the tombs of the Valley of the Kings that can be visited would require much more space than provided by a simple introductory guide, we shall of necessity operate a choice based upon criteria of artistic value and of general interest.

29 top left A peculiar moment of the funerary ritual was the ceremony of the "Opening of the Mouth" in which the officiating priest magically restored to the deceased the use of speech and senses. In this scene painted on the northern wall of Tutankhamun's tomb (KV no. 62), it is the Pharaoh Ay, dressed as a sem-priest, who performs the ceremony of the "Opening of the Mouth" in front of Tutankhamun, shown as Osiris.

29 top right In this scene painted in Sennedjem's tomb (TT no. 1), Anubis "the Divine Embalmer" is bent over the deceased's body, while performing his skills. Anubis was not only the protector of the necropolis but also, according to tradition, the inventor of the embalming process, which was placed under his guardianship.

TOMBS OF THE EIGHTEENTH DYNASTY

TUTHMOSIS III
1479 - 1425 BC

KV no. 34

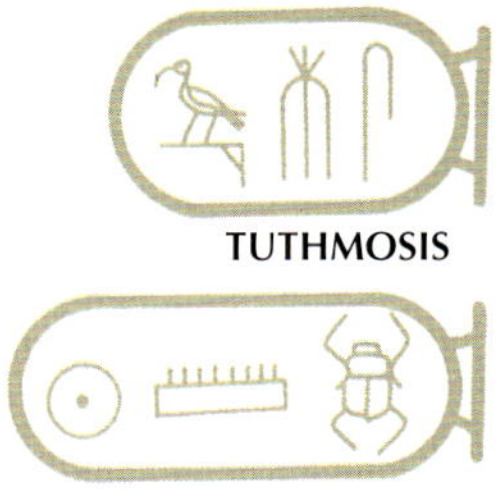

The tomb of Tuthmosis III is located in a narrow gorge at the bottom of the Valley of the Kings, a real fold of the rocky wall forming the flank of the main wadi, which has to be climbed on a small metal ladder in order to reach the tomb's entrance, located at an altitude of about thirty meters above ground level.
The tomb of the great pharaoh, who officially mounted the throne rather young, at the death of Tuthmosis II, but was able to assume power only at the death of Hatshepsut, his father's sister (who at first undertook the regency and later succeeded in having herself enthroned), was discovered in 1898 by Victor Loret, then director of the Antiquities Service. An exceptional ruler, considered, along with Ramesses II, to be one of Egypt's greatest pharaohs, Tuthmosis III, besides being a very great strategist who led glorious military campaigns in the East, consolidating a huge empire, was an innovator in the religious field, as he knew how to recover the tradition of the ancient Heliopolitan worships. It was under his reign that the Valley of the Kings definitely assumed the character of a royal necropolis. The tomb, notwithstanding its position which rendered it almost inaccessible, did not escape looting by the necropolis robbers and was found by Loret deprived of great artistic treasures but still with part of its funerary furniture.
The tomb begins with a double succession of steps and a corridor. The second corridor leads to a quadrangular shaft which in its turn ends in a two-pillar vestibule, at 90° to the corridor axis and decorated with reproductions of the 765 divinities that daily generate the sun. The shaft's purpose, a structure found in many, though not in all the royal tombs, is subject to debate, but it is highly probable that the shafts had above all a ritual meaning as an evocation of Sokar's cavern, a very ancient funerary deity protectress of the deceased king, and possibly also had the practical aim of physically protecting the sarcophagus hall, both from profanations and from flooding following torrential rains.
From the vestibule, a few steps lead into the oval-shaped burial chamber, with two pillars at the center and four lateral annexes opening into the eastern and the western sides.
The large burial chamber, holding a wonderful sarcophagus of red quartzite on which an image of the goddess Nut is carved, was conceived as a huge ornamental scroll inside which the complete texts of the *Book of Amduat* were written as on a papyrus, while on the pillars there are passages taken from the *Litanies of Re*. By the name of "Book of Amduat" (this last word meaning "that which there is in the Afterlife"), we refer today to a collection of magical and religious texts, called by the ancient Egyptians the "Book of the Secret Room", subdivided into twelve parts corresponding to the night's twelve hours and dealing with Afterlife's sacred geography and with the sun's nightly course. The *Amduat* is the oldest of all the texts transcribed on the tomb walls of the Valley of the Kings. Tuthmosis III's mummy was found in 1881 inside tomb no. 320 at Deir el-Bahri.

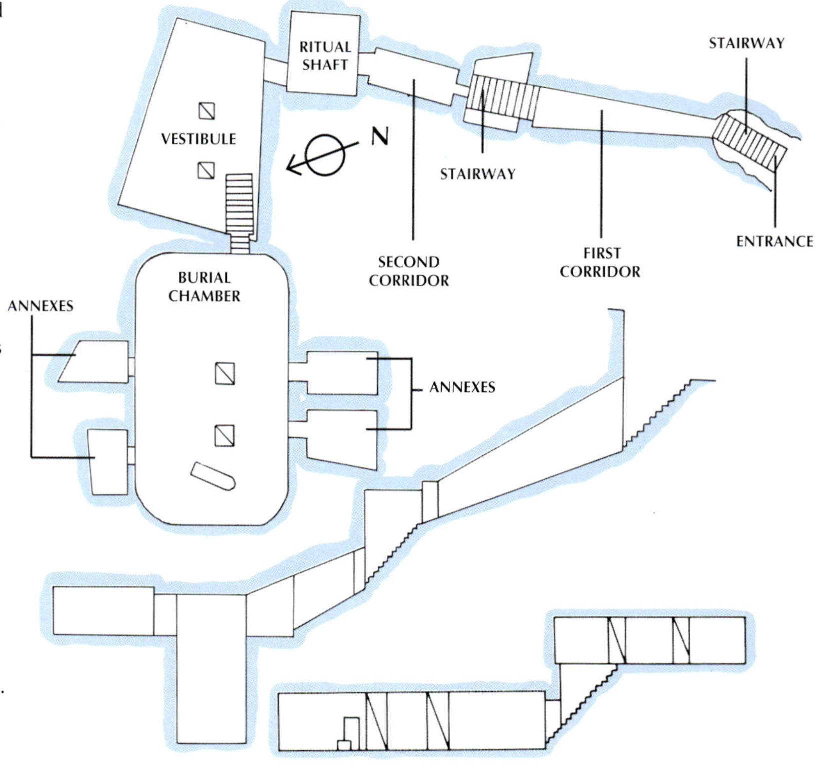

30 top Tuthmosis III officially mounted the throne in 1479 BC at the death of his father Tuthmosis II, but he really assumed power only at the death of his aunt and wife Hatshepsut in 1457 BC, then maintaining it for thirty-two years, until his death in 1425 BC. A great conqueror and shrewd politician he turned Egypt into the greatest power of the time. (Luxor Museum)

***a**- Astronomical ceiling*

***b** - Scenes with deities*

c - Scenes with deities and Litanies of Re *on the pillars;* Book of Amduat *on the walls*

A - Overall view of one of the walls of the oval-shaped burial chamber, reminiscent of a cartouche, on which are transcribed in cursive hieroglyphs the complete texts of the Book of Amduat, *an Egyptian word meaning "that which there is in the afterlife", a collection of magic-religious texts subdivided in twelve parts, corresponding to the twelve hours of the night. The* Book of Amduat *is the oldest among the texts transcribed in the tombs of the Valley of the Kings.*

B - Representation of the pharaoh breast-fed by the goddess Isis in the shape of a tree, followed by the pharaoh holding in his hands the sceptre and the ceremonial mace, accompanied by his spouses Merit-re and Satioh and by his daughters.

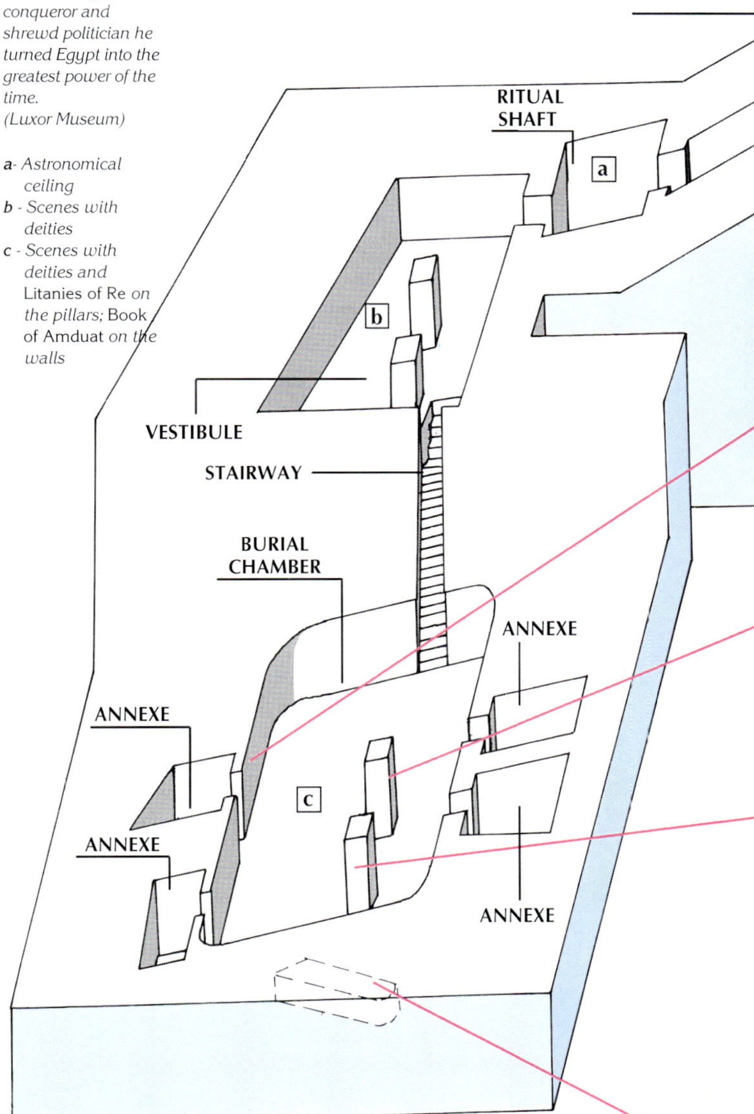

A

B

C

D - The cartouche-shaped sarcophagus of red quartzite of the king is found in the north-western side of the burial chamber. At the moment of discovery in 1898 by Victor Loret, then director of the Egyptian Antiquities Service, the cover of the sarcophagus was on the ground, broken. Tuthmosis III's mummy had already been found in 1881 by Gaston Maspero in the Deir el-Bahri cache. In the detail of the sarcophagus can be seen the goddess Isis, kneeling on a large neb-*sign.*

C - Representation of the Litanies of Re, *the name by which a religious composition, probably contemporary with the* Book of Amduat, *is referred to, in which are described the seventy-five transformations of the sun god in his journey to the afterlife, followed by a series of litanies in which the king is assimilated to the sun and to other deities.*

D

AMENOPHIS II

1427 - 1397 BC

KV no. 35

AMENHOTEP HEQAIUN

AKHEPERURE

A - On the walls of the burial chamber the texts of the Book of Amduat *are transcribed with a decorative program analogous to that of the tomb of Tuthmosis III, by whose style it is quite evidently inspired. The texts in cursive hieroglyphs are arranged in vertical columns and are simply painted on the smoothed wall and not engraved in bas-reliefs.*

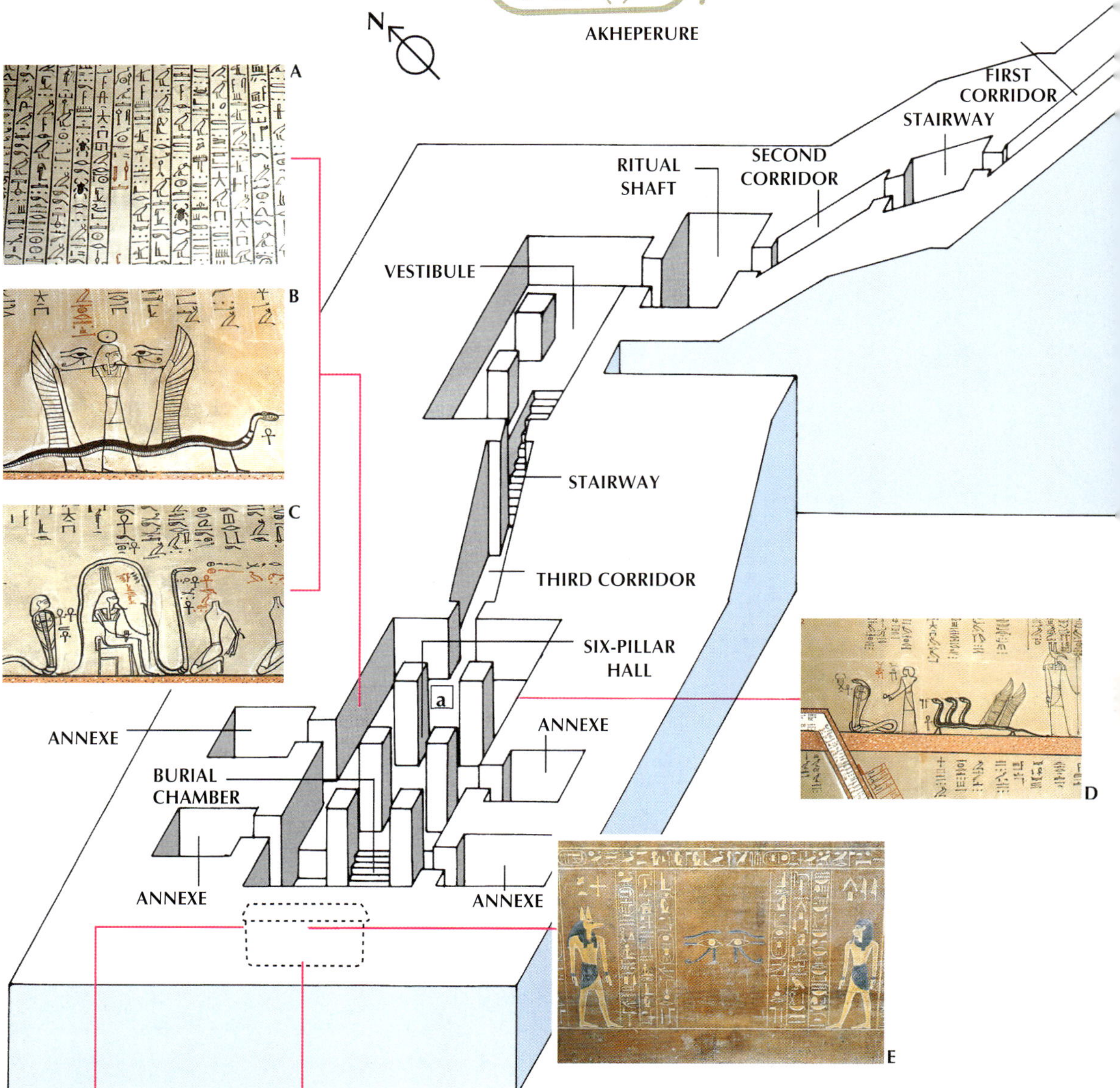

F

G

B - Representation of the Eleventh Hour of the Book of Amduat *in which the earth snake provided with wings carries to the heavenly kingdom the king's mummy.*

C - Detail of the Seventh Hour of the Book of Amduat *in which Osiris, seated on his throne and surrounded by the* mehen-snake, *attends his enemies' torture.*

D - Detail of the Fourth Hour of the Book of Amduat *in which is ilustrated the descent of the sarcophagus escorted by snakes into the tomb.*

The tomb of Amenophis II, Tuthmosis III's successor, is no doubt one of the most beautiful achievements of Eighteenth Dynasty funerary architecture. Located on the slope opposite the Valley's main wadi, this tomb was discovered by Loret in March 1898 and, like the other tombs in the valley, it had been savagely looted.
The tomb's structure is complex and its dimensions impressive, but there are many similarities with the tomb of Tuthmosis III, both structurewise and from the point of view of the decorative style. A double succession of steps and corridor lead to the shaft room opening into the two-pillars vestibule with a main axis set at 90° to the corridors. From the vestibule a third flight of steps and a third corridor lead to a large rectangular room supported by six pillars, on which the king is shown in the presence of different deities. The room extends to the south, beyond the last pair of pillars, into the burial chamber, in which a quartzite sarcophagus is found which, at the time of discovery, contained the pharaoh's intact mummy with a garland of mimosa flowers at his neck. The mummy remained exhibited in the tomb until 1928, when it was transferred to the Cairo Museum.
The six-pillar room and the burial chamber are both provided with two lateral annexes placed along the eastern and the western sides.
The wall decorations are similar, from the stylistic and the content points of view, to Tuthmosis III's tomb, even though here the ornamental scroll-shaped oval form of the burial chamber, which had characterised the tombs of the first Tuthmosides, is definitely abandoned.
The six-pillar room's walls are decorated with the complete texts of the *Book of Amduat* and with the corresponding illustrations, as if they were a large mural papyrus. In the western lateral annexe, which was carefully closed by a stone wall, Loret made another extraordinary discovery: here were found nine royal sarcophagi with the mummies of Tuthmosis IV, Amenophis III, Merneptah, Sethos II, Siptah, Setenakhte, Ramesses IV, Ramesses V and Ramesses VI. The sarcophagi had been carried here probably at the beginning of the Twenty-First Dynasty, at the time of the high priest Pinudjem I (1070-1037 BC), as Pinudjem II (990-969 BC) later did, when he decided to transfer the remaining pharaohs' sarcophagi to the Deir el-Bahri cache. It is not clear why the ancient desecrators of the tomb did not violate this easily found cache too, nor is it clear why they did not violate Amenophis's mummy, as they used to do searching for gold amulets and other precious objects which were laid on the deceased's corpse.

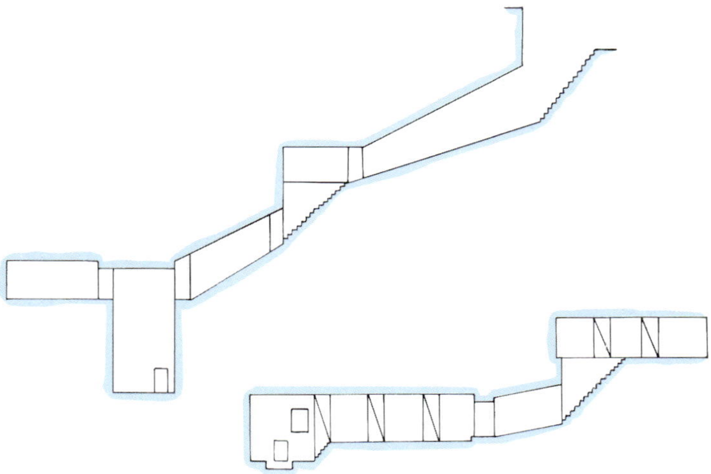

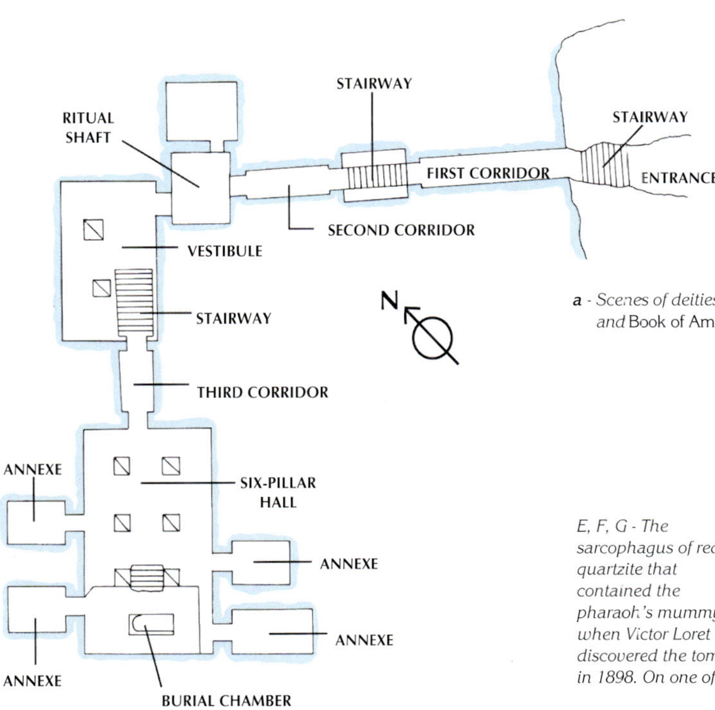

***a** - Scenes of deities and* Book of Amduat

E, F, G - The sarcophagus of red quartzite that contained the pharaoh's mummy when Victor Loret discovered the tomb in 1898. On one of the sides of the sarcophagus two udjat*-eyes with protective functions and Anubis in human shape with a doglike head can be seen at the center.*

TUTANKHAMUN
1333-1324 BC

KV no. **62**

TUTANKHAMUN HEQAIUNUSHEMA

NEBKHEPRURE

In November 1922 Howard Carter discovered the intact tomb of a practically unknown pharaoh whose name, Tutankhamun, pretty soon became so famous that it obscured those of the other pharaohs. Carter, who worked on behalf of Lord Carnarvon, a wealthy British landowner who had obtained from the Antiquities Service the concession to dig in the Valley of the Kings formerly granted to Theodore Davis, was digging from 1917 in the area between the tomb of Ramesses II and that of Ramesses IV. After years of research as unfruitful as it was expensive, Lord Carnarvon was about to give up the concession, as Davis had already, done declaring the valley an exhausted site from the archaeological point of view, when on November 4, 1922 a workman uncovered a stone step, the first of a flight descending into the mountain. Carter, perhaps guessing he was at the threshold of the much expected discovery, covered the find and sent Carnarvon a telegram to England informing him of the event and asking him to come over immediately. On November 24 work was briskly resumed, the steps were freed of debris and Carter and Carnarvon found themselves facing a first walled door followed by a second inner door: both carried the necropolis seals and the long sought name, Tutankhamun. On November 26, 1922 Carter, Carnarvon, his daughter Lady Evelyn and Callender, the engineer who had been engaged to assist with the work a short time before, succeeded at last in digging a little hole in the second door and observing the tomb's interior and the treasures it contained.

It was the first, and to this day the only royal tomb in the history of Egyptology to be found practically untouched, even though, in ancient times, it had been the object of no less than two attempts at robbery, luckily without serious consequences. The emptying of Tutankhamun's tomb lasted several years and made possible the recovery of about 3,500 articles, confirming that the matter at hand was the most exceptional archaeological discovery ever made in Egypt. The tomb presents a plan simple and typical of the Eighteenth Dynasty's tombs: at the bottom of the stairs, a short corridor ends inside a rectangular vestibule with a small annexe. The vestibule leads to the burial chamber on whose eastern wall opens a second annexe, called by Carter "the Treasury". The burial chamber, in the middle of which the large red quartzite sarcophagus occupies the place of honor, is the only room of the whole tomb decorated with paintings. Inside the quartzite sarcophagus, on whose corners four protecting deities are carved (Isis, Nephthys, Selkis and Neith), there is a wooden anthropoid coffin, covered with gold leaf, the first of three anthropoid coffins originally enclosing the mummy of the king, who, even though in poor condition as the result of a clumsy autopsy, rests in his tomb to this day. The decoration is rather simple, and the paintings, well preserved, show signs of Amarnan influence: the young king, son of Amenophis IV / Akhenaten, the heretical pharaoh who introduced the cult of Aten, the only solar god, was brought up and lived until he mounted the throne at the court in Akhetaten (Amarna), the new capital founded by his father.

The scenes represented describe the funerary procession with Tutankhamun's sarcophagus carried by the court's dignitaries and the ceremony of the mouth opening performed by Ay, his successor, both scenes being quite uncommon in a royal tomb. The other paintings represent Tutankhamun with his *ka* welcomed by Nut in front of Osiris (north wall), and again the young king, with Anubis and Isis following in his footsteps, in the presence of Hathor (south wall) and in the act of sailing in his boat for the Afterlife world (east wall): the texts painted on the walls are taken from the *Book of Amduat*, from which some of the wall paintings also draw inspiration.

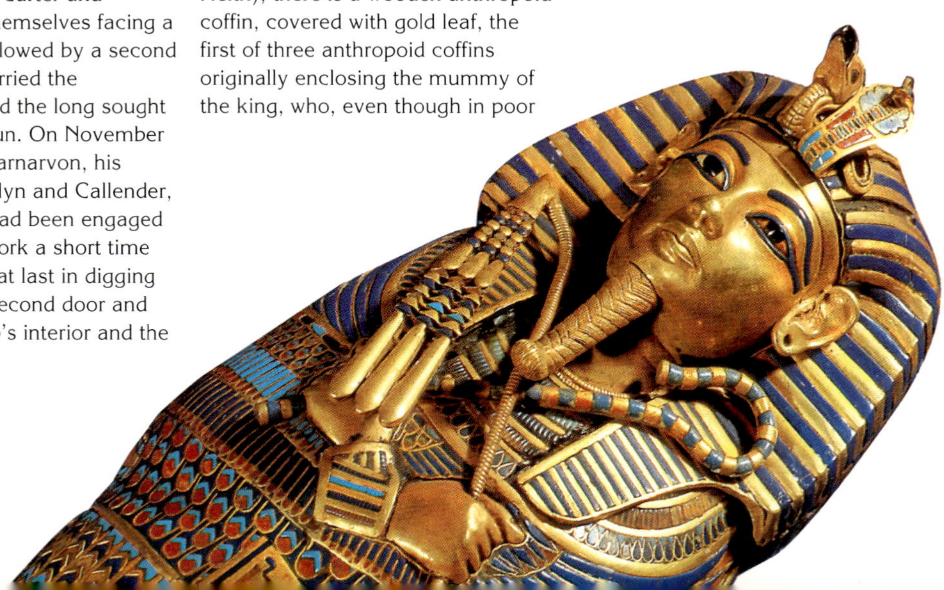

34 This miniature model is a small-scale but extremely accurate reproduction of the second coffin. Found with three other identical ones inside the canopic shrine made of calcite, it contained the viscera of the king (his intestines, to be precise) and had been placed under the protection of Qebhsenuef, one of the four sons of Horus. (Cairo Museum)

35 right The famous gold mask weighing ten kilos that rested directly on the the pharaoh's mummy inside the third coffin. The pharaoh wears the classic nemes *headdress striped with transversal bands of glass paste imitating lapis lazuli, and is adorned with a wide collar composed of streaks of semi-precious stones and colored glasses, while the eyes are of quartz and obsidian. (Cairo Museum)*

35 left The second coffin, also referred to as the intermediate coffin, of gilded laminated wood with inlayings of polychrome glass pastes. The coffin cover was attached by ten silver strips kept in place by as many silver nails. (Cairo Museum)

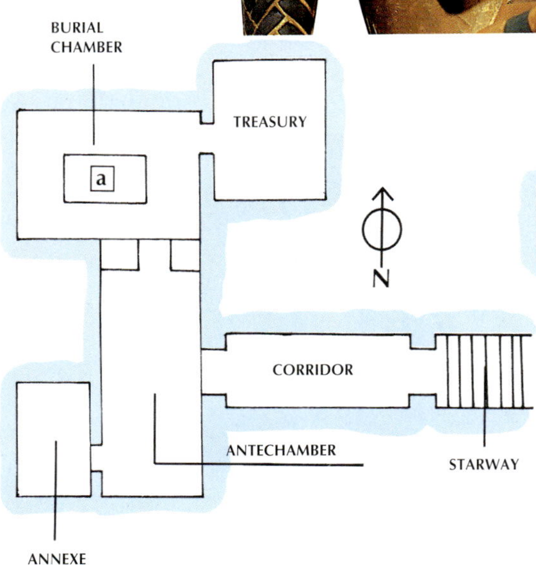

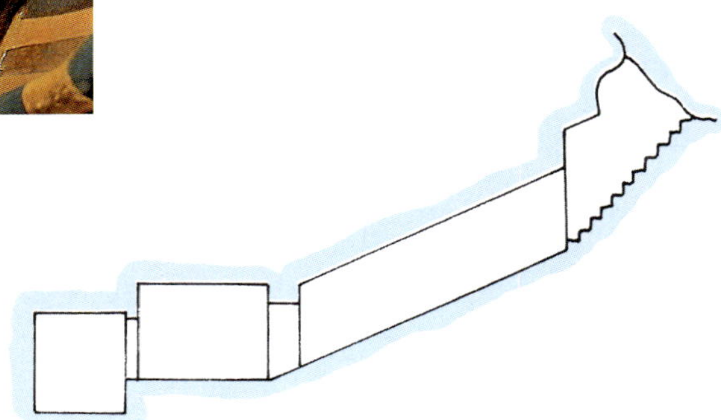

a - *Funerary procession, "Opening of the Mouth", scenes with deities and* Book of Amduat

A - The three ritual beds of gilded wood were decorated with the effigies of three deities: Isis Mehet, lion-headed, Meheret Weret, cow-headed with lyre-shaped horns framing a solar disc (in the photo), and Ammit, a creature made up of a hippopotamus head and a crocodile's body. (Cairo Museum)

B - This small wooden naos *covered with a gold lamina mounted on a sledge was found in the antechamber and was probably meant to contain a little statue of the king, removed during the episodes of partial plundering of the tomb in antiquity. The walls of the* naos *are decorated with splendid scenes of hunting and of daily life. (Cairo Museum)*

C - The so-called "ecclesiastic throne" of ebony with gold inlayings, semi-precious stones and polychrome glass pastes was found in the annexe. In the texts painted on the back panel, whose upper part is decorated with an Amarnan type solar disc, the pharaoh is quoted both with his original name of Tutankhaten and with the later and better known one of Tutankhamun. (Cairo Museum)

D - Tutankhamun's royal throne is, after the mortuary mask, the best known object found in the tomb. The throne of engraved wood is covered with sheet gold and adorned with semi-precious stones and polychrome glass pastes. Its back panel is decorated with a beautiful scene strongly influenced by the Amarna style, in which the royal spouse Ankhesenamun can be seen standing in front the pharaoh while she puts her hand on his shoulder: a solar disc, a reminder of the Aten cult, spreads its rays on the royal couple. (Cairo Museum)

C

D

E

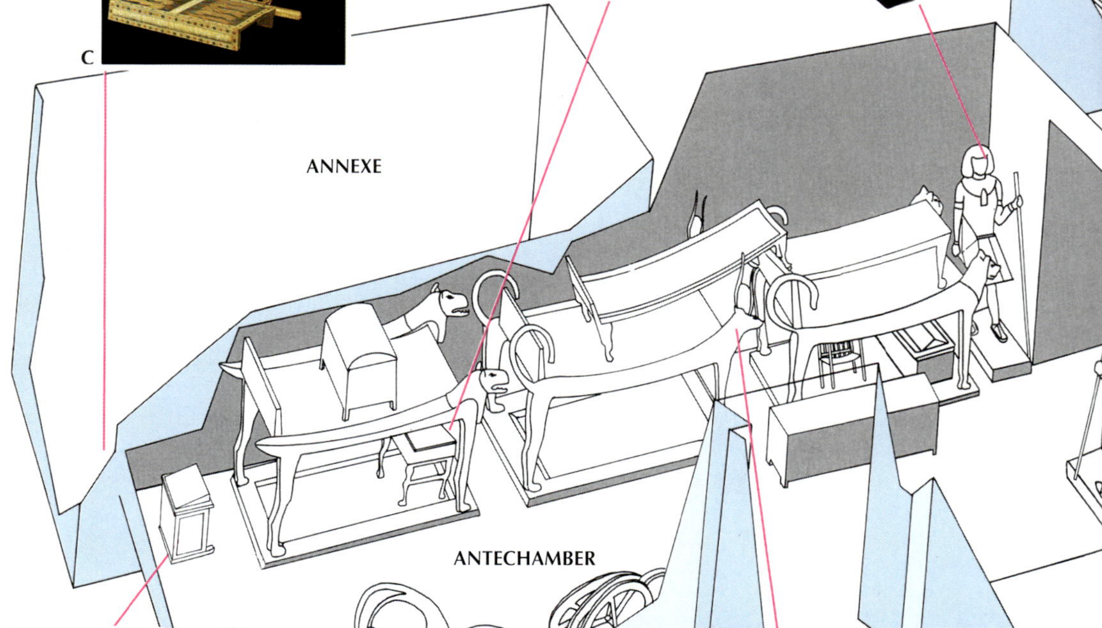

B

A

E - One of the two wooden and painted sentry-statues posted in the antechamber to the sides of the walled door that led into the burial chamber: these life-sized statues were a figuration of the royal ka. *(Cairo Museum)*

F - The third coffin, made of solid gold.

G - The burial chamber as it appears today with the large red quartzite sarcophagus containing inside the first wooden coffin and the king's mummy. On the background wall Tutankhamun is shown with his ka *facing Osiris and the ceremony of the "Opening of the mouth" celebrated by his successor Ay. (Cairo Museum)*

H - The gilded wood canopic shrine.

I - In the antechamber in front of the shrine of the canopic chest was found a statue of Anubis, originally covered with a linen cloth, on a little chapel of gilded wood mounted on a palanquin so that it might be carried on arms during the funeral procession. (Cairo Museum)

F

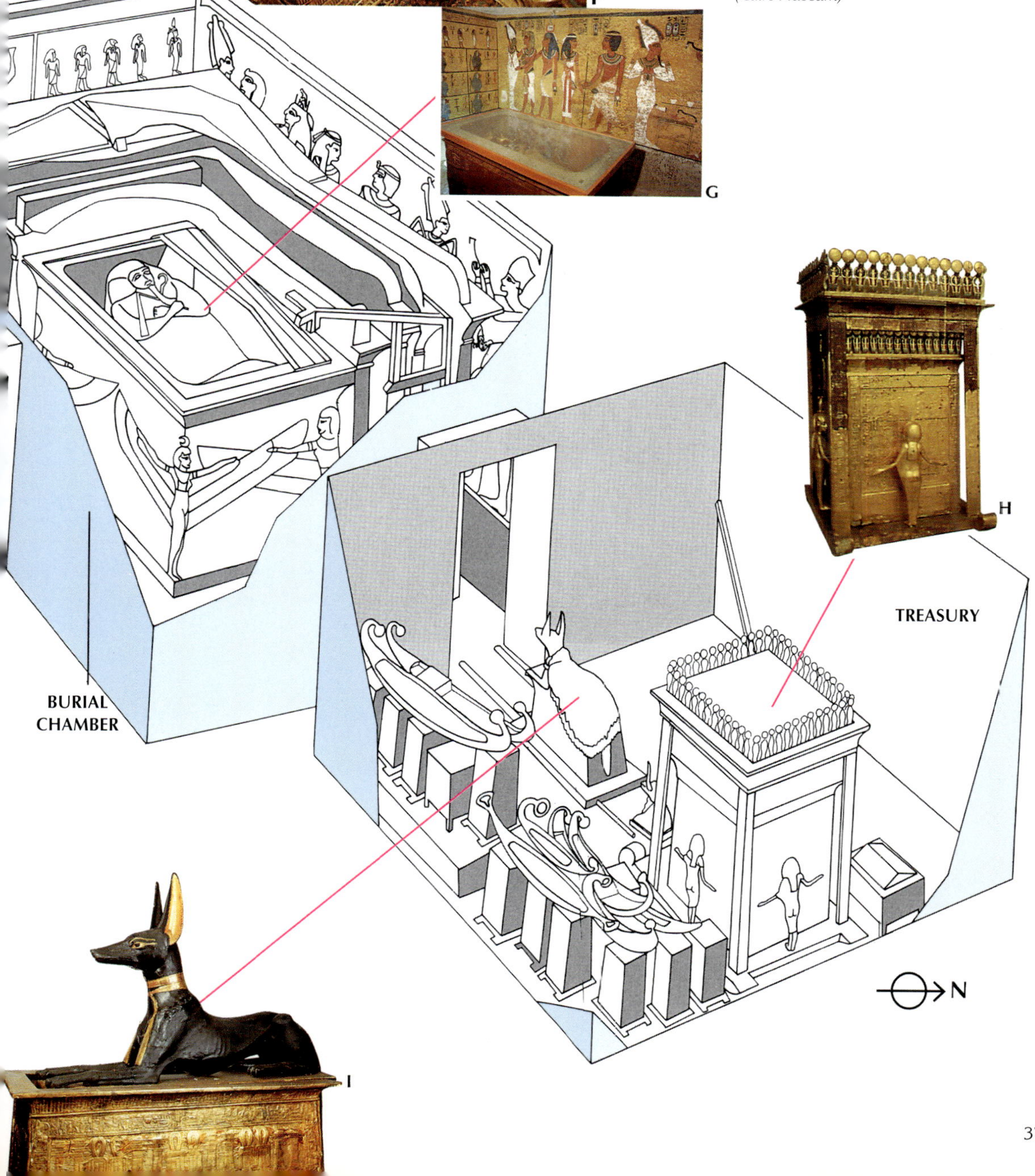

G

H

I

38 left and top right
Tutankhamun, originally called Tutankhaten, was the son of Amenophis IV/ Akhenaten, the heretic pharaoh who enforced the worship of Aten, the sole solar god, moving the state's capital from Thebes to Amarna. Tutankhamun, a name meaning "the living image of Amun", mounted the throne in 1333 BC assuming the praenomen of Nebkheprure and in year 2 of the reign changed his name from Tutankhaten to Tutankhamun: he died in year 9 or perhaps 10 of his reign at the age of about seventeen in circumstances that haven't yet been elucidated. Before the discovery of his tomb, Tutankhamun was a practically unknown pharaoh. (Cairo Museum)

38 bottom right
The large sarcophagus of red quartzite, inside which were the three anthropoid coffins, is still in the tomb today. It was adorned on the corners with the images of four protecting deities with spread out wings: Nephthys (in the photograph), Isis, Selkis and Neith.

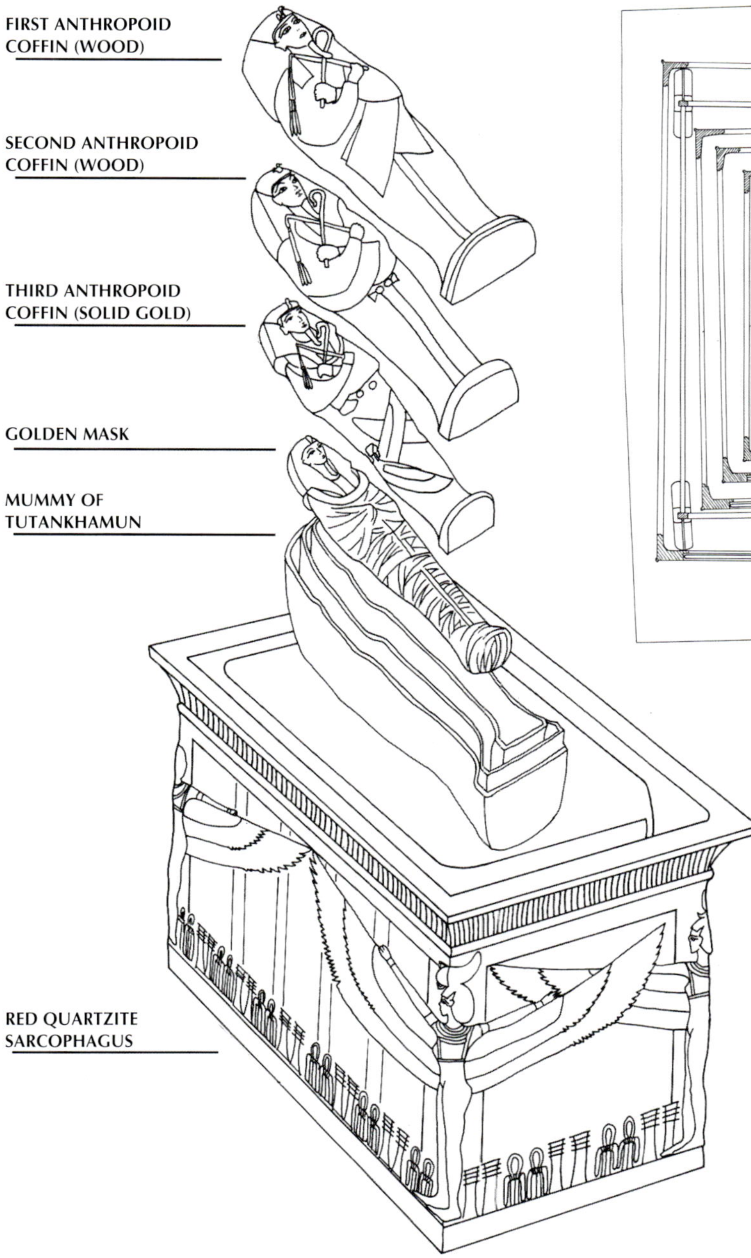

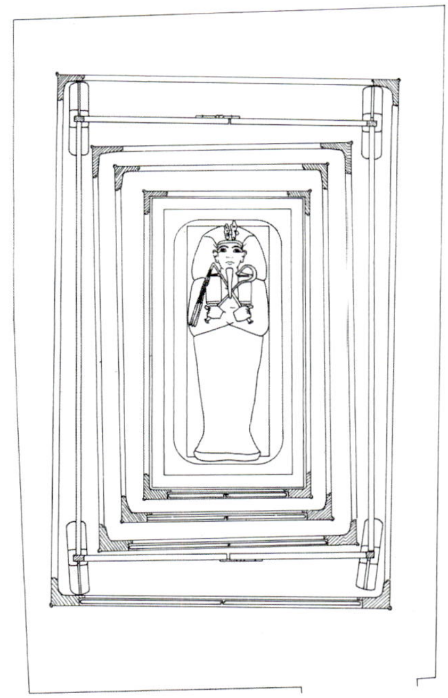

39 top right Vertical plan of Tutankhamun's coffins and shrines.

39 bottom The third solid gold coffin weighing about 110.4 kilos, contained the royal mummy. In all three anthropoid coffins, the king is represented in an identical way, with the nemes-headdress, the ceremonial beard and folding his arms as his hands grasp the insignia of the royal power: the heqa-sceptre in the left and the nekhakha-flail in the right. From the king's forehead a snake and a vulture stand out, emblems of Wadjet and Nekhbet, the two tutelary deities of Lower and Upper Egypt. (Cairo Museum)

40 top Extremely refined scenes of hunting and of the sovereign's daily life inspired by the amarnian style, decorate the walls of this little naos about fifty centimeters high found in the annexe. Tutankhamun is shown together with the royal spouse Ankhesenamun hunting. In the lower scene, the king sitting on a high-backed chair shoots with a bow at the birds rising in flight from a thicket of papyri, while his wife holds out an arrow to him. (Cairo Museum)

40 bottom left Gilded wood statuette of Sokar, a funeral divinity in the form of a falcon whose role was to protect the dead. This statuette was one of a group of thirty-two found in the "Treasury", most of them depicting gods and goddesses. (Cairo Museum)

40 bottom right Detail of the third solid gold coffin on which the goddess Isis is shown with her wings spread out in a protective attitude, as she appears to be embracing the mummy's feet. (Cairo Museum)

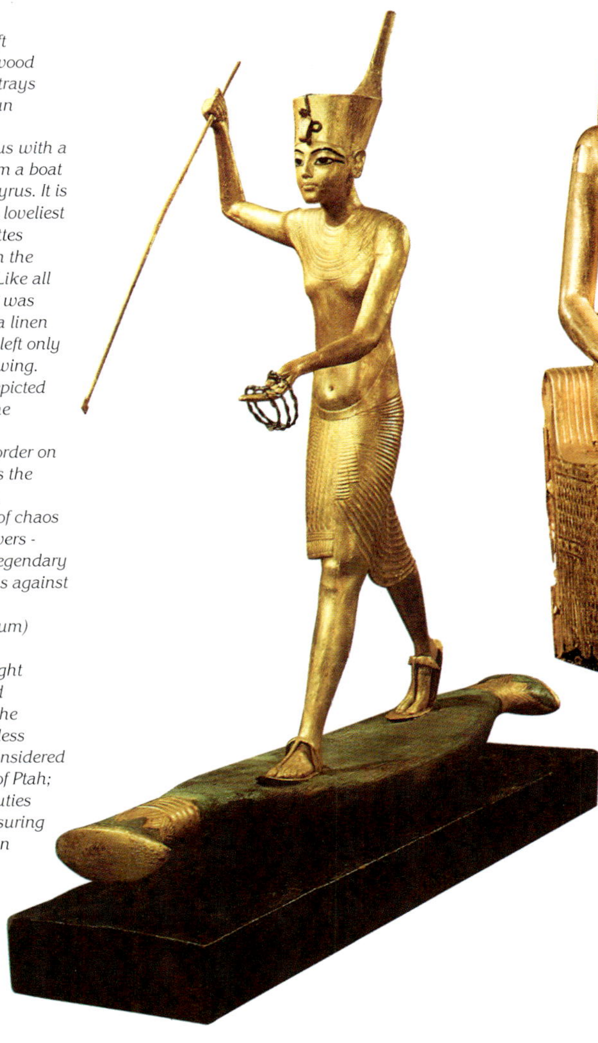

41 top left Golden fan decorated with a hunting scene: the pharaoh on his chariot, to which are attached two fiery horses "strong as bulls" - so goes the text -, is hunting ostriches. Two servants carry on their shoulders birds already shot down. (Cairo Museum)

41 top right Short dagger with gold blade and a haft decorated with gold granulations and glass paste stripes and mounted semi-precious stones, reproducing floral motifs. On the sheath there are relief representetions of oryxes, of a bovine, of a bull attcked by a dog and of a leopard. (Cairo Museum)

41 bottom left This gilded wood statuette portrays Tutankhamun hunting hippopotamus with a harpoon, from a boat made of papyrus. It is certainly the loveliest of the statuettes discovered in the "Treasury". Like all the others, it was wrapped in a linen cloth which left only the face showing. The scene depicted - in which the pharaoh, protector of order on Earth, spears the hippotamus, incarnation of chaos and evil powers - evokes the legendary fight of Horus against Seth. (Cairo Museum)

41 bottom right Gilded wood statuette of the lioness-goddess Sekhmet, considered the consort of Ptah; her many duties included ensuring the protection of the king. (Cairo Museum)

42 top Pectoral in the shape of a hawk with its wings spread out and the head surmounted by a solar disc and with claws holding two shenu-*signs, powerful protecting amulets related to the concept of eternity, surmounted by two* ankh-*signs, amulets related to the vital breath and to life. (Cairo Museum)*

42 centre Pectoral in the shape of a winged scarab with a solar disc resting on a neb-*sign. The scarab, an animal emerging from the earth as he pushes forward a little sand ball, evokes for the ancient Egyptians the image of the sun god Re on his morning rising. The combination solar disc* (Re) ⊙*, scarab* (khepru) *and* neb-*sign allows the reading of the pharaoh's name Nebkheprure. (Cairo Museum)*

42 bottom left Ear-rings of gold and polychrome glass pastes with pendants. (Cairo Museum)

42 bottom right Alabaster cover of one of the four canopic jars modelled after the image of the king: the king's viscera were enclosed in four miniaturized coffins placed in four cells of a box, made of alabaster as well, each one of them closed with such covers. (Cairo Museum)

43 top left Gold ointments holder in the shape of a double cartouche surmounted by solar discs and plumes with representations of the king, sitting on a large neb-*sign, in the different moments of his life: young man, adult, deceased and after his rebirth. (Cairo Museum)*

43 centre Pectoral in the shape of a chapel with a vulture inside with its wings spread out, holding two shenu*-signs in his claws, found by Carter in the annexe. The analysis of the hieroglyphs in the cartouches, oriented in an unusual way, has led to the opinion that this jewel had originally been prepared for pharaoh Akhenaten and later reused by his son Tutankhamun. (Cairo Museum)*

43 bottom left This object of outstanding beauty was found by Carter among the debris that partially obstructed the descending corridor; it shows a lotus flower carved in wood and painted, surmounted by the head of the pharaoh as a boy, evoking the rebirth of Tutankhamun, like the sun being born from the lotus. (Cairo Museum)

43 bottom right Unusual calcite model of a boat with double oryx-headed prow resting on a little alabaster basin. At the centre of the boat a baldachin can be noted, supported by four double-capital pillars in the shape of lotus and papyrus, under which a kind of sarcophagus is found. At the stern a woman with clear signs of nanism of the acondroplastic type steers the boat, while at the prow a naked young woman holds in her hand a lotus flower. The meaning of this object is not yet quite clear. (Cairo Museum)

AY
1324-1321 BC

WV no. 23

AY ITNETER

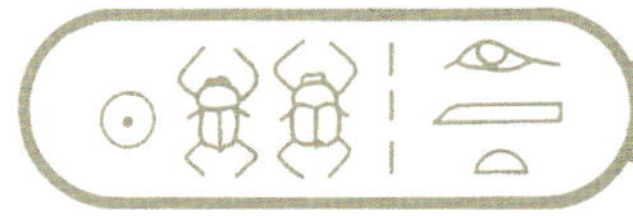

KHEPERKHEPERURE

A - Passages from the Book of Amduat *in vertical columns of text: in the upper register there are a first boat with standards carrying the emblem of the falcon, the goddess Nephthys and the boat of the Ennead.*

B - The entrance door to the little room annexed to the burial chamber: above the architrave four deities can be noticed (perhaps they are Horus' Four Sons) facing a table of offerings.

E

F

G

D

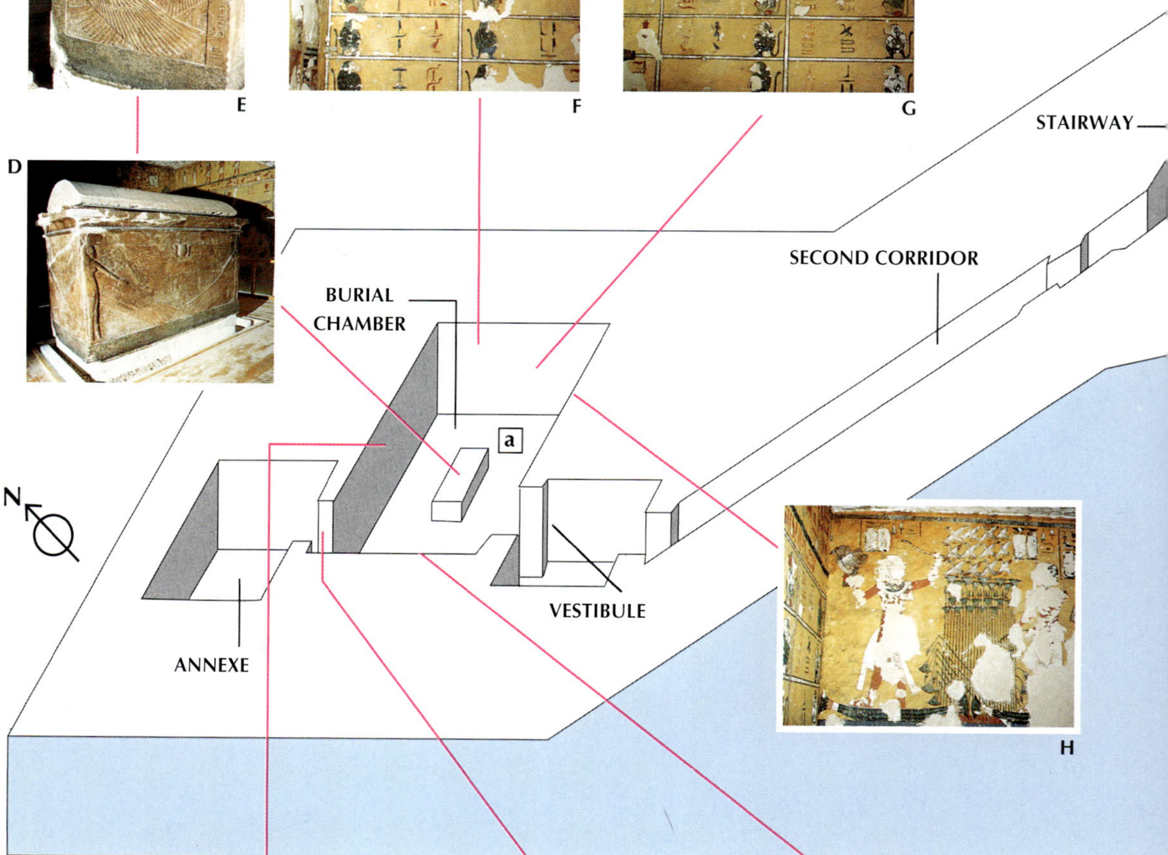

H

C

B

A

C - Ay and his ka *are in the presence of (from left to right) Osiris and the goddesses Hathor-Imentit, Nut officiating the* njnj *rite and Hathor.*

D, E - Sarcophagus of red quartzite analogous in shape and decorative program to that of Tutankhamun. At the corners the four tutelary deities are carved in relief: Isis, Nephthys, Selkis and Neith.

The tomb of Ay, Tutankhamun's successor who mounted the throne at the death of the young king whose authoritative counsellor and vizier he had been, is found in the Western Valley, whose entrance is located near the new rest-house of the Valley of the Kings. From here starts the track which, after passing close to Amenophis III's tomb (WV no. 22), follows the bottom of this wonderful and wild valley and after about two kilometers reaches Ay's tomb, which was recently opened to the public for the first time.
The tomb, which not only had already been looted in antiquity, but appears to have been the object of deliberate mutilations, was discovered in 1816 by Belzoni, who carved his name and the date on the rock at the side of the entrance: inside, he recovered only fragments of a sarcophagus while the king's mummy was never found.
The tomb of Ay has a linear architectural structure that curiously seems to anticipate the typical plans of the Twentieth Dynasty's tombs, and includes a descending stairway leading to the first corridor, a second flight of steps giving access to the second corridor which, in its turn, ends a vestibule followed by the burial chamber from which opens a small annexe.
Even though quite damaged, the tomb is interesting both because it presents a beautiful bird hunting scene in the marshes, an absolutely unique depiction for a royal tomb, and because it continues a decorative design already found in the tomb of Tutankhamun featuring for example, the representation of the twelve monkeys symbolizing the night hours on one of the burial chamber's walls, from which originates the name of *Bab el-Gurud* "tomb of the baboons" given to the tomb by the natives and then, by extension, to the Western Valley: *Wadi el-Gurud*, namely "Valley of the Monkeys".

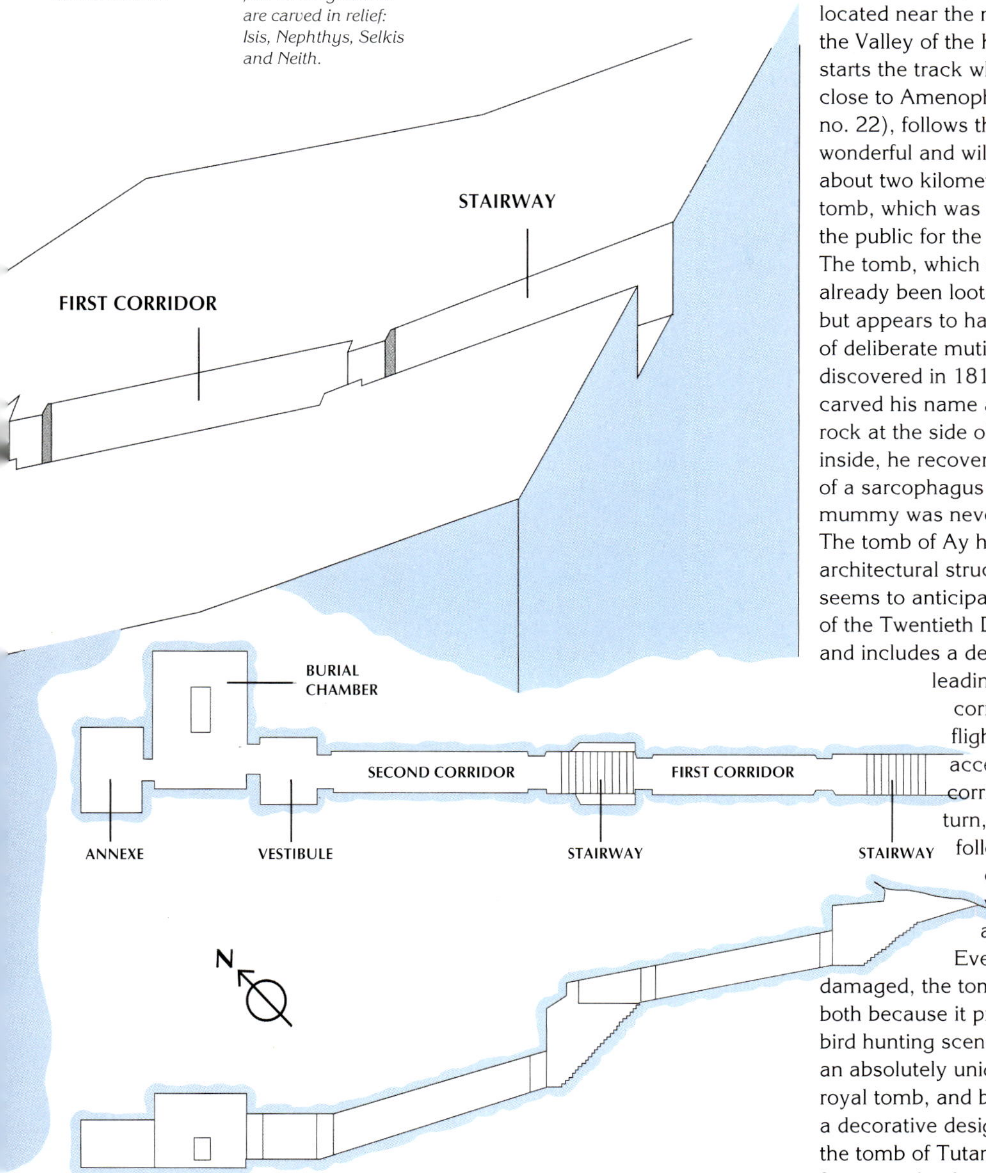

F, G - Passages from the Book of Amduat, *analogous to those of Tutankhamun's tomb, are transcribed and illustrated in the wall paintings of the sarcophagus hall. In the photograph, Khepri's solar boat preceeded by five deities can be seen and in the lower registers twelve baboon deities corresponding to the twelve hours of the night.*

a *- Birds hunting scenes,* Book of Amduat *and scenes with gods*

H - The pharaoh (the image is irremediably lost) on a papyrus boat is hunting birds in the marshes using a hunting club.

HOREMHEB

1321-1295 BC

KV no. 57

HOREMHEB MERIAMUN

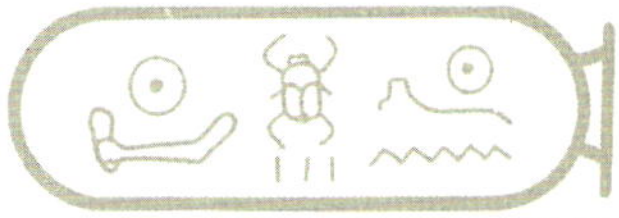

DJESERKHEPERURE SETEPENRE

The tomb of Horemheb, Ay's successor, was discovered in February 1908 by the young British egyptologist Edward Ayrton, who worked under orders from Theodore Davis, a wealthy American passionately fond of archaeology. As a result of its position the large tomb was full of debris, carried by the waters of the rushing torrents developing within a very short time during the rare but torrential rains falling from to time in the region of Thebes. Horemheb had served at Amenophis IV's court, continued under Tutankhamun and finally under Ay's orders, before himself ascending the throne. Horemheb, royal scribe and general of the armies, on whom had also been bestowed the title of *erpa* (prince) and who, at the time of the Ramessids was regarded as Amenophis III's direct descendant, from a religious point of view is essentially an energetic restorer of Amun's old worship, and from a political point view a restructurer of the provincial administration and of the military cadres.

A great builder (he enlarged the Karnak temple, erecting the Second, Ninth and Tenth pylons and dismantling the Aten temples in order to reuse their materials), he ordered the construction of a new tomb in the Valley of the Kings, as requested by tradition, even though he already had a high dignitary's tomb of his own at Saqqara.

With Horemheb, the Eighteenth Dynasty traditionally ends even though, from the point of view of dynastic right, it had already ended several decades before with Tutankhamun, the last real royal blood pharaoh of the Amenophis stock. However, one may also say that with Horemheb, a transition pharaoh, begins the Nineteenth Dynasty and his tomb seems to reflect this major change.

The architectural structure of the Horemheb tomb presents two stylistic innovations that will characterize the large Nineteenth Dynasty hypogeums: the disappearance of the right angle between the end of the descending corridor and the vestibule preceding the burial chamber, and the introduction of the use of painted bas relief instead of the simple painting in the decorations of the walls.

In addition, for the first time, passages from the *Book of the Gates*, a religious composition (so called with reference to the "gates" that separate the

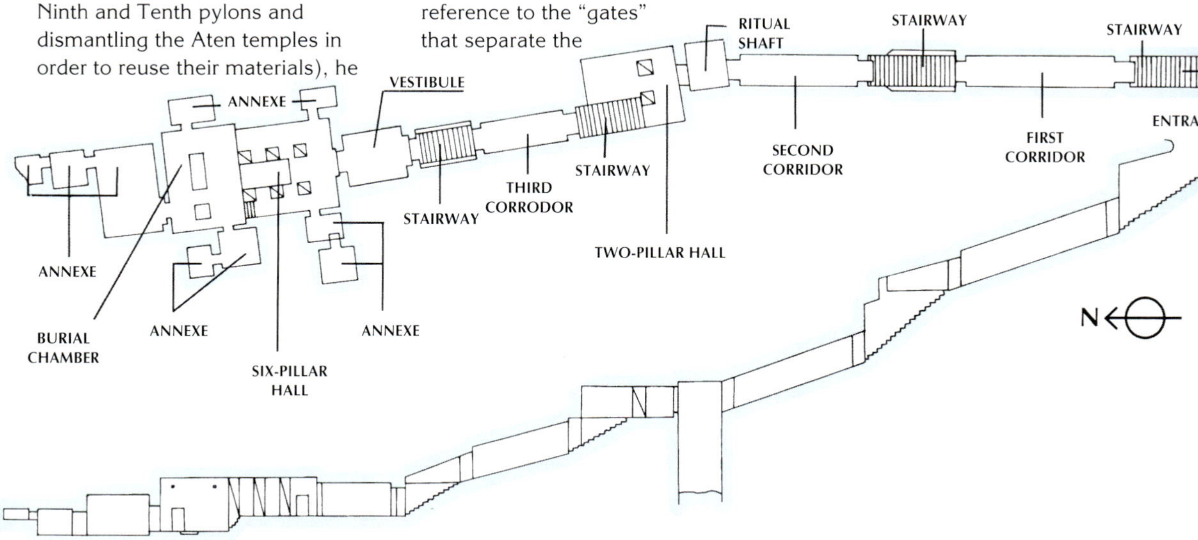

night's twelve hours), appear in the texts transcribed on the walls, an evolution from the *Book of Amduat*. The first descending stairway ends in the first corridor, interrupted by a second stairway, the starting point of a second corridor leading to a room with a shaft on whose walls appear the first paintings showing two groups of deities: Hathor, Isis, Osiris and Horus to the left, and Hathor, Anubis, Osiris and Horus to the right. The tomb continues with a two-pillar hall where the third corridor starts leading to the vestibule, which, in its turn, leads to the burial chamber, supported by six pillars. In the burial chamber, into which open four lateral and one back annexe, a large sarcophagus, still in place, can be observed and, on a wall, a scene recalling the Fifth division of the *Book of the Gates* with the figure of Osiris in whose presence are carried presented nine personages. One of the most interesting aspects of Horemheb's tomb is that many wall decorations were interrupted at different stages of the work, and thus afford an exact idea of the techniques used by Deir el-Medina's artists. At certain points the drawings are just sketched, at others the grids used for calculating the proportions of the illustrations or the corrections of the chief artist can be seen, in others still the sculptor's work begins as he incises the plaster layer in order to obtain the bas relieves which will be later painted... The fact that the tomb was not finished is all the more unusual if we realise that Horemheb had reigned for not less than twenty eight years, a period more than sufficient to complete the decoration of any tomb and we almost have the impression that all of this had been done on purpose, as if to leave a message.

46 top Several parts of Horemheb's tomb were left unfinished at different stages of the decoration: in this case the painters were spreading the grey-blue background that characterizes this tomb. The motive of the presence of these unfinished parts is obscure, particularly if we take into account that the tombs were being prepared in rather short spaces of time and that Horemheb reigned for about 30 years.

46-47 In this double scene located in the south-eastern corner of the antechamber, Horemheb performs a wine offering to Anubis by holding out to him ritual nu- *vases, while to the right the pharaoh stands between Hathor-Imentit and Harsiesis.*

47 top left
The pharaoh in the presence of Harsiesis, one the forms of the god Horus, "Son of Isis", represented in a hawk-headed human shape with the double crown of Upper and Lower Egypt.

47 top right In the scenes located on the western wall of the antechamber the pharaoh performs a ritual offering to Hathor-Imentit, then finds himself in the presence of Harsiesis and, successively, performs offerings to Isis and finally he faces Anubis.

47 bottom
General view of the antechamber: in the background to the sides of the door, the pharaoh can be seen in front of Hathor-Imentit, to the right, and between Hathor-Imentit and Harsiesis, to the left.

A - Detail of the astronomical ceiling of the six pillars room: in the blue background the yellow five-point stars symbolize the heavenly vault.

B - The texts in vertical columns reproduce passages from the Book of the Gates, *a magic-religious anthology used towards the end of the Eighteenth Dynasty, dealing with the twelve doors, corresponding to the night hours the sun has to cross. In the upper register the First Hour of the* Book of the Gates *is illustrated: ram-headed Re moves forward on his boat in the world of the Afterlife hauled by four genii, while in the lower register the god Atum can be seen facing four men lying down, defined by the text "those who are exhausted" and that may be an embodiment of the four cardinal points (necessary only in the earthly world) followed by the enemies of the light with their hands tied behind their back.*

C - The sarcophagus of Horemheb, in red quarzite and similar in form to that of his predecessors Tutankhamun and Ay, was found open with the lid broken: inside were fragments of bone belonging to several people; it was impossible to identify those of the king.

A

C

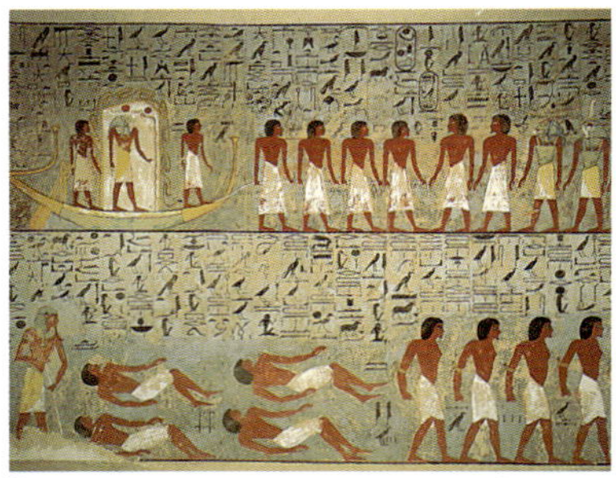

B

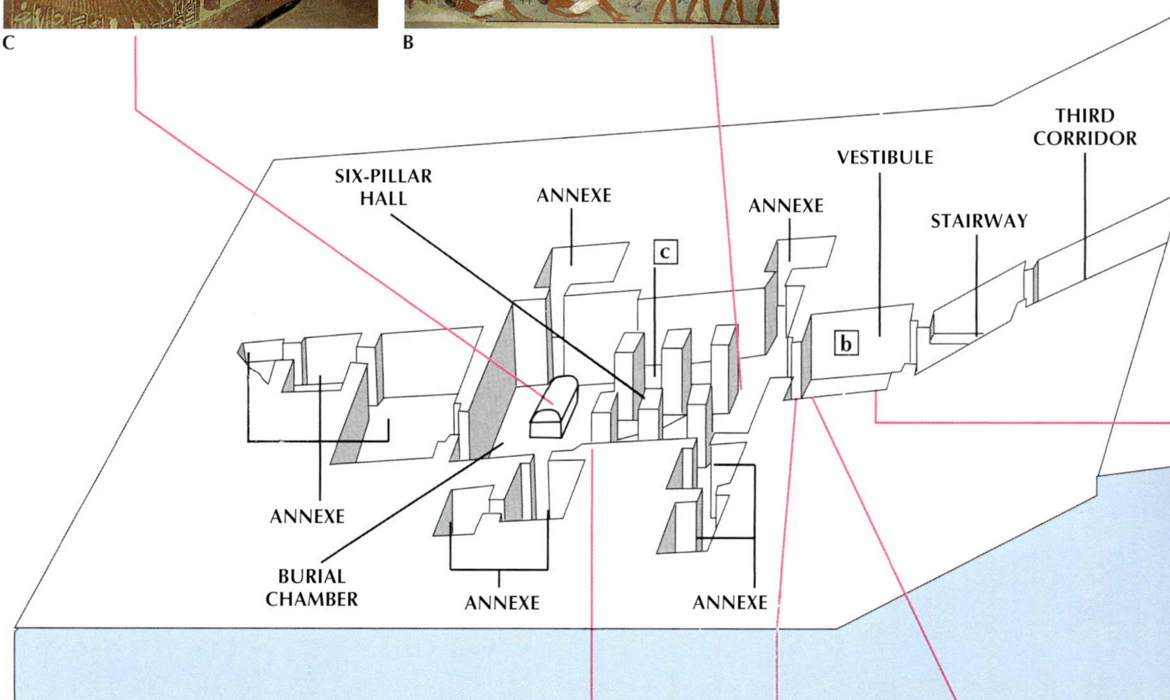

D

E

F

D - A part of the wall remained unfinished and only the red and black signs drawn by the draftsmen and by the correctors can be seen.

E, F - Details of the western wall of the antechamber: the god Harsiesis, hawk-headed with the double crown of Upper and Lower Egypt, and the goddess Isis, here represented in a form analogous to Hathor's with two lyre-shaped horns framing a solar disc on her head.

G - Horemheb is taken by the hand by Anubis who displays the classic attributes of the deities: the long was-*sceptre in his right hand and the* ankh-*cross in his left.*

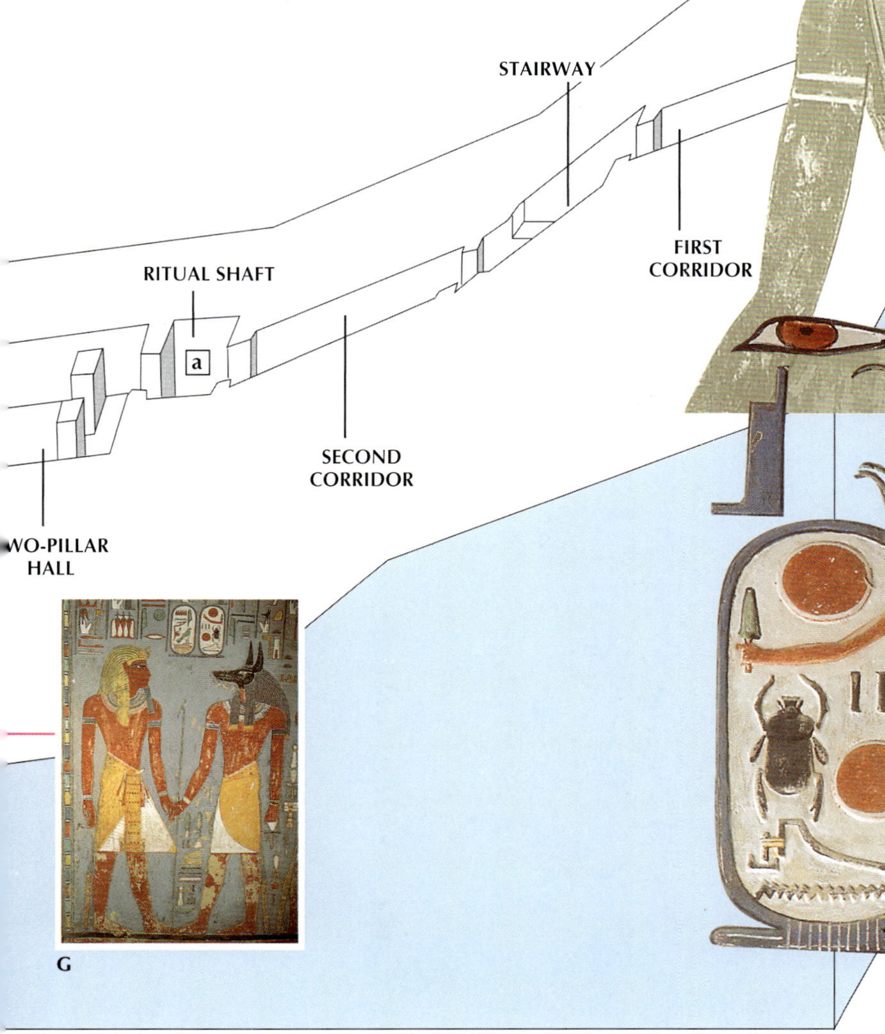

G

a - *Scenes with gods*
b - *Scenes with gods*
c - Book of the Gates

49 bottom
The pharaoh's cartouches transcribing his praenomen and his name: Djeserkheperure - Horemheb. The praenomen was taken up by the pharaoh at the moment of his crowning since it designated the king of Upper and Lower Egypt.

TOMBS OF THE NINETEENTH DYNASTY

RAMESSES I
1295-1294 BC

KV no. 16

A - This scene illustrates on a passage of the Book of the Gates *reproduced in the vertical registers above the god Atum as he fights the malevolent snake Apophis.*

B - The boat of Re, shown with a ram's head inside a tabernacle surrounded by the mehen-*snake, moves ahead in the Afterlife, hauled by four deities.*

C - Iun-Mutef dressed in the characteristic leopard skin hide facing the pharaoh and diverse deities (not seen in the photograph). The Iun-mutef, a name meaning "(Horus) support of his mother", is a form of Horus related to ancient priestly functions and was at the same time a priestly charge.

D - In the little niche opening on the south-western wall of the burial chamber, a scene related to the Third Hour of the Book of the Gates *shows Osiris between a ram-headed deity and the snake goddess Nesert.*

B

A

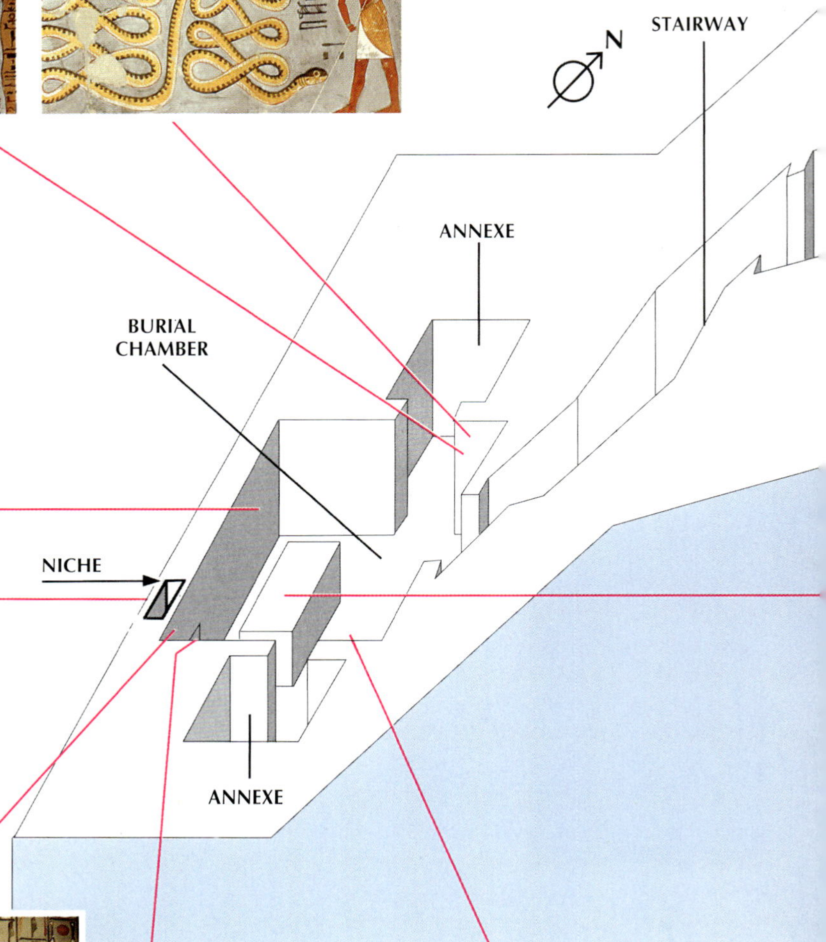

C

D

E

F

G

E - The pharaoh kneeling among the Souls of the towns of Pe and of Nekhen, (ancient towns of the Delta and of Upper Egypt) embodying the souls of the deceased kings, performs the henu-*gesture, that expresses prayer and joy.*

F - The Fourth Hour of the Book of the Gates*: above, nine mummies in black anthropoid coffins, that will be revived by the passage of the solar boat. At the centre, in a ditch, a snake with multiple coils is related to the eternity of time. Beside him are two groups of six goddesses embodying night's twelve hours.*

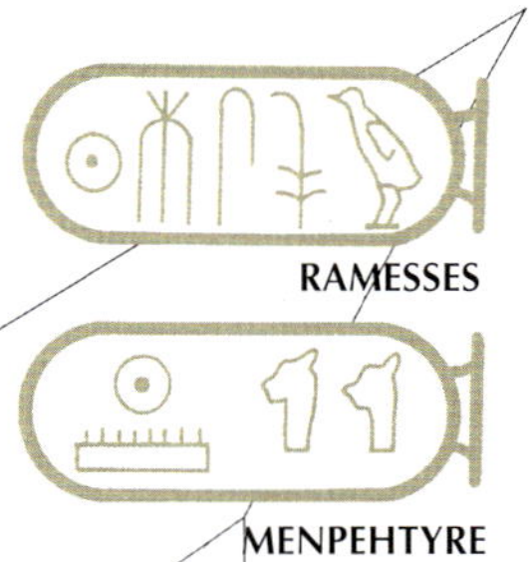

The tomb of Ramesses I, located in a small lateral valley perpendicular to the main wadi and discovered by Belzoni in October 1817, is of small dimensions but exhibits wall paintings of excellent workmanship strongly reminiscent, from the stylistic point of view, of those in the tomb of his predecessor, Horemheb. Ramesses I (a Greek transliteration of the Egyptian name *Ra-mes-su*), regarded as the first king of the Nineteenth Dynasty and founder of the glorious lineage of the Ramessids, was a soldier and was chosen by Horemheb as a successor to the throne of Egypt. The short duration of his reign (less than two years) forced the Deir el-Medina craftsmen to complete his eternal dwelling quickly and accounts for the unusually small dimensions of the corridor and the burial chamber.

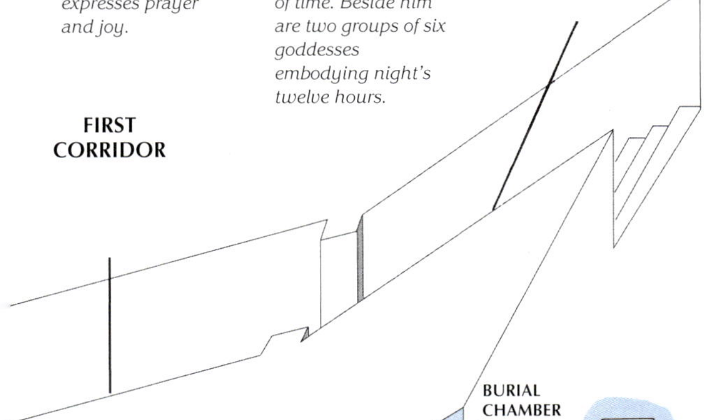

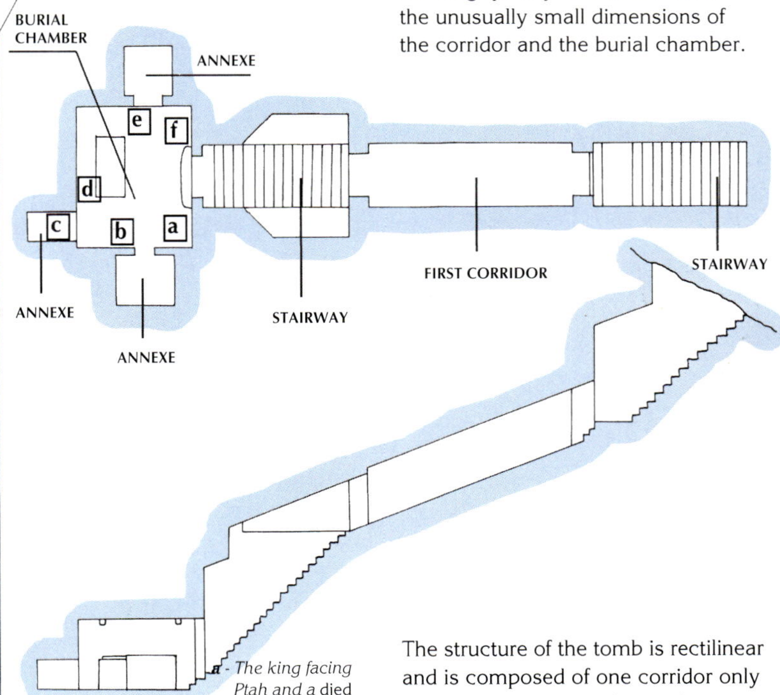

H

a - The king facing Ptah and a djed pillar
b - The king facing Harsiesis and Anubis; Book of the Gates
c - Niche featuring a ram-headed deity with Osiris in a chapel and the snake Nesert; Book of the Gates
d - The king with the souls of Pe and Nekhen, facing Aton and other deities
e - Book of the Gates
f - The king offering wine to Nefertum

G - Ramesses I is welcomed in the Afterlife by Anubis shown, as usual, in a jackal-headed humane shape and Harsiesis.

H - Overall view of the sepulchal chamber with, at the centre, the great sarcophagus of red quartzite. This hall is the only decorated part of the whole tomb, whose small dimensions and the simplicity of its decorative program are explained by the very short reign of Ramesses I, that lasted about 16 months. Since his tomb is 29 meters long, it is inferred that the workmen proceeded in the preparation of the tomb at the incredible speed of 1.80 meters per month.

The structure of the tomb is rectilinear and is composed of one corridor only located between two descending sets of steps, the second of which opens directly into the burial chamber, taken up for the most part by a large granite sarcophagus and flanked by two small annexes. As in the tomb of Horemheb, here too the scenes and the texts painted on the walls are related to the *Book of the Gates*. In the burial chamber, Ramesses presenting offerings to Atum-Re-Khepri, is led into the presence of Osiris by Horus, Atum and Neith, while in the lateral annexe to the left there is a representation of the souls of Pe and Nekhen.

SETHOS I
KV no. 17

Menmaatre
1294-1279 BC

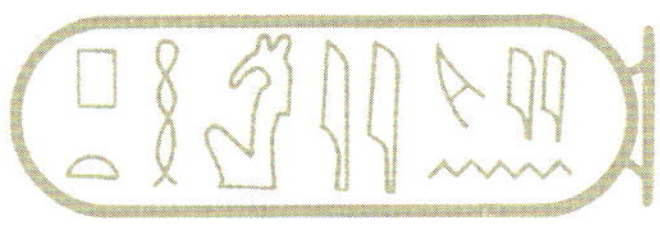

SETHOS MERIENPTAH

MENMAATRE

The tomb of Sethos I, Ramesses II's father, was discovered in October 1817 by the Italian Giovanni Battista Belzoni, a few days after that of Ramesses I. Even though this tomb, still called by the British "Belzoni's tomb" was closed to the public in 1991 owing to a real danger of collapse in the burial chamber and in an annexe room, its importance is such that we cannot omit its description.
Located in a small lateral wadi in the Valley of the Kings, the tomb of Sethos I is more than 120 meters long and is decorated with colorful paintings and with highly refined bas reliefs. The structure of the tomb is particularly complex: after a first descending flight of steps, a corridor leads to a second hall followed by another corridor, into which opens a square hall with a ritual shaft.

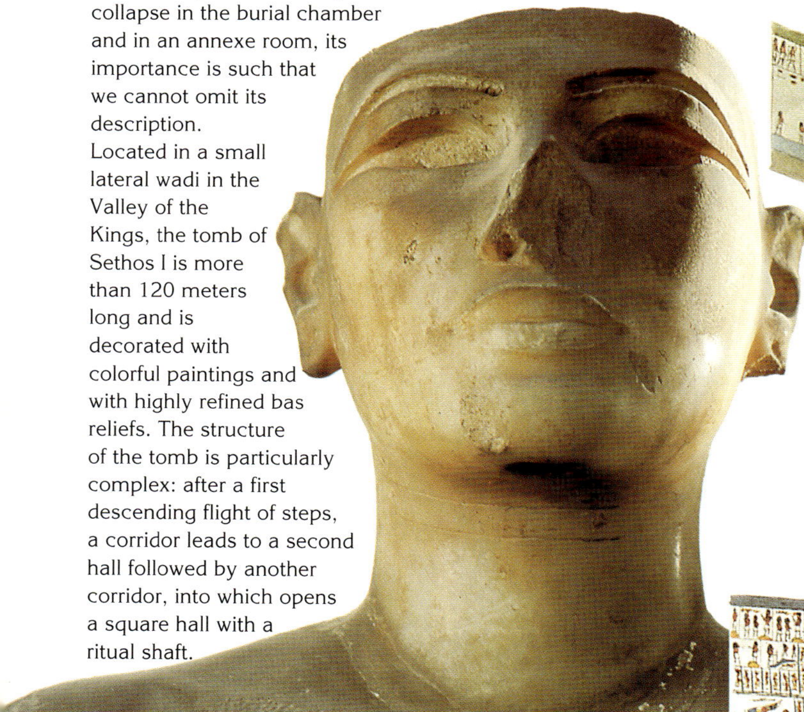

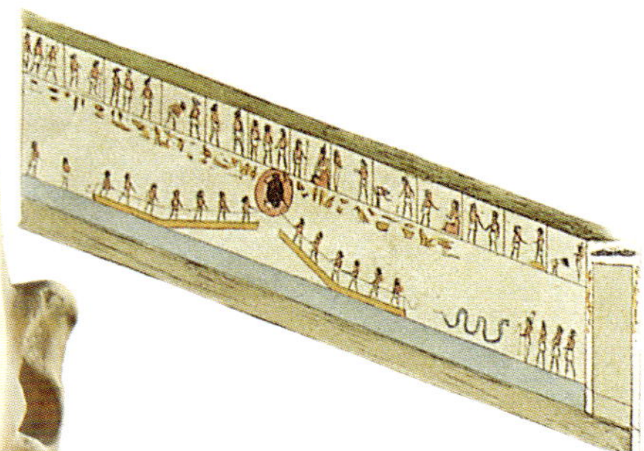

Beyond the shaft, there is a room eight meters wide, with four pillars, to which another hall of similar dimensions is attached: from the four-pillar hall a second lateral stairway descends, leading to a series of three corridors and thence to a large six-pillar hall with two small lateral chapels. From the six-pillar hall one finally reaches the burial chamber, whose astronomical ceiling symbolizes the vault of heaven and the main constellations. In this hall Belzoni found a beautiful empty alabaster sarcophagus, a little less than three meters long, on which were engraved passages from the *Book of the Gates*, a text of magical character which relates the journey of Osiris' solar boat through the night's twelve hours, sailing the underworld river crowded with demons, and lists the magic formulas required to cross the twelve gates guarded by genii and snakes.
This sarcophagus, made of alabaster so thin that it is translucent (it is just five centimeters thick), was brought to England and, subsequently, purchased by a British collector, Sir John Soane, who put it in his London museum-house, in Lincoln's Inn Field, where it still is today.
The mummy of Sethos I was found only in 1881 in the Deir el-Bahri cache.

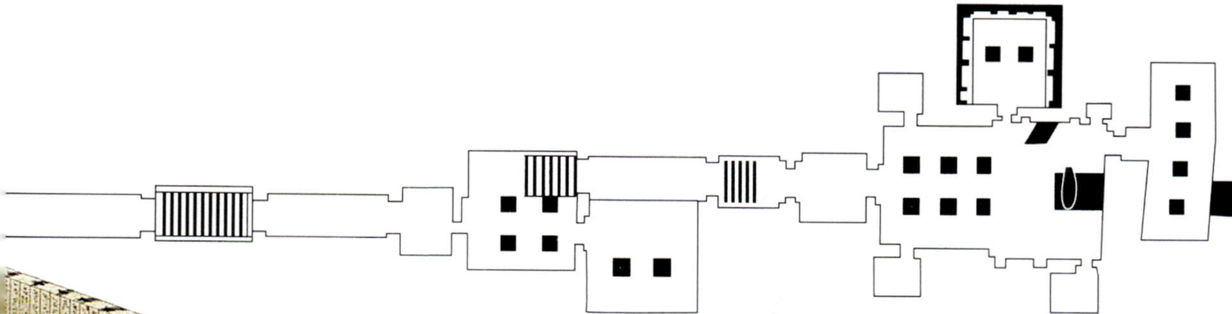

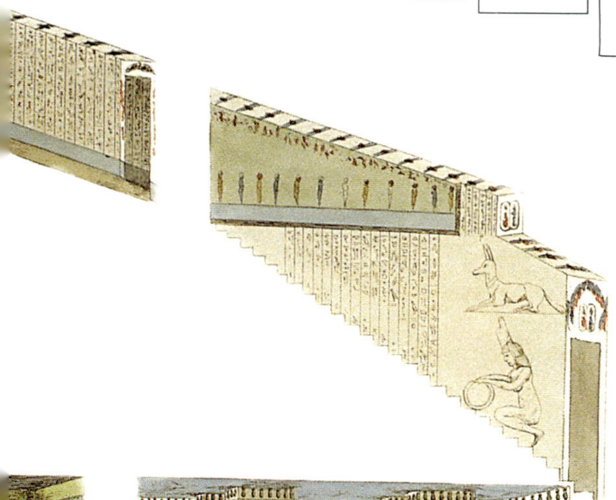

52-53 Sethos's tomb was discovered by Belzoni on October 18, 1817, a few days after that of Ramesses I. Belzoni, assisted by Alessandro Ricci of Siena, worked for several months in this tomb, carrying out a survey of its wall paintings and drawing this section. Since at the time the hieroglyphic writing still was a big mystery, Belzoni attributed the tomb to a hypothetical pharaoh called Psammuthis and only later, in 1828, was it identified by Champollion as that of Sethos I.

52 Alabaster statue of Sethos I son of Ramesses I, the founder of the Nineteenth Dynasty. His reign was characterized by a high artistic level and by a great building fervour, of which the hypostyle hall of Amun's temple at Karnak, the Osireion and the great temple of Abydos and the mortuary temple of Qurna are splendid witnesses. (Cairo Museum)

F

D

A - In the hall of four pillars the pharaoh is shown in the presence of diverse deities; in the photograph, Sethos is in the presence of Ptah, the demiurge god of the Memphis theology.

B - The hall of two pillars annexed to the four-pillar hall was called by Belzoni "Hall of Drawings", since it has remained unfinished. On the walls the Ninth, the Tenth and the Eleventh Hour of the Book of Amduat *are represented. In the photogaph Sethos can be seen in the presence of Re-Harakhty.*

E

C

G

H

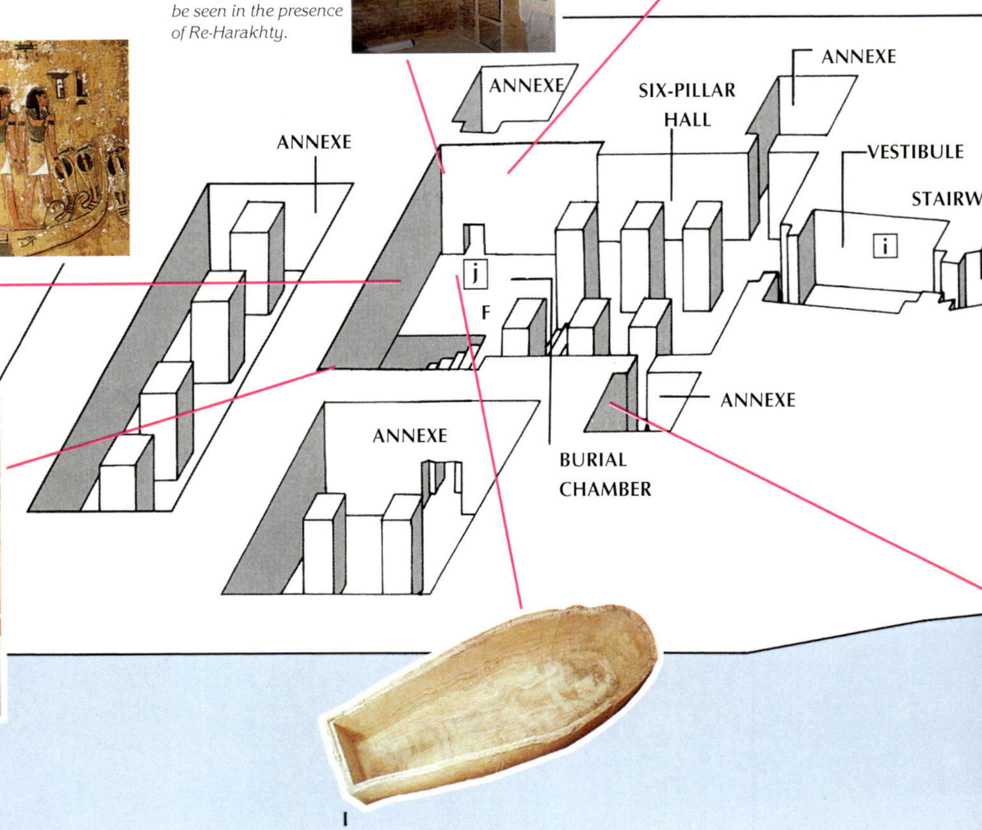

C - On this wall the Second and the Third Hour of the Book of Amduat *are illustrated, with the related accompanying texts, describing the journey in the waters of the Afterlife of the solar deity on his boat escorted by a procession of other boats.*

D - Tympanum of the western wall of the burial chamber: Nephthys, at the centre of the wall among the royal cartouches, spreads her wings out in a protecting sign.

E - South-western corner of the burial chamber with representations of Second and Third Hour of the Book of Amduat.

F - Detail of the northern heaven in the famous astronomical ceiling of the burial chamber in which are illustrated the main constellations and the heavenly stars. This is the only part of the tomb, apart from the "Hall of Drawings", in which the decorations are not in bas-relief.

G - The boat of Re, shown with a ram's head, accomplishes its night journey in the Underworld.

H - In this little niche Anubis performs the ceremony of the "Opening of the Mouth" in front of Osiris, represented between two Imiut-*symbols, fetishes of Anubis consisting of an animal's hide attached to a pole placed in a vessel.*

I - The beautiful alabaster sarcophagus on which were delicately engraved passages from the Book of the Gates, *was found by Belzoni in the burial chamber and was brought to London. After having been rejected by the British Museum, the piece was bought by Sir John Soane, a private collector, and placed in his museum house, where it is still found.*

J - On this side of the tomb the Fourth Hour of the Book of the Gates *is described: the genii feed the fire of the "burning wells" into which the damned shall be thrown.*

K - On the south-eastern side of the "Hall of Four Pillars" we find the representation of the Fifth Hour of the Book of the Gates*: a huge snake crosses several figures dressed in white tunics and identifiable as resuscitated mummies.*

L - The boat of Re during its night sail.

a - Litanies of Re
b - *Personalities drawn from the* Litanies of Re, Book of Amduat, *deities*
c - Book of Amduat
d - *Scenes with deities*
e - *Book of the Gates and chapel of Osiris*
f - Book of Amduat
g - *Opening of the mouth*
h - *Opening of the mouth*
i - *Scenes wih deities*
j - Book of the Gates, Book of Amduat *and astronomic ceiling*

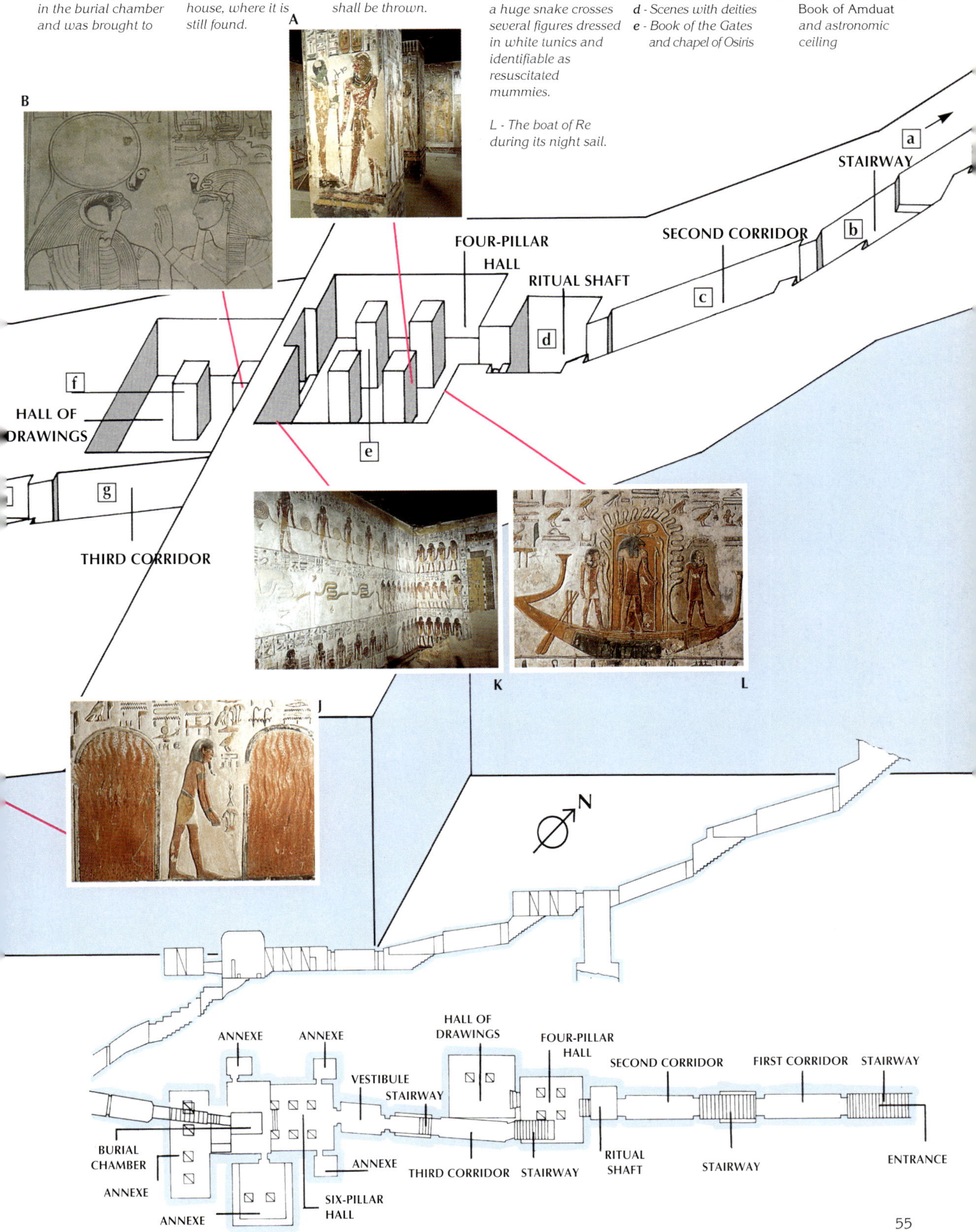

56 top left Detail of the "Hall of Four Pillars": Sethos is in the presence of Atum.

56 top right Royal cartouches bearing the name and praenomen of the pharaoh: Sethos Menmaatre.

56-57 Texts and illustrations relating to the Second Hour of the Book of Amduat *decorate the south wall of the burial chamber.*

57 top Four deities pull the barque in which Re journeyed by night.

57 bottom Detail from a bas-relief in the "Hall of Four Pillars", showing Iun-mutef wearing a leopard skin.

MERNEPTAH

1213-1204 BC

KV no.8

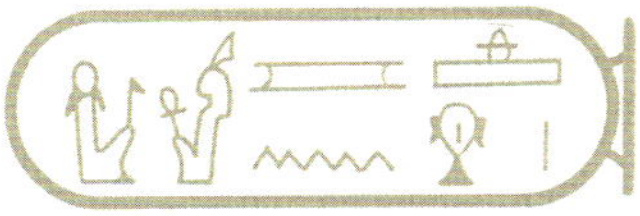

The tomb of Merneptah, son of Ramesses II and of queen Isis-Nofret, known since antiquity, is located in a little lateral valley opening to the right side of the main wadi at a short distance from his father's huge tomb (KV no. 7), located a little beyond the access gate to the Valley. The tomb, which was full of debris at the beginning of the century, was excavated in 1903 by Carter, who found only scanty elements of the funerary furniture. This hypogeum, interesting from the architectural and decorative points of view, marks a distinct evolution as compared with that of Ramesses II and constitutes a transition point between the complex tombs of the Nineteenth Dynasty and the Twentieth Dynasty's rectilinear ones, with a decrease in the number of the lateral rooms and a sharp increase in the height of the corridors and the rooms. The plan is simple and includes three corridors, the central with a stairway, leading to the shaft hall set in front of a hall with a two-pillar annexe in which the cover of the outer sarcophagus is located. A forth corridor leads to a vestibule and, thence, to the large rectangular-shaped

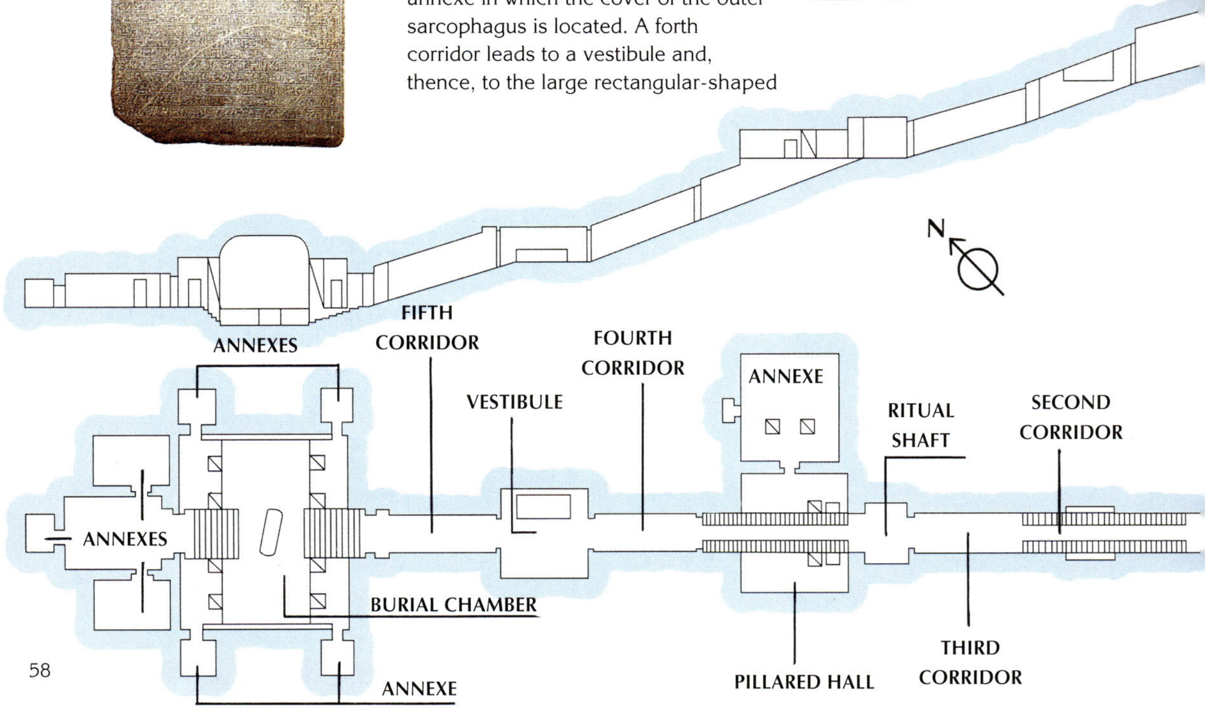

burial chamber, whose astronomical vaulted ceiling is supported by eight pillars arranged in two lines: at the center there is the impressive cover of the king's inner ornamental scroll-shaped sarcophagus of pink granite, resting above a wide cavity in the floor, symbolizing the so-called "pit of gestation", which precedes the regeneration of the deceased king and his subsequent transfiguration. With regard to the decorative plan in the first corridor, the first scene portrays the king in the presence of Re-Harakhty. Then there are passages from the *Litanies of Re*, continuing also in the second corridor, where also appear texts and images related to the *Book of Amduat*, which constitute the subject of the third corridor. As we penetrate deeper inside the tomb, into the four-pillar hall, we notice that the texts of *Amduat* are replaced by the *Book of the Gates*, and in the vestibule, by the *Book of the Dead*, while on the walls of the burial chamber there are passages from the *Book of the Gates*. In its first part, the tomb of Merneptah reminds us of the impressive tomb of his father, with regard to both its architectural and the decorative aspects, while it considerably differs from it in the second part where a marked tendency to simplification appears. Likewise, with regard to the decoration, we notice at the beginning bas reliefs of elegant workmanship and subsequently the use of less sophisticated but much faster techniques. The tomb probably reflects a certain anxiety on the part of Merneptah to complete quickly the work and the consciousness that his reign would be inevitably short.

Merneptah mounted the throne at the death of Ramesses II, late in life, as he was probably about seventy years old, and ordered the immediate start of the works, both for the construction of his tomb and of his temple of the millions of years, trying to speed up their completion to the utmost.

Moreover, during his reign which lasted only about ten years, he was unable to take care exclusively of his personal monuments since he also had to face an attack on the part of the Libyans against Egypt and to subdue an uprising of the Nubians, reaffirming Egypt's sovereignty and the strength of pharaonic power and continuing in this way his father's political line. With his death the last great pharaoh of the Ramessid family, already drawing to a close, disappeared. After the brief reigns of his successors (the obscure Amenemesses of unknown origin, his son Sethos II, Merneptah-Siptah and finally queen Twosret) who overall ruled about 15 years, the glorious Nineteenth Dynasty left the stage of the history of Egypt.

58 top Merneptah, thirteenth son of Ramesses II, whose enormous tomb (not open to the public) is situated only a few meters away from that of his son and successor. During his ten-year reign he organized numerous military campaigns in the Orient, in Nubia and against the Libyans. The famous "Israel stela", one of the texts carved to commerate the victory against the Libyans in the fifth year of his reign, contains the only known reference to the Hebrews in Egyptian literature. Merneptah was the last great pharaoh of the Nineteenth Dynasty.

58 bottom The "Israel stela" discovered in the memorial temple of Merneptah, in Western Thebes.

58-59 Deities pull the barque of Re, during his passage through the night.

59 top General view of the corridors of the tomb of Merneptah, leading to the chamber containing the sarcophagus (the straight layout of the corridor is typical of the Twentieth Dynasty tombs): the tomb's total length is 115 meters. Above the architrave of the door is a dual representation of the king as Osiris welcomed by Anubis and Harsiesis.

A - Prominent between the two goddesses Isis and Nephthys, above the architrave at the entrance to the tomb, is a disc representing the sun, painted - unusually - in yellow. At its centre are the kheper-*scarab and the deity with the head of a ram, pratically identical to the one on the corridor wall at the beginning of the* Litanies of Re.

B - The tomb of Merneptah is characterised by a series of straight corridors leading to the burial chamber. This architectonic style is typical of the Twentieth Dynasty.

On the walls of the corridors can be found passages from different compositions like the Litanies of Re, *the* Book of Amduat, *the* Book of the Gates *and the* Book of the Dead.

D

C

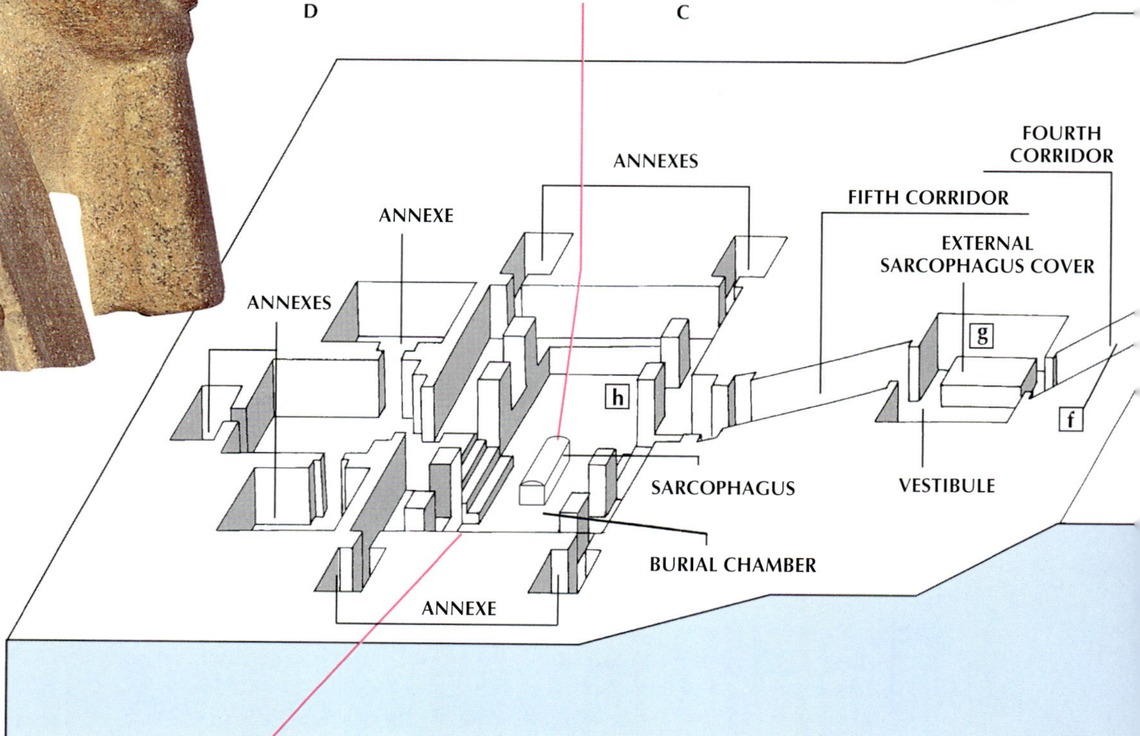

E

D - At the centre of the large burial chamber is the magnificent sarcophagus of the king. Made from granite, it is carved in the shape of a cartouche on which the dead king is depicted with his arms crossed, holding the heqa-*sceptre and* nekhakha-*flail. Surrounding this image is the uroboros, the serpent which encircles the world in relation to the cycles and infinity of time, and which expresses the concept of resurrection and rebirth.*

E - Portrayed on the upper part of the south-west wall of the burial chamber is a scene related to the Book of the Caverns and the nighttime passage of the solar star. Above a creature with a ram's head and outstretched wings, there are two pairs of arms which push the sun, depicted as a young boy, a black scarab with the head of a ram and a red disc surmounting the royal cartouche. At the sides and bottom the deceased pharaoh and his ba *worship this triple representation of the solar deity.*

C - The sun god Re, depicted with a ram's head, wanders through the night on his boat pulled by divinities.

B

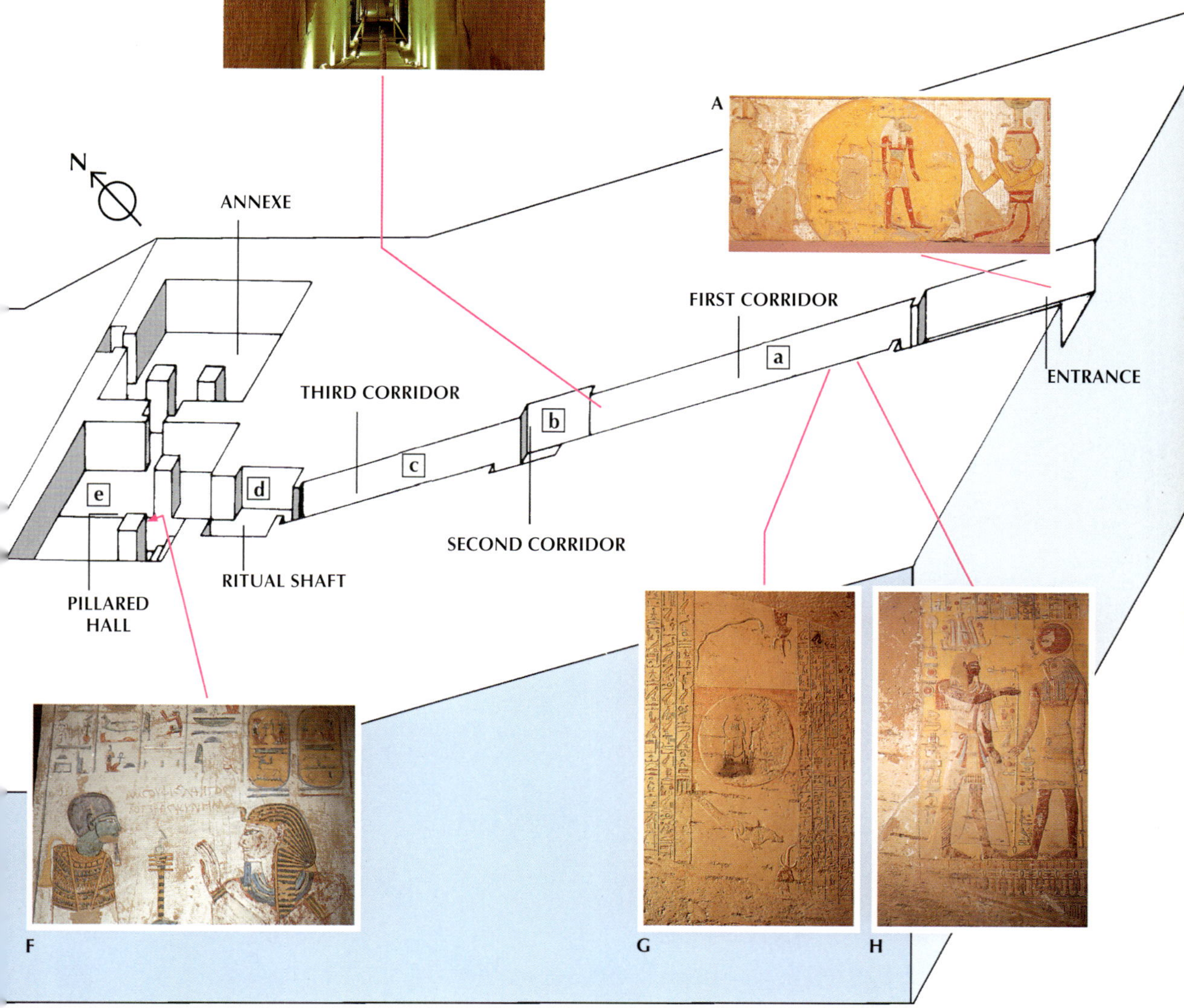

F - Wearing a nemes *headdress on his head, the pharaoh stands before the Memphite god, Ptah. It is interesting to note the numerous graffiti between the two figures, left by visitors who came here in far-off Greek and Roman times.*

G - The Litanies of Re *are inscribed along the first corridor. The initial part of the text can be seen in this photo: at its centre is the disc of the sun, encompassing a* kheper-scarab *symbolizing the morning sun, and a deity with a ram's head, which personifies the sun at night. The disc puts to flight the enemies all around it (crocodile, serpent and a monstrous creature with horns).*

H - This multicolored bas-relief marks the start of the decorative scenes along the first corridor of the tomb. Here the king, wearing an ornate atef-crown, is in the presence of Re-Horakhtis.

a - Litanies of Re
b - *Figures taken from the* Litanies of Re, Book of Amduat, *divinities*
c - Book of Amduat
d - *Scenes portraying deities*
e - Book of the Gates and shrine of Osiris
f - *Opening of the mouth*
g - *Pharaoh with deities and* Book of the Dead
h - Book of the Gates *and astronomical ceiling*

TOMBS OF THE TWENTIETH DYNASTY

RAMESSES III
1186 - 1154 BC

KV no. 11

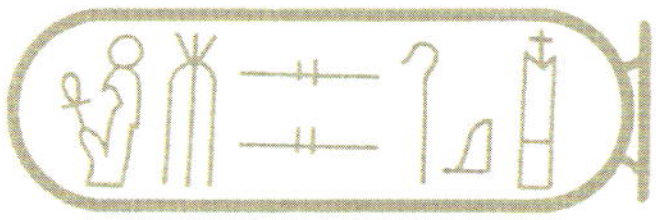

RAMESSES HEQAIUNU

USERMAATRE MERIAMUN

A - Jugs, pots and amphorae are drawn on the walls of this small side room.

B - Representation of the Nile god and of the deities that personified some of the names of Egypt or some cities. Each deity bears a rich offering table and carries on his head the name of the nomos that he represents.

D

C

The tomb of Ramesses III, known since antiquity, was explored for the first time in modern times by the Scottish traveler James Bruce in 1768, during an adventurous journey which took him all the way to Abyssinia. Bruce named this tomb "tomb of the harpists", on account of a marvelous bas relief representing two blind harpists.
The tomb, decorated with beautiful paintings which have preserved their lively colors, is of imposing dimensions, being 125 meters long, with the typical plan of the Nineteenth Dynasty's royal hypogea, even though it presents some peculiarities both in the decorations and in the internal setting. Into the second corridor, on whose walls are transcribed extracts taken from the *Litanies of Re*, open eight small cells, arranged in two groups of four on each side, decorated with a series of scenes quite uncommon and interesting, such as the procession of Egypt's protecting deities, the preparation of food, the funerary furniture and the weapons of the king, the food offerings to the god Hapy, embodiment of the Nile as bearer of plenty, and the famous pair of harpists, who gave their name to the tomb, singing the praises of the ruler in front of Atum, Shu and Onuris.
The representation on the walls of objects and scenes magically assured their eternal existence or accomplishment, at the same time sheltering the deceased from the ravages of ever likelier looting.
At the end of this corridor, a little hall marks a sharp change of

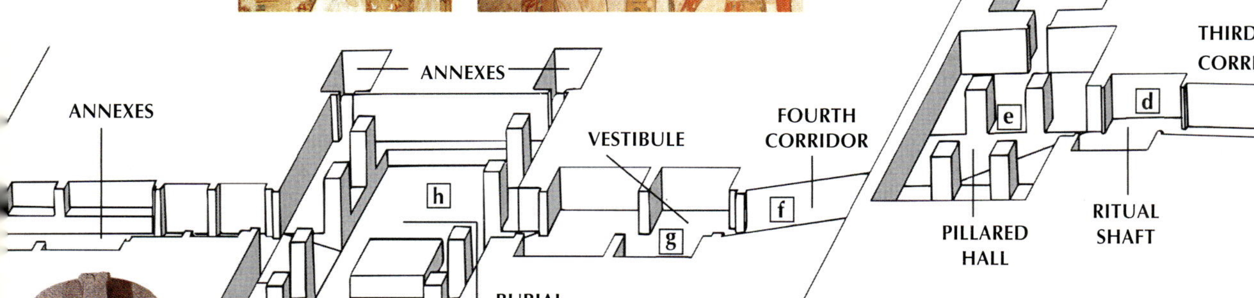

E

F

G

C - The pharaoh with the crown of Lower Egypt offers a candle to the god Atum

D - The Memphite demiurgic god Ptah with his composite sceptre that combines an ankh-*cross, a* was-*sceptre and a* djed-*pillar, and a rare headdress made up of two curved plumes and a solar disc placed upon his habitual blue or black cap.*

E - Belzoni retrieved the lid of the sarcophagus of Ramesses III in 1818. It is conserved at the Fitzwilliam Museum in Cambridge and depicts the pharaoh in relief as Osiris with the atef-*crown flanked by Isis and Nephthys. The sarcophagus is in the Louvre Museum.*

F - The pharaoh, with a short, blue knitted wig called ibes *encircled by a* seched-*diadem with* uraeus, *offers incense.*

G - The pharaoh, wearing a ceremonial headdress called a khepheresh, *offers a torch.*

H - One of the two blind harpists behind the name given to the tomb by Bruce in 1768.

I - View of the hall of the pillars with scenes illustrating the Sixth Hour of the Book of the Gates. In foreground, on the pillar, Ramesses II is making an offer.

direction in the axis of the tomb, owing to the fact that during the excavation, carried out according to the preestablished plan, the workmen came across the nearby tomb KV No. 10 of Amenemesses (a pharaoh who ruled for a short period of time between Merneptah and Sethos II) and had therefore to change the general direction of the tomb: a case quite unusual but not unique, that happened also in the Valley of the Queens during the building of Nefertari's tomb, where a similar change in the axis is noticed, due to the presence of Tuya's tomb. The third corridor, out of its axis but parallel to the first, is decorated with passages from the *Book of the Gates*, in addition to texts from the *Book of Amduat*, and leads to a ritual shaft and, thence, to a four-pillar hall in which, beside chapters Four and Five of the *Book of the Gates*, there is a representation of the known human races and scenes of offering to Re-Harakhty, Khepri and Atum, the three forms of the solar godhead. In the lateral annexe, opening to the right side of this hall, there is a scene in which Ramesses III finds himself facing Osiris who holds out a feather to him, the feather symbolizing the order and justice of Maat. Here ends the part of the tomb open to visitors.
The tomb continues with a fourth corridor leading to a vestibule and, thence, to the eight-pillar burial chamber which sheltered the red quartzite sarcophagus: it was sold to the king of France and is now in the Louvre Museum, while its cover, recovered by Belzoni, was transferred to England and purchased by the Fitzwilliam Museum in Cambridge. The mummy of the king was found in the Deir el-Bahri cache and is now in the Cairo Museum. Ramesses III, the builder of the temple at Medinet Habu, was the last of Egypt's great pharaohs: during his thirty two year reign, he succeeded in defending Egypt's borders against external attacks, such as those originating from the Peoples of the Sea in year 8 or from the Libyans in year 11, but his rule ended at an extremely difficult moment from the economical point of view and one of great political uncertainty: with him an entire world, that had experienced transitory crises but also long periods of great splendour, ends forever.

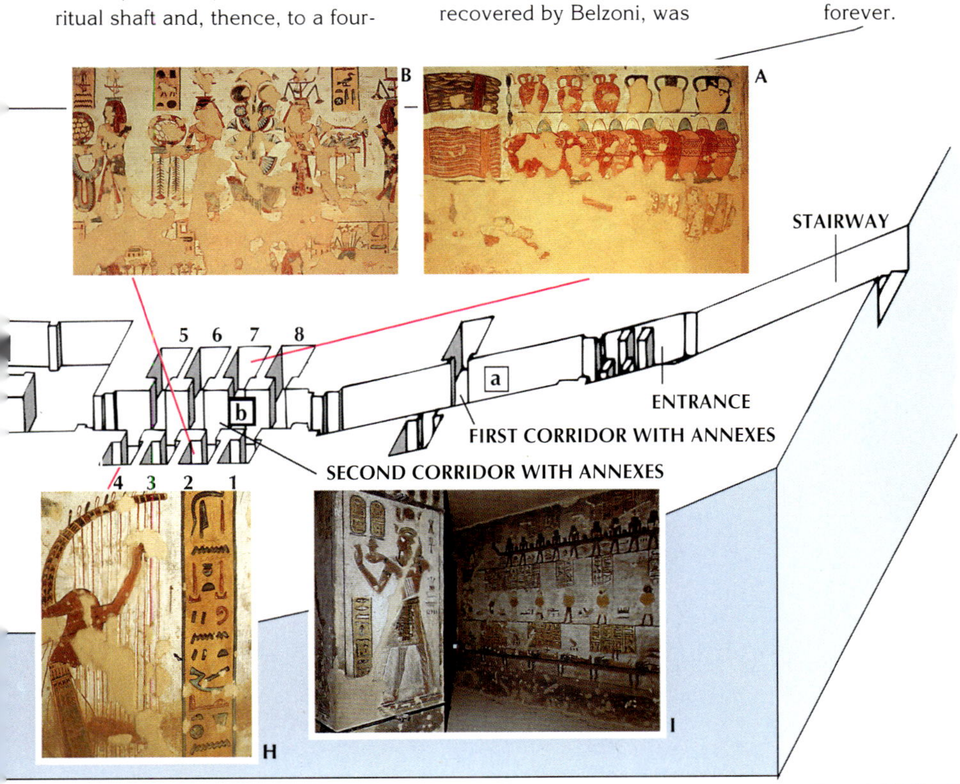

a - Litanies of Re
b - *Personalities drawn from the* Litanies of Re

Left lateral annexes
1 - *The Nile god presenting offerings to deities*
2 - *Procession of the Nile god and of the deities of the nomoi*
3 - *The bull and the heavenly cows*
4 - *Harpists facing the deities*

Right lateral annexes
5 - *Osiris on the throne*
6 - *Fields of Iaru*
7 - *Pitchers, pots and vessels*
8 - *Standards, bows and vessels*

c - Book of Amduat
d - *Divine scenes*
e - *Book of the Gates and chapel of Osiris*
f - *Opening of the mouth*
g - Book of the Dead *and divine scenes*
h - Book of the Gates, *deities, divine scenes and* Book of the Earth

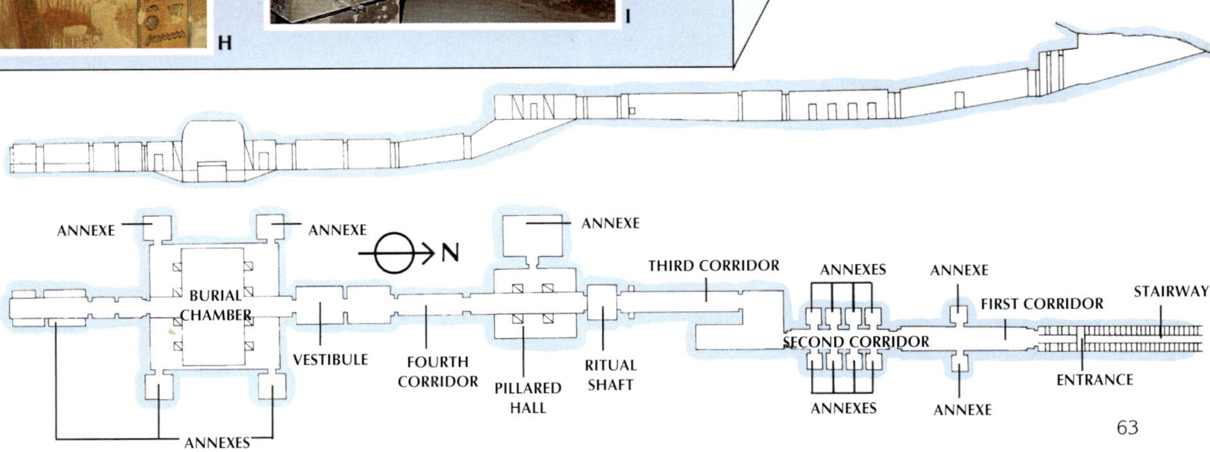

RAMESSES VI
1144 - 1136 BC

KV no. 9

RAMESSES AMUN-HER-KHEPSHEF-NETER-HEQAIUNU

NEBMAATRE MERIAMUN

The tomb of Ramesses VI, even though known and much visited in antiquity, as attested by the numerous graffiti engraved on its walls, was excavated and freed from the debris that took up a great part of its rooms only in 1888 by Georges Daressy on behalf of the Antiquities Service. Actually, this burial site had been prepared and taken up previously by Ramesses V, Ramesses VI's predecessor, who ruled only four years, and was subsequently extended by Ramesses VI. We do not know the precise reason why Ramesses VI preferred to use his brother's tomb, rather than have a tomb of his own dug, as tradition requested, but it is logical to assume that this decision was dictated by reasons of an economical character and also by the brothers' unquestionable identities of theological-religious outlook. The tomb exhibits the typical classic plan of the Twentieth Dynasty, with a considerable architectural simplification as compared to that of Ramesses III, while the decoration is extremely complex and sophisticated. The tomb of Ramesses VI encloses a sort of treatise on theology in which the fundamental elements are the sun and its daily journey in the world of darkness, from which it emerges perpetually victorious, and the light which is its main emanation. The meaning of the wall paintings in the tomb, which have preserved their splendid colors, among which prevail the reds and the yellows, is sometimes obscure and enigmatic in its details. In general, however, it is an analysis of the origins of heaven, of earth and of the creation of the sun, of the light, and of life. In the first, second and third corridors, texts from the *Book of the Gates* and from the *Book of the Caverns*, a collection of texts dealing with Afterlife's sacred geography and with the caverns the sun has to cross during its nightly journey, are painted on the walls. The third corridor ends in a ritual shaft and in a four-pillar room from which a corridor starts, emerging inside a second vestibule: the walls of this entire sector of the tomb take up again and continue with the texts of the *Book of the Gates* and the *Book of the Caverns*, begun in the precedent corridors. In the fourth and fifth corridors there are passages from the *Book of Amduat* and, in the second vestibule, passages from the *Book of the Dead*. The second vestibule precedes the burial chamber, where the broken sarcophagus is found: the walls are decorated with the *Book of the Earth*, while on the astronomical ceiling the *Book of Day* and the *Book of Night*, illustrated by a double image of Nut in the shape of goddess of the daily and nightly heavens, are represented. It is here that the mystery of the creation of the solar disc and of its daily revival took place, in addition to the regeneration of the pharaoh himself, assimilated to the sun.

64 Ramesses VI, represented in this statue as the victor subjecting a Libyan prisoner, succeeds his brother Ramesses V, for whom the tomb KV no. 9 had originally been prepared, in rather unclear circumstances. The story of the reign of Ramesses VI is little known, but his tomb is perhaps the one with the most sophisticated and complete decorative plan of all the tombs of the valley, and its walls constitute a veritable library painted in the rock. The mummy of the pharaoh was discovered in 1898 in the tomb of Amenophis II. (Cairo Museum)

64-65 The burial chamber of the tomb of Ramesses VI is decorated with texts and illustrations related to the Book of the Earth *or* Book of Aker *that deals with the theme of the creation of the solar disk. The* Book of the Earth *is one of the great anthologies of religious magic texts which describes the journey of the sun god Re in the underworld and his going out into the light.*

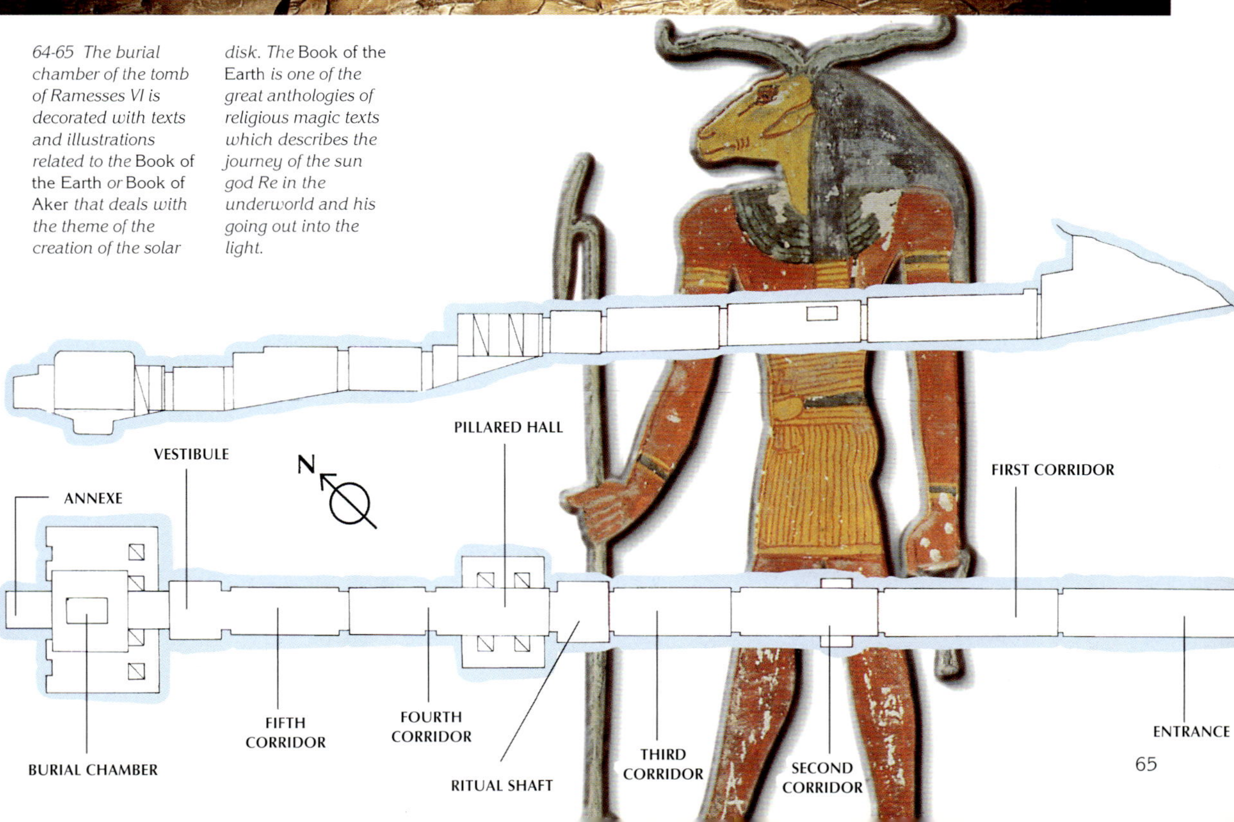

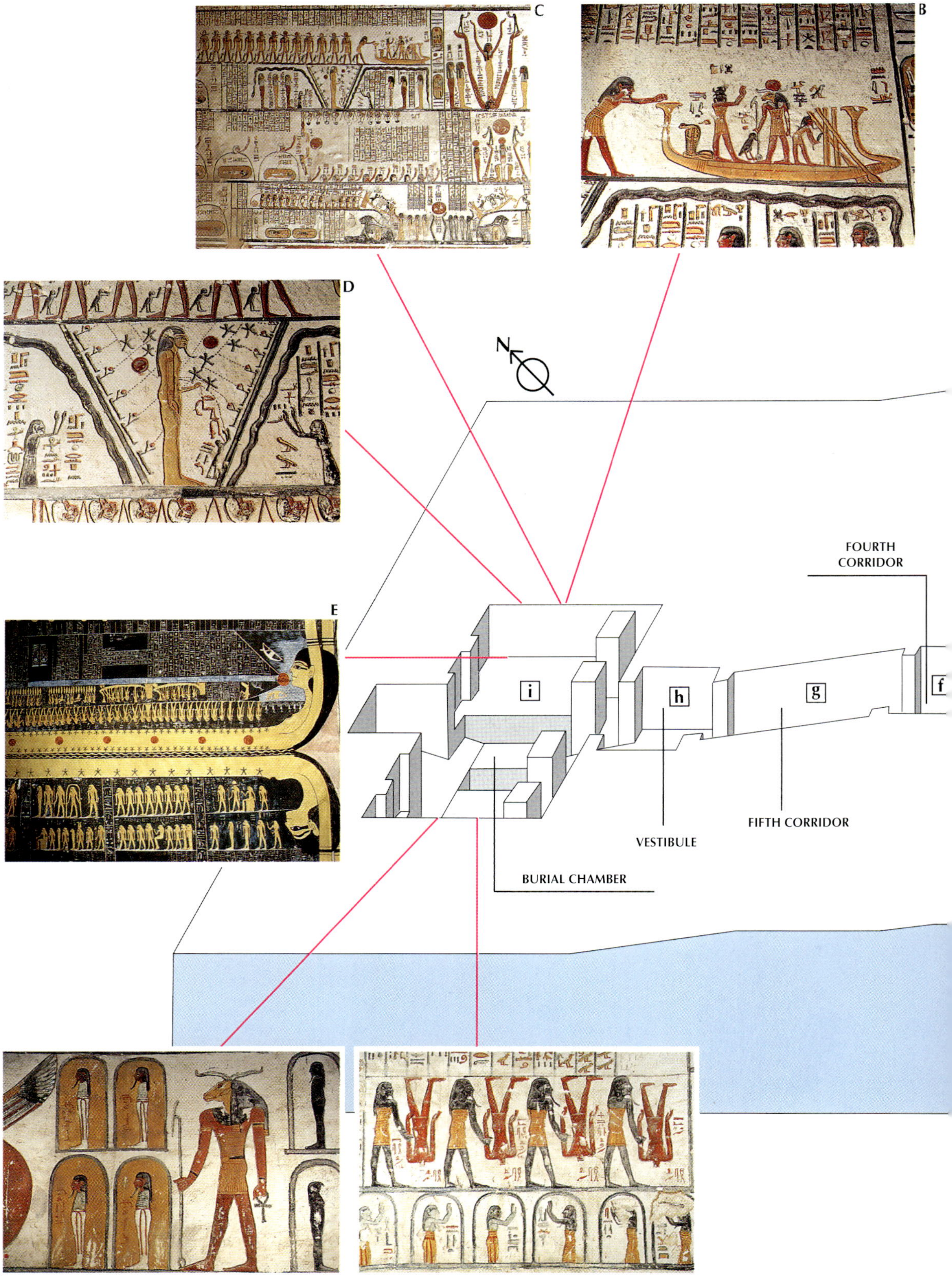
C
B
D
N
E
FOURTH
CORRIDOR
i
h
g
f
VESTIBULE
FIFTH CORRIDOR
BURIAL CHAMBER
F
G

A - Details of the east wall of the burial chamber: the solar disc is raised from the depths of the underworld by the arms of the goddess Nut, "Lady of the Sky and the Stars, Mother of the Sun", who regulates the movement of the stars and daily gives life back to the sun, renewing the creative act of the world.

B - The barque of the ram-headed sun god Re with his ba *and Khepri, personification of the morning sun.*

C - Details of the wall of the burial chamber: the sun god Re during his celestial navigation is accompanied by the representations of Osiris and of the deity that personifies the hours.

D - A deity named "He who hides the hours", with his phallus erect in an attitude of procreation, is joined by dotted lines to the twelve gods that personify the hours with which the sun continually re-creates.

E - The astronomical ceiling of the burial chamber is decorated with scenes illustrating the Book of the Day *and the* Book of the Night. *A double representation of the goddess Nut, personification of the celestial vault and "Mother of the solar star", goes along the major axis of the room: the goddess is represented in the act of swallowing up the sun in the evening and regenerating it in the morning; she thus assumes the role of a life-giving and regenerating force that shines down on the dead pharaoh, assimilated with Re with whom he shares the rebirth.*

F - The mummies in their chapels are brought back to life by the energy of the endlessly reborn sun.

G - The damned who symbolize the destructive forces, beheaded and painted blood-colored red, are seized and turned upside down by black executioners.

a - Book of the Gates, Book of the Caverns *and astronomical ceiling*

b - Book of the Gates, Book of the Caverns *and astronomical ceiling*

c - Book of the Gates, Book of the Caverns, *astronomical ceiling and* Book of the Heaven

d - Book of the Gates, Book of the Caverns, *astronomical ceiling and* Book of the Heaven

e - Book of the Gates, Book of the Caverns, *chapel of Osiris and astronomical ceiling*

f - Book of Amduat, *on the ceiling the* Book of the Heaven

g - Book of the Amduat, *on the ceiling the* Book of the Heaven *and cryptographic texts*

h - Book of the Dead, *divine scenes and on the ceiling*

i - Book of the Earth *and on the ceiling* Book of Day and Night

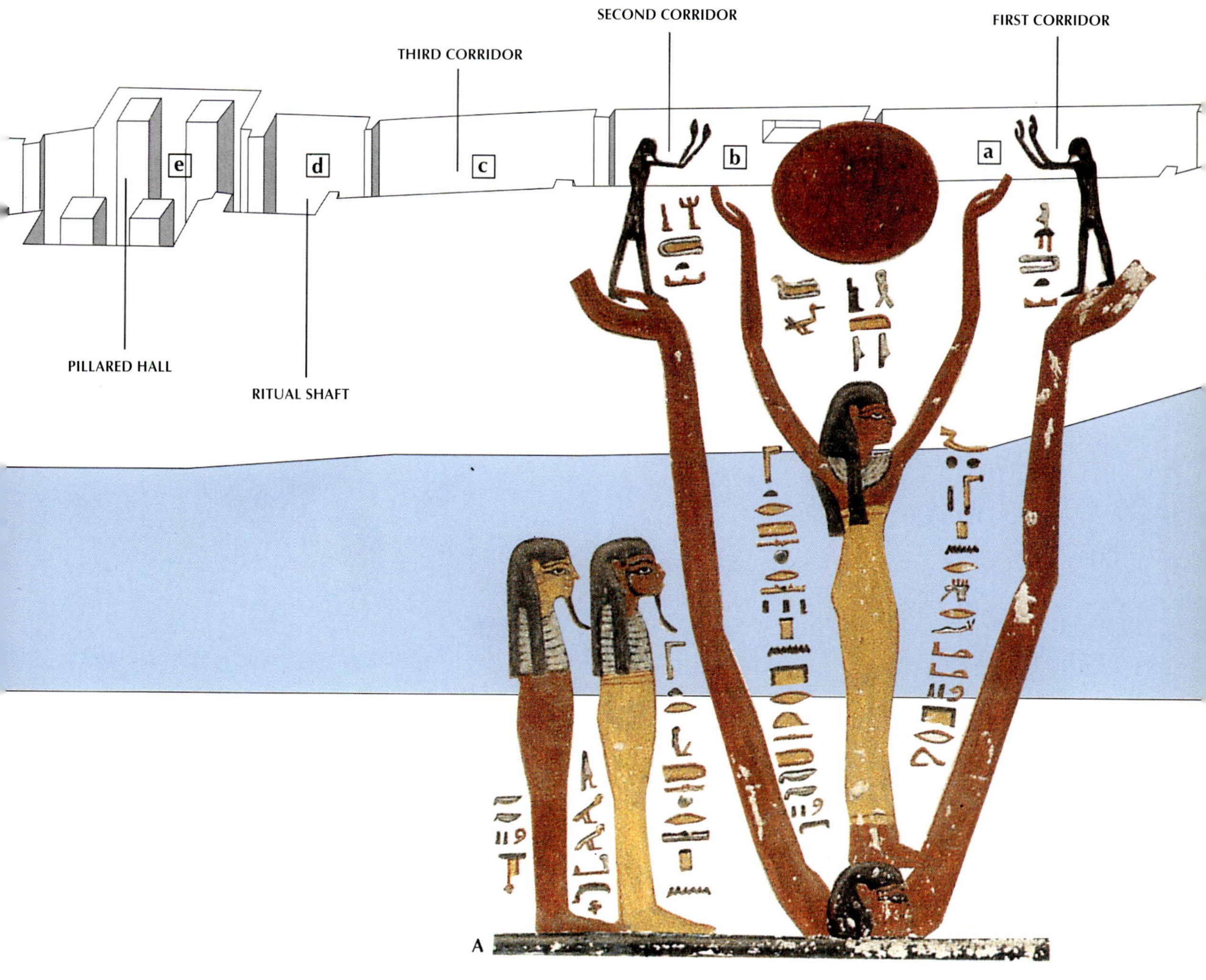

A

RAMESSES IX
1125 - 1107 BC

KV no. 6

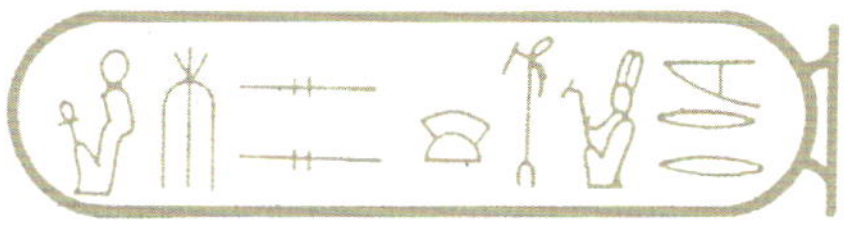

RAMESSES KHA-EM-WASET MERER-AMUN

NEFERKARE SETEPENRE

A - A double image of the pharaoh worshipping the solar disc, inside which the ram-headed god Atum and an udjat-*eye are depicted, decorates the architrave of the door at the beginning of the second straight corridor that leads to the burial chamber.*

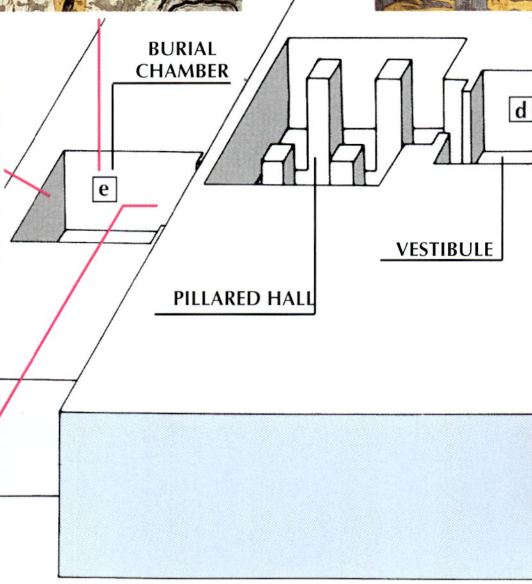

D

C

E

B

F

B, C - Details of the astronomical ceiling of the corridor: against a blue background divine boats and processions of deities are depicted in yellow.

D - Scene that illustrates passages from the Book of the Earth, *dealing with the birth of the sun. In the upper register, Re and Khepri hold up a scarab which represents the rising solar disc. In the lower register a deity called "He who conceals the hours" makes fruitful the deity who personifies hours engendering the sun.*

E - General view of the burial chamber with an astronomical ceiling similar to that of the tomb of Ramesses VI, inspired by, and perhaps completing its plan.

F - Details of the astronomical ceiling of the burial chamber, decorated with an abbreviated version of the Book of Day and Night, *a veritable treatise on cosmogony and theology that appeared in the Ramessid age: the goddess Nut swallows up the solar disc, to regenerate it the following morning.*

a - Litanies of Re *and* Book of the Caverns
b - Litanies of Re, Book of the Dead *and* Book of the Caverns
c - Book of Amduat, *divine scenes and deities*
d - *Divine scenes*
e - Book of the Caverns, Book of the Earth, Book of Amduat *and on the ceiling* Book of Day and Night

The tomb of Ramesses IX, excavated on the left bank of the Valley of the Kings, is the first tomb met by the visitor, after passing through the entrance gate to the site. The tomb is interesting on account of the topics of the wall paintings, taking up again some of the motifs and themes conveyed in the tomb of Ramesses VI, even if here, on the walls of the first two corridors, the *Book of the Gates* is replaced by the *Litanies of Re*, a religious composition celebrating the solar deity in its 75 different transformations during its nightly journey, and its morning resurrection with which the resurrection of the pharaoh himself is identified.

In the second and third corridors, which precedes a little quadrangular vestibule, there are passages from the *Litanies of Re*, from the *Book of the Dead*, the *Book of the Caverns* and, in the last part, from the *Book of Amduat* with representations of underworld deities. The corridor and the vestibule are decorated with astronomical ceilings extremely interesting but not yet really elaborate in their details. The vestibule emerges inside a four-pillar hall whence a very short corridor leads to the burial chamber which has a vaulted ceiling with a double representation of Nut and passages from the *Book of Day* and the *Book of Night*, as in the tomb of Ramesses VI.

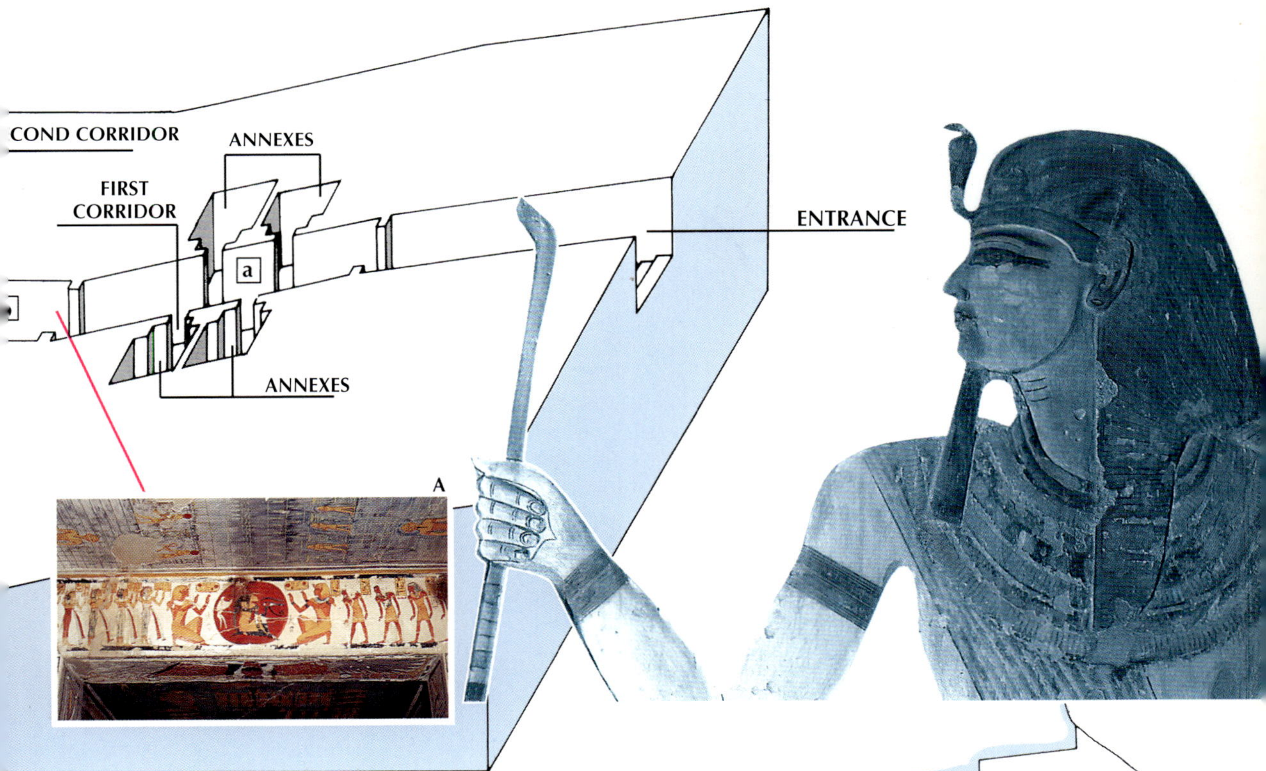

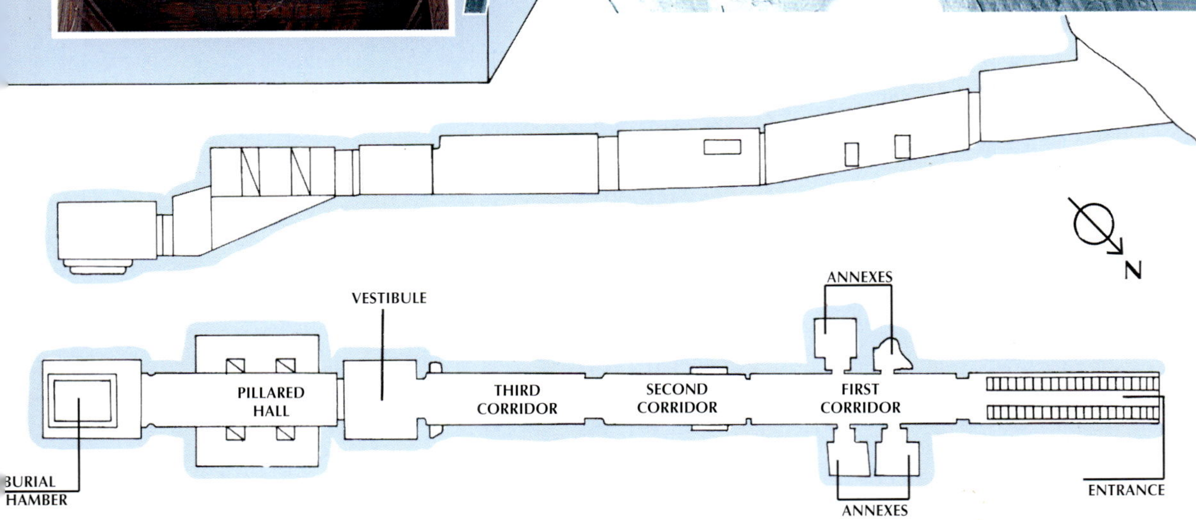

THE VALLEY OF THE QUEENS

The Valley of the Queens is the southernmost of the Theban necropolises and is the place where, starting from the Eighteenth Dynasty (about the sixteenth century BC), the first princes and princesses of the royal blood were interred together with personages living in the court circles and, subsequently, starting from the times of Ramesses II, the queens on whom the title of "royal bride" had been bestowed.
Later, during the Twentieth Dynasty, Ramesses III renewed the tradition and had the tombs of some of his children prepared in the Valley.
The Valley of the Queens or *Wadi el-Melikat*, as the natives call it in Arabic, was so named by Champollion, but originally the Egyptians referred to it as *Ta-set-neferu*, an expression which admits of various interpretations but which can in all likelihood be translated as "the Place of the Children of the Pharaoh", clearly referring to the tombs of the royal princes, rather than "the Site of Beauty", this interpretation being generally more widespread. The site was regarded as sacred, hence suitable for its function of royal necropolis, both for its proximity to the Theban Peak and for the presence at the bottom of the valley of a cave waterfall, whose shape and the natural phenomena connected with it could suggest a religious and funerary concept. In fact, the cave would have represented the belly or the womb of the Celestial Cow (one of the figurations of the goddess Hathor) from whom the waters gushed out which foretold the impending revival of the deceased buried in this privileged site.
From a typological point of view the burials of the Valley of the Queens can be divided into two large groups: the first includes the funerary shafts (over sixty) going back to the Eighteenth Dynasty, the second the large Ramessid tombs of the Nineteenth and Twentieth Dynasties, which exhibit a complex structure and constitute real funerary apartments modelled on the type of those existing in the nearby Valley of the Kings, of which they would appear to be "simplified versions".
Only starting from the beginning of the Nineteenth Dynasty, with the inhumation of Sat-Re, wife of Ramesses I and mother of Sethos I, did the Valley of the Queens begin to harbour the mortal remains of the royal brides. After the end of the Ramessid period and the subsequent systematic looting of the site by grave robbers, as proven by numerous juridical papyri, burials in the Valley were resumed: starting from the Twenty-First Dynasty and in the Third Intermediate Period the tombs became a burial site for personages of non-royal blood and essentially linked to the tilling of the soil in the huge estates of the priests.
Turned into a popular cemetery at the beginning of the Roman Empire, the Valley of the Queens kept this status until the mid-fourth century AD, when the Copts settled in the site, burning and irretrievably disfiguring numerous tombs and founding a monastery, the Deir Rumi, whose ruins can still be seen today. Many of the tombs excavated in the Valley of the Queens suffered already in antiquity from serious, so to say "constitutional" problems, linked to the hydrogeological and petrographical characteristics of the site. The pharaoh's craftsmen, who 3500 years ago were working to prepare the royal burials in this valley, no doubt realized that they had to work on bad rock which forced them to make use of peculiar technical devices such as the massive use of *muna*, a special plaster often covering the entire walls and ceilings of the hypogeum.
Sometimes the rock became of such poor quality that the ancient architects chose to interrupt the work and start it over again at a new, more suitable site: this explains the high number of unfinished tombs found in the valley.

70 top Overall view of the Valley of the Queens: this was the name given by Champollion to this wide wadi located in the southernmost part of the Theban necropolis, where, starting from the Eighteenth Dynasty, princes and princesses, royal brides and high dignitaries of the court were buried, and which continued to be used as a burial place in the Ptolemaic and the Graeco-Roman age as well.

70-71 The Valley of the Queens, called by the ancient Egyptians Ta-set-neferu, *a toponym that may be translated as "the Place of the Children of the Pharaoh" or "the Place of the Royal Harem". In the Valley of the Queens there are over one hundred tombs and simple funerary wells.*

Besides, plentiful signs have been discovered of the advent of a period of torrential rains in the post-Ramessid era, which no doubt had devastating effects on the tombs themselves. The first archaeologist who conducted systematic excavations in the Valley of the Queens was the Italian Ernesto Schiaparelli, director of the Egyptian Museum in Turin, who worked on the spot between 1903 and 1906 assisted by Francesco Ballerini an Egyptologist from Como. To Schiaparelli's excavations we owe the discovery of all the most important tombs of the site, such as those belonging to the children of Ramesses III, Seth-her-khopshef, Khaemwaset and Amun-her-khepshef. But the most extraordinary discovery was the tomb of Nefertari, Ramesses II's "great royal bride", regarded by many as the most beautiful of all Theban tombs. It was only in 1970 that a series of annual missions began, carried out by the Centre National de la Recherche Scientifique (CNRS) of Paris, the Louvre Museum and the Centre d'Etudes et Documentation sur l'Ancienne Egypte (CEDAE) of the Egyptian Antiquities Organisation.
The works made possible the cleaning and a complete survey of the site, in addition to a systematic study of all the burials in the valley, whose original aspect was restored thanks to the removal of backfill materials and of the debris from Schiaparelli's excavations, which had changed the morphological characteristics of the valley.

*71 top left
A photograph of the burial chamber of prince Khaemwaset's tomb (QV no. 44), one of the sons of Ramesses III, taken at the moment of its discovery in February 1903.
The tomb, used again in a later period, was encumbered with mummies and piled up sarcophagi.*

*71 bottom left
One of the members of the Italian Archaeological Mission, headed by Schiaparelli, at work in the tomb of Nefertari (QV no. 66), Ramesses II's great royal bride, discovered in 1904.*

71 right Ernesto Schiaparelli (1856-1928), director of the Egyptian Museum at Turin, headed two excavation campaigns in the Valley of the Queens between 1903 and 1906, with the assistance of Francesco Ballerini, the Egyptologist from Como. To Schiaparelli and his team we owe the discovery of the most beautiful and the most important tombs of the Valley.

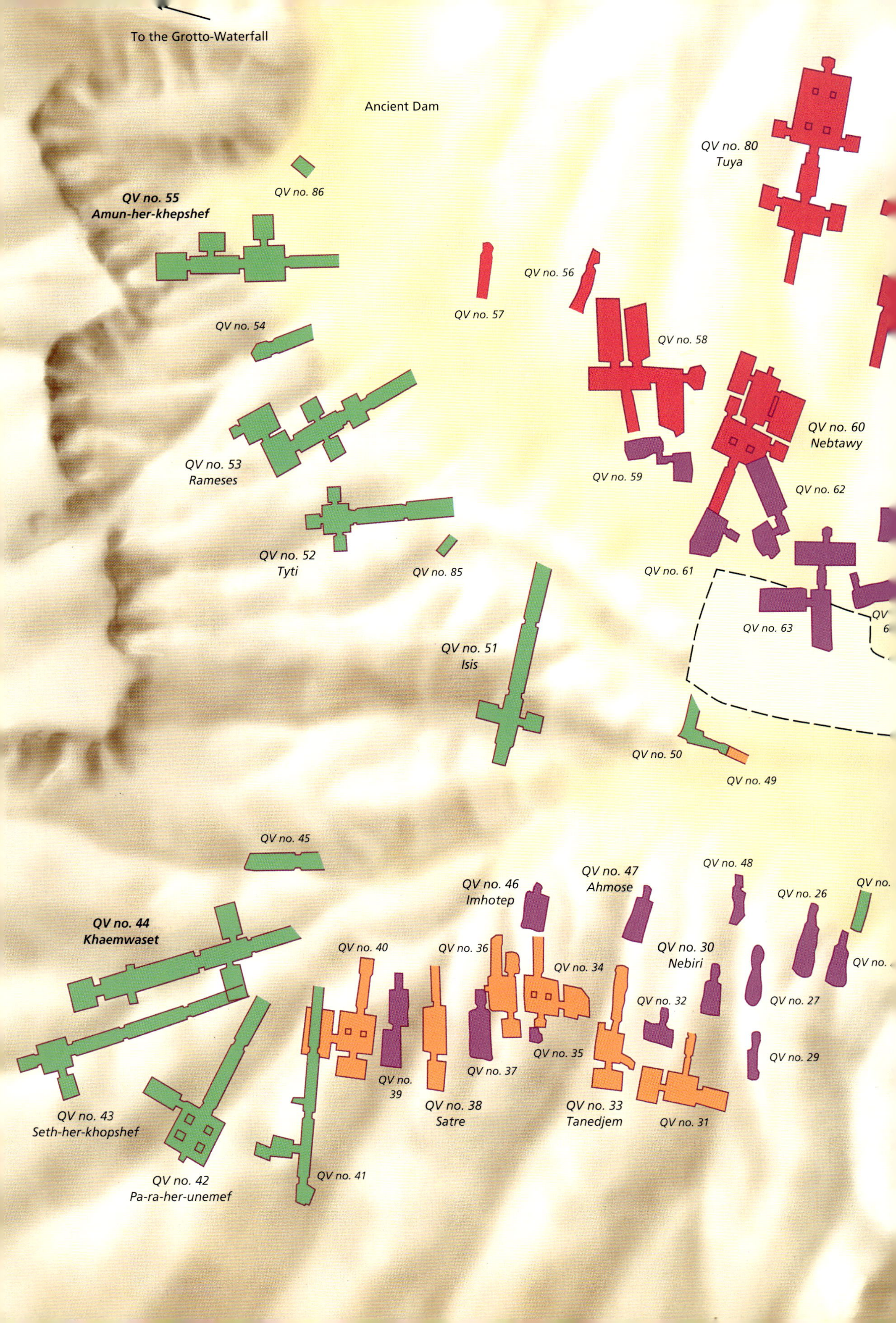

To the Grotto-Waterfall
Ancient Dam
QV no. 80
Tuya
QV no. 86
QV no. 55
Amun-her-khepshef
QV no. 56
QV no. 57
QV no. 54
QV no. 58
QV no. 53
Rameses
QV no. 60
Nebtawy
QV no. 59
QV no. 62
QV no. 52
Tyti
QV no. 85
QV no. 61
QV no. 63
QV no. 51
Isis
QV no. 50
QV no. 49
QV no. 45
QV no. 48
QV no. 46
Imhotep
QV no. 47
Ahmose
QV no. 26
QV no.
QV no. 44
Khaemwaset
QV no. 40
QV no. 36
QV no. 34
QV no. 30
Nebiri
QV no. 27
QV no.
QV no. 32
QV no. 35
QV no. 37
QV no. 39
QV no. 29
QV no. 43
Seth-her-khopshef
QV no. 38
Satre
QV no. 33
Tanedjem
QV no. 31
QV no. 42
Pa-ra-her-unemef
QV no. 41

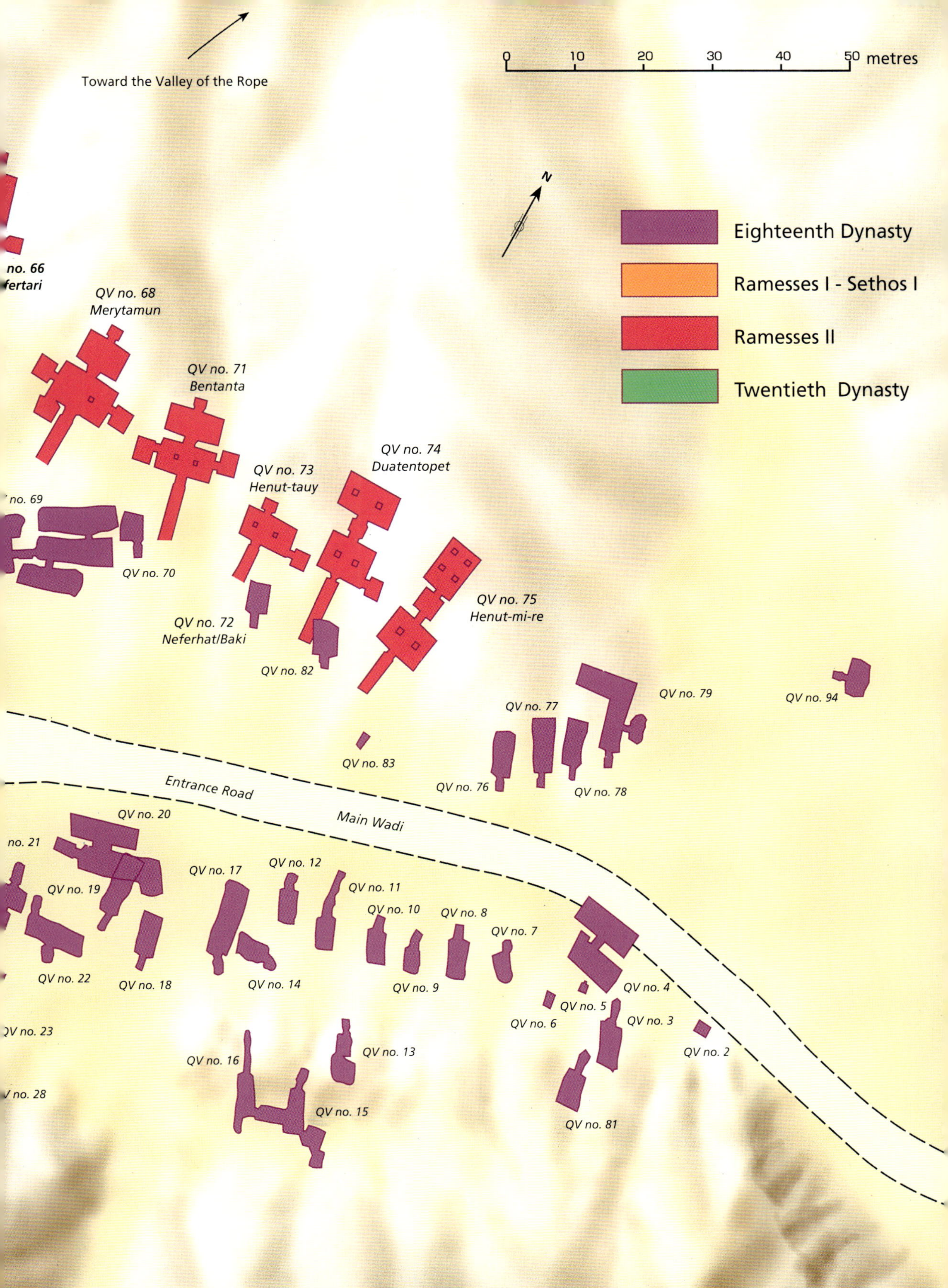

THE VALLEY OF THE QUEENS

THE TOMBS OF RAMESSES III'S SONS

The tombs of the Valley of the Queens intended for Ramesses III's five sons (Seth-her-khopshef no. 43, Pa-ra-her-unemef no. 42, Khaemwaset no. 44, Ramesses no. 53, Amun-her-khepshef no. 55) are located on the southwestern side of the main wadi and no less than three of them were discovered by the Schiaparelli Mission. It is not clear who these princes really were, how old they were, when and how they died. We know that Ramesses III issued the orders to prepare these tombs in the year 28 of his reign, four years before his death. Were the princes therefore already dead at that time or perhaps were they doomed to die because of an incurable disease? And why were these princes buried in the Valley of the Queens? Perhaps in order to be reconnected with a tradition dating back to the time of the Eighteenth Dynasty? In the nearby temple of Medinet Habu, on the western wall of the second yard, there is a portrait of the royal offspring: thirteen princes and fourteen princesses. As far as the princes are concerned, ten among them are named, a rather unusual feature since at that time such representations were generally anonymous. The princes, all bearing the common title of "standard bearer to the right of the king", are distinguished from each other by their other titles and by their dress. It seems, however, that those lying in the tombs in the Valley of the Queens are not identical with those shown at Medinet Habu.
From a chronological point of view it would follow that the tombs of Seth-her-khopshef and Pa-ra-her-unemef are earlier than Khaemwaset's and Amun-her-khepshef's: these last would appear to have been built in succession as proved by the complementary sequences of the funerary genii in chapter 145 of the

74 top This splendid painted bas-relief shows Prince Khaemwaset (QV no. 44) with a typical children's hairstyle: the long hair is collected in a tress, fastened with a braid which falls sideways, covering an ear.

74 bottom On the eastern wall of the antechamber of tomb QV no. 55, Ramesses III introduces his son Amun-her-khepshef, holding a flabellum in his right hand, into the presence of the principal gods of the Afterlife: Ptah, Ptah-Tatenen, Duamutef and Imset.

Book of the Dead, which preside over the twenty-one gates of Osiris' dwelling in the Fields of Iaru.
The tomb of Seth-her-khopshef never contained the mummy of the prince, who mounted the throne under the name of Ramesses VIII and was buried in the Valley of the Kings.
The tombs of Ramesses III's sons all have a so-called "syringe-shaped" structure: they are essentially a rectilinear corridor with lateral annexes arranged in various ways, leading into the burial chamber, sometimes provided with a small room opening on the rear wall.
The tomb of Pa-ra-her-unemef (No. 42) alone substantially differs from this plan, having a structure by far more complex with the room of the sarcophagus supported by pillars.
It is very similar to the tombs in the Valley of the Kings.
One of the more typical characteristics of the tombs of Ramesses III's sons is that in the decorations the princes are almost always preceded by the king, the real protagonist of the scenes carved on the walls. It is Ramesses who, sumptuously dressed, accomplishes the ritual sacrifices and it is always he who introduces the sons to the different deities, this being a task normally fulfilled by a god not by a living ruler. The polychrome bas-reliefs decorating the tomb walls show considerable similarities and comply with a precise decorative plan which expresses belief in a ritual course accomplished by the soul of the prince who descends into the world of the Afterlife, symbolically represented by the tomb. Welcomed by friendly deities, he crosses the doors and the gates of the kingdom of Osiris, watched by different guard genii, who bar whoever does not resort to the magical formulas prescribed in chapters 145 and 146 of the *Book of the Dead*. Finally the deceased regenerates himself and, by transfiguring himself "comes out to the light" assimilated to the everlasting stars. At present the two most beautiful tombs, those of Khaemwaset and that of Amun-her-khepshef are open to the public.

75 top Ramesses III with Lower Egypt's red crown in a bas-relief of the tomb of prince Amun-her-khepshef (QV no. 55), one of Khaemwaset's brothers. In the tombs of his sons Ramesses III, omnipresent, is always depicted in a sumptuous way with manifold crowns and headdress.

75 centre In this scene located on the northern wall of the western lateral annexe of the tomb of Khaemwaset (QV no. 44), the prince is in the presence of Ismet, one of Horus's Four Sons.

75 bottom In this scene, which follows the preceding one, Khaemwaset is in the presence of Duamutef, another one of Horus' Four Sons. The decorative program of the tombs of Ramesses III's sons illustrates a kind of ritual journey of the souls of the princes. In this case Khaemwaset, after having been introduced by his father into the world of the Afterlife, finds himself alone in front of the gods and afterwards, in the burial chamber, he starts his gestation that comes to an end with his regeneration and the tranfiguration thanks to which he "comes out into the light" assimilated to the heavenly stars.

KHAEMWASET
QV no. 44

Eldest son of the King
Sem-priest *of Ptah*
Twentieth dynasty

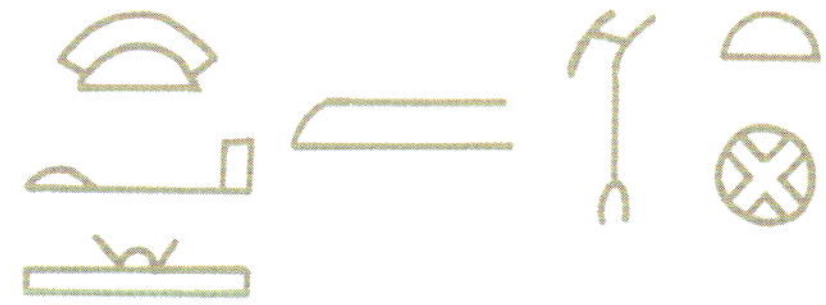

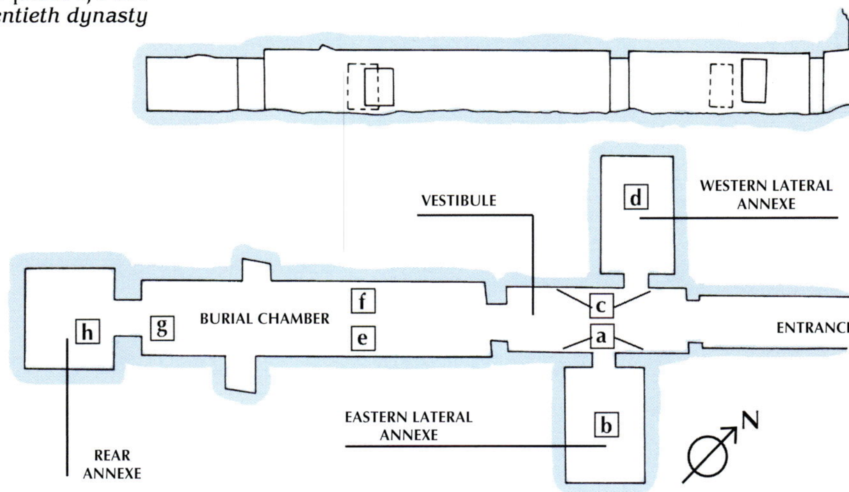

A - The goddesses Isis and Nephthys painted in yellow, a color typical of the female deities.

B - This deity with a doggish face is the embodiment of the Ennead of the Duat, the nine deities of the kingdom of the dead, followed by the god Horus-em-nekhu, Horus in the shape of a youth

C - Dendeni, "the furious", is the watchman of the Ninth gate of the kingdom of Osiris in Chapter 145 of the Book of the Dead.

E

D

C

F

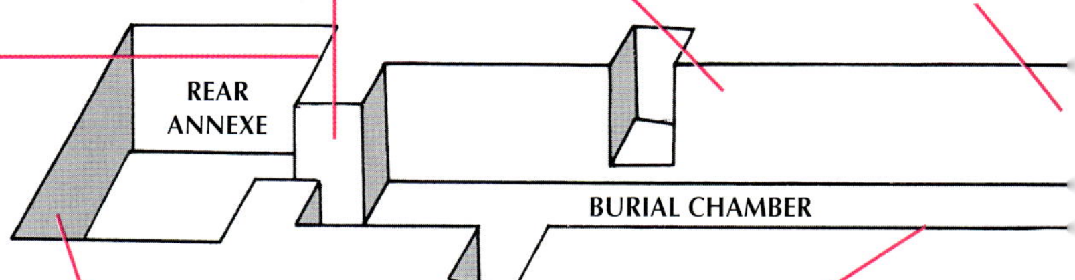

D - Ramesses III followed by his son heads towards the Fifteenth gate of the kingdom of Osiris where he will have to confront the genius Nehes-her-per-em-duat, "He whose face is dark, coming from the Duat"; it is only by reciting the magic formulas prescribed in the Book of the Dead *that the deceased was able to surmount the numerous intervening obstacles, and thus to accede to the kingdom of Osiris.*

E - View of the burial chamber and of the door leading inside the rear annexe, on whose wall appear two representations of Osiris. The door is watched by two genii mentioned in Chapter 146 of the Book of the Dead: *to the right there is Nehes-her-per-em-duat and to the left Dikesu-uden-bega-per-em-mut, watching respectively the Fifteenth and the Sixteenth gates of the kingdom of Osiris.*

G

H

The tomb of Khaemwaset was discovered in February 1903 and when the archaeologists entered it, the corridor was encumbered with countless piled up sarcophagi, a clear sign that the tomb had been put to use again as a site of common burial. Since the inscription engraved on the cover of the prince's sarcophagus, found in a fragmentary condition, dates from the times of Ramesses IV, it may logically be assumed that Khaemwaset had been buried at that period, during the reign of his brother. The bas reliefs on the walls of the tomb have preserved their colors practically untouched and are of elegant workmanship.
In the vestibule, on whose walls two lateral annexes open to the left and to the right, there is to the left a representation of Ptah followed by an image of the king and of Khaemwaset in front of Anubis and Re-Harakhty, while on the right side is the king bringing offerings to Ptah-Sokar and, together with his son, presenting Geb with offerings of incense before being welcomed by the god Shu. In the lateral annexe to the left (annexe east) we see again Horus-Inmutef, Isis and Nephthys and Neith with Selkis. The prince alone is found in the presence of Anubis, of Horus's Four Sons and, finally, of Selkis and Neith. The lateral annexe to the right (annexe west), shows Horus-Inmutef and two groups of deities, Isis and Nephthys and Neith and Selkis, while the prince is shown alone in the act of greeting the personification of the Ennead of Duat and of Horus-em-nekhu, evocation of Horus as a child.
In the second corridor, corresponding to the burial chamber, the wall decorations are related to chapters 145 and 146 of the *Book of the Dead*, as in the room of the sarcophagus of Amun-her-khepshef's tomb, the continuation of which it seems to represent. Indeed, we observe the king followed by the prince in front, to the right the genii watching the Ninth, Eleventh, Thirteenth and Fifteenth doors of the kingdom of Osiris and, to the left, the genii of the Tenth, Twelfth, Fourteenth and Sixteenth doors.
The watchmen of the Fifteenth and Sixteenth doors, bird-headed Nehes-per-em-duat and Dikesu-uden-bega-per-em-mut are found to the sides of the door leading to the rear annexe, whose steps are adorned with two *djed*-pillars. In the rear annexe, on the northern wall, to the left are the jackal Anubis and the lion, and then the king alone presenting offerings to Thoth and to Harsiesis, while to the right are the genii Nebneru and Hery-maat and then the king in the act of accomplishing offerings in front of Horus and Shepes. Finally, on the rear wall there is a double scene in which the king makes offerings to Osiris, preceded by Isis and Neith (left side) and Nephthys with Selkis (right side).

B

A

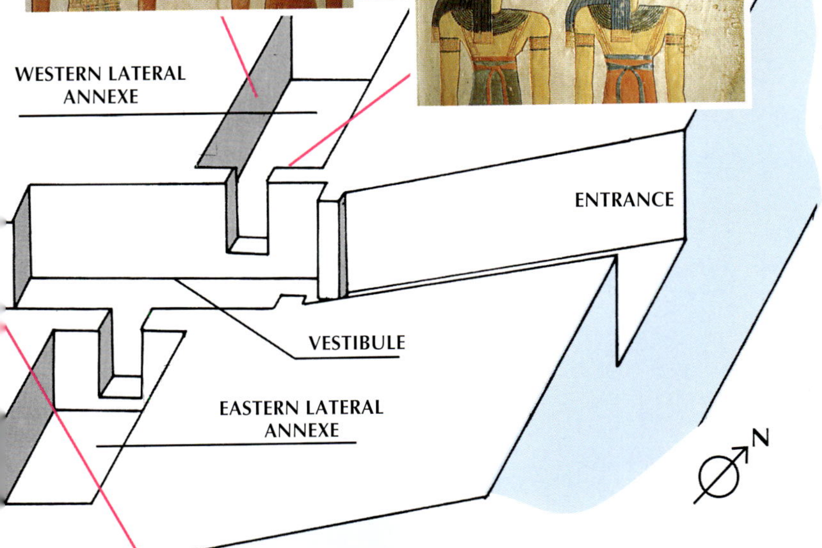

I

F - Two genii depicted in the rear annex of the burial chamber: Neb-neru "the Lord of Terror", lion-headed, and Hery-maat "He who Commands the Truth", appearing as a young man wearing a khayt*-headdress.*

G - Osiris, "Lord of the Afterlife", with his face painted in green, color of regeneration, wears the atef*-crown and displays his classic attributes: the* heqa*-sceptre and the* nekhakha*-flail.*

H - Miu, the "cat", holding in his hands two knives, was the watchman of the Twelfth gate of Osiris' kingdom, in Chapters 145 and 146 of the Book of the Dead.

I - Ramesses III wearing a short wig with blue knots, called ibes.

***a** - (from left to right) Ptah, Ramses III followed by Prince Khaemwaset before Thoth, Anubis, Re-Harakhty*
***b** - The prince before deities (Anubis, Sons of Horus, Selkis, Neith); Nephthys and Isis in the presence of Osiris*
***c** - (from right to left) The pharaoh followed by the prince before Ptah-Sokaris, Geb, Shu, Atum (fragment)*
***d** - The prince before deities (Hapy, Qebhsenuef, Ptah, Horus the Young, Imset, Duamutef, etc.); Isis in the presence of Osiris and Nephthys opposite Ptah-Sokaris*
***e** - (from left to right)* The Book of the Dead *(Chapters 145-146): the pharaoh followed by the prince before texts, gates and the genies of the Tenth, Twelfth, Fourteenth and Sixteenth Gates*
***f** - (from right to left)* The Book of the Dead *(Chapters 145-146): the pharaoh followed by the prince before texts, doors and the genies of the Nineth, Eleventh, Thirteenth and Fifteenth Gates*
***g** - The winged solar disk Behedety*
***h** - (clockwise) Guardian genies (jackal and lion); the king before Thoth, Harsiesis, Neith, Isis, Osiris, Nephthys, Selkis; lion-headed Neb-neru and Heri-maat.*

AMUN-HER-KHEPSHEF
QV no. 55

Son of the King
Heir to the throne
Charioteer-in chief
Twentieth dynasty

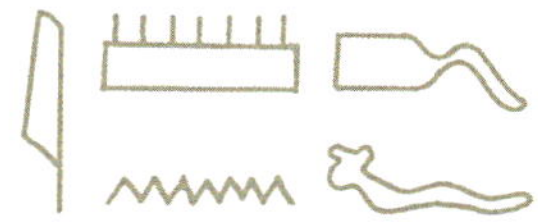

79 top The cartouche of Ramesses III in the tomb of Amun-her-Khepshef (QV no. 55).

G

H

F

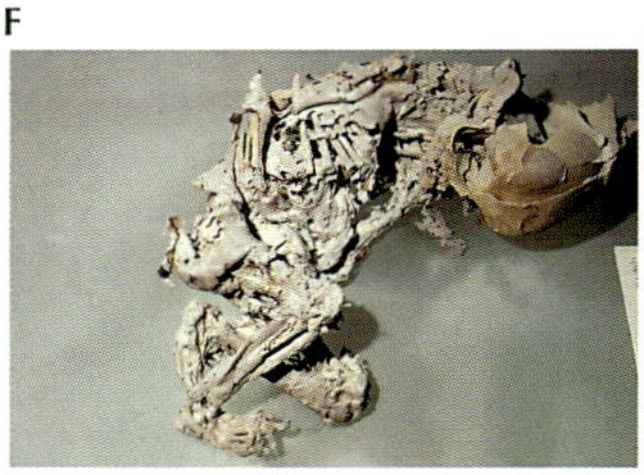

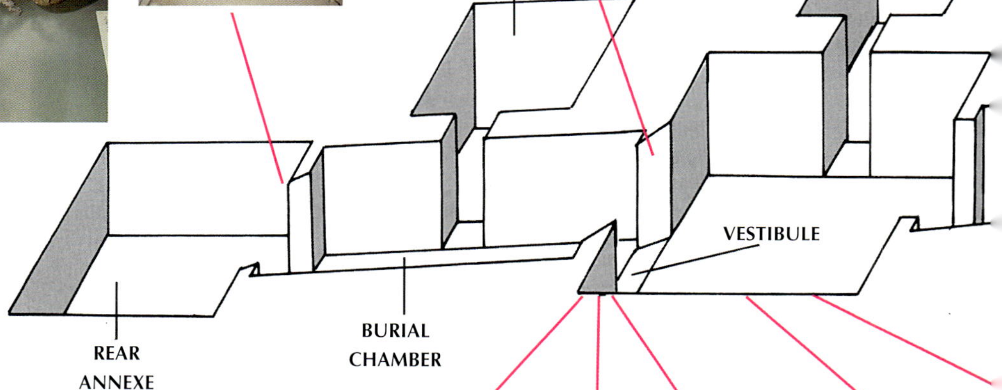

E

D

C

A - Detail of the god Ptah-Tatenen.

B - Ramesses III introduces his son Amun-her-khepshef into the presence of Duamutef.

C - The pharaoh with the classic nemes-*headdress, made of material with blue and yellow stripes that wraps up the head, falling back on both sides of the neck.*

D - Detail of Ramesses III's sumptuous ceremonial dress.

E - The pharaoh wearing a decorated helmet with gold rings.

F - Skeleton of a foetus, now preserved in a case in the rear annexe of the burial chamber, discovered by Schiaparelli wrapped up in linen bandages in a little box found in the lateral wadi to the south of the Valley of the Queens.

G - The door leading into the rear annexe of the burial chamber, where the sarcophagus is found, has an architrave decorated with the royal names protected by two big winged snakes and by two shenu-*signs. A solar winged disc, a representation of the god Horus-Behedety, sits above this scene.*

H - On the rear wall of the vestibule the pharaoh introduces his son Amun-her-khepshef into the presence of the goddesses Isis (to the left) and Hathor (to the right).

a *- (from left to right) Ramesses III between Isis and Thoth (fragment), the pharaoh followed by Prince Amun-her-khepshef before Ptah, Ptah-Tatenen, Duamutef, Imset, Isis* **b** *- (from right to left) The pharaoh followed by the prince before Shu, Qebhsenuef, Hapy and Hathor* **c** *- Isis and Nephthys perform the* njnj *rite* **d** *- Horus Iun-mutef* **e** *- (from left to right) Chapters 145 and 146 of the* Book of the Dead*: the pharaoh followed by the prince before texts, doors and the genies Iukenty and Qutgetef, related to the Seventh, Eighth Gates of the kingdom of Osiris*

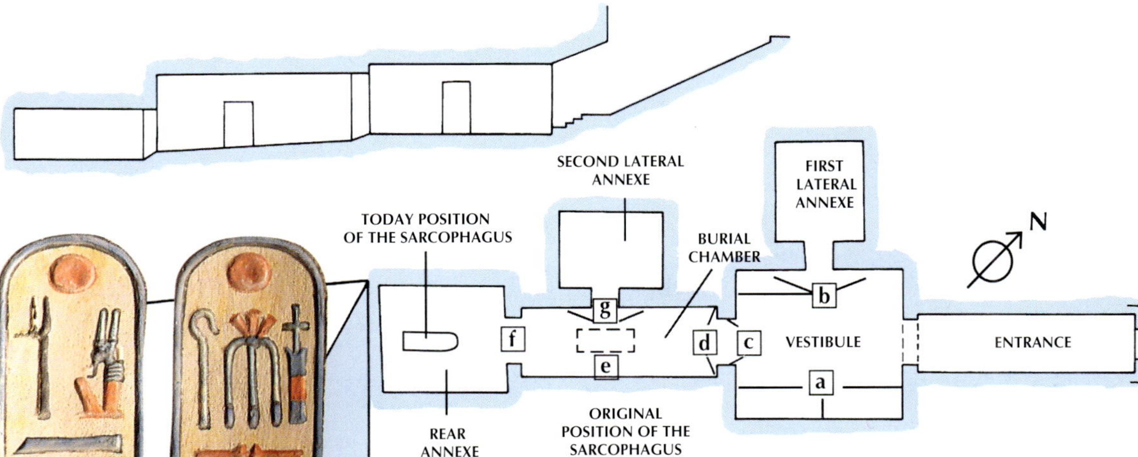

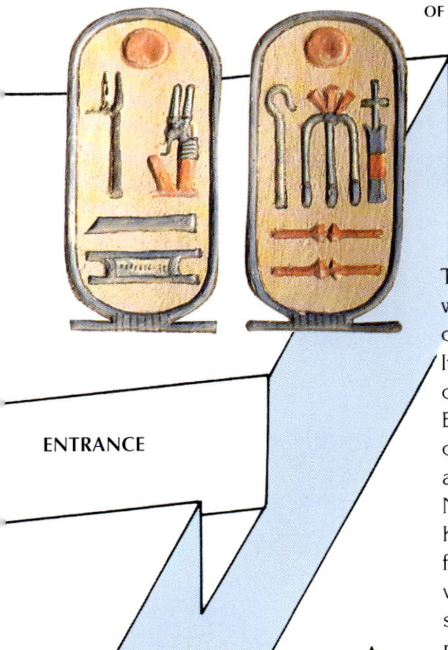

The tomb of Amun-her-khepshef was discovered during the second campaign of excavations by the Italian Archaeological Mission conducted between 1903 and 1904. Even though this burial too had been completely looted already in antiquity, probably at the end of the Nineteenth Dynasty, unlike Khaemwaset's tomb it was totally free of sarcophagi or debris and the wall decoration was in an excellent state of preservation. Due to the refined and elegant style of its bas-reliefs this tomb, like Khaemwaset's, is regarded as one of the masterpieces of the art of the Twentieth Dynasty. It appears that prince Amun-her-khepshef, who bore among numerous titles also that of "Heir to the throne", was about fifteen years old at the time of his death, and he may have been the son of Queen Isis.

A steep, yet short flight of steps leads to the first corridor which leads into the first hall, or antechamber, where the king, followed by Amun-her-khepshef carrying a broad fan of feathers, pays homage to the gods so that they may kindly welcome his son and he intercedes on his behalf by accomplishing rites of purification. To the left are Ptah, Ptah-Tatenen, Imsety and Duamutef, on the right Shu, Qebhsenuef and Hapy are represented, while on the rear wall, beside the door, the king and the prince greet the goddesses Isis (to the left) and Hathor (to the right).

On the northern side of the antechamber opens the first lateral, undecorated annexe. On the doorstep separating the antechamber from the second hall are Isis and Nephthys accomplishing a purifying rite (*njnj* rite), while the king and his son are led by Horus Iunmutef into the adjacent second hall, or hall of the sarcophagus. This, of elongated shape, where originally the rose granite sarcophagus was found, is adorned with wall bas-reliefs related to chapters 145 and 146 of the *Book of the Dead*. Here Ramesses III and his son introduce themselves to the watching genii of the Fifth, Sixth, Seventh, and Eighth gates of the kingdom of Osiris: to the right Heneb-reku (Fifth gate) with a black dog's head and Sematy (Sixth gate) with a ram's head, while to the left are Iukenty (Seventh gate) with an ox's head and Qutgetef (Eighth gate).

On the northern side of the hall of the sarcophagus there is a second lateral annexe lacking decorations just like the first. The hall of the sarcophagus extends into a small room or rear annexe, which is also without decorations, into which the sarcophagus has been moved.

Also in this annexe is found a little urn holding a foetus, which had originally been wrapped in the bandages used for the process of embalming. It was discovered by Schiaparelli inside a little wooden casket in the so-called Valley of Prince Ahmes, a lateral wadi opening into the lowest part of the southern side of the Valley of the Queens.

A

B

f - The winged solar disk Behedety and the winged uraei *which frame the cartouche of the king*
g *- (from right to left) Chapters 145 and 146 of the* Book of the Dead*: the pharaoh followed by the prince before texts, doors and the genies Heneb-reku and Sematy*

NEFERTARI
QV no. 66

Meri-en-mut, heir to the throne,
Bride of the King, Great Royal Bride
Lady of the Two Lands
Twentieth Dynasty

80 top The cartouche encloses the name of Ramesses II's great royal bride in full: Nefertari Meri-en-Mut, meaning "the Lovely One, Beloved of Mut".

80 centre At the time of its discovery, the tomb of Nefertari was practically empty and the archaeologists of the Italian Mission found only a few objects, including parts of the cover of the granite sarcophagus, several shawabti, *fragments of little wooden boxes and this pair of sandals of palm fiber. (Egyptian Museum, Turin).*

80 bottom Among the finds brought to light was this djed-pillar, *originally walled up in the walls of the burial chamber, together with three other amulets, for a protective purpose. The* djed-pillar *symbolizes Osiris' spine and is linked to the concepts of stability, duration and resurrection. (Egyptian Museum, Turin)*

The tomb of queen Nefertari, discovered by Ernesto Schiaparelli in 1904, is regarded by many specialists as the most beautiful tomb of all Egypt. Owing to the countless and serious problems that affected its wonderful paintings, the tomb was closed to the public in the '50s and only in 1986, on the initiative of the Egyptian Antiquities Organization and the Getty Conservation Institute, was a first emergency intervention carried out in order to stabilize the paintings. Then, in February 1988, the real restoration started, preceded by multidisciplinary studies performed by an international team of scientists. First of all the plastering was strenghthened, then the fragments of the paintings which had been detached from the walls were pasted back and finally the restorers proceeded to clean the paintings and remove old retouches badly executed, replacing them with a mortar similar to the one used in the pharaonic era.
In April 1992, the restoration of the tomb was completed, but only in November 1995 was the tomb reopened to the public, whose admission is subject to very severe regulations, drastically limiting the number of daily visitors in order to preserve as much as possible the fragile microclimatic balance.

Nefertari, the Lovely One, Beloved of Mut
Nefertari Meri-en-mut (a name meaning "the Lovely One, Beloved of Mut") most probably married the great pharaoh Ramesses II before he mounted the throne and she held a position altogether peculiar and unequalled in the history of Egypt. Numerous epithets define her as the "sweet of love", the "pretty-looking", the "rich in charm". This leading role, compared with the other numberless wives of pharaohs, is confirmed by the fact that she was always in Ramesses' retinue, not only during civil and religious ceremonies, but even in the course of important journeys, like the one made to Nubia in the year 24 of his reign (around 1255 BC), on the occasion of the inauguration of the little temple of Abu Simbel dedicated to the goddess Hathor and to Nefertari herself: the queen is represented in large statues equal in size with those of the pharaoh, an extraordinary fact, considering that generally the wife was shown at the side of the pharaoh hardly coming up to his knee.
Nefertari played her own role in foreign policy too, as attested by a letter she sent to Pudukhepa, queen of the Hittites (a people against whom Ramesses had bitterly fought), in which she declared all her sisterly friendship to the "great ruler of Hatti".
Nefertari's origins remain clouded in mystery: certain evidence points to her family having come from the

81 top left The wall paintings of the vestibule have recovered their original splendour after the restoration and the colors do not seem to have suffered from the effects of the thirty centuries and more that have elapsed. In the image the goddess Neith welcomes Nefertari, whom the god Harsiesis leads by the hand to Re-Harakhty and Hathor-Imentit, his daughter and wife, who carries on her head the symbol of the West, both seated on archaic thrones. The paintings of the tomb of Nefertari occupy a surface of over 500 square meters.

81 bottom left One of Nefertari's splendid portraits, here wearing a wig in the shape of a vulture's skin topped by a feathered crown with solar disc, an ample usekh*-collar and a white linen tunic painted so as to give an impression of transparency.*

81 right A restorer at work in the tomb of Nefertari. Owing to infiltrations of water which had caused a crystallization of salts on the walls, a detachment of the paintings had taken place. The work of restoration, carried out by an international team headed by Paolo and Laura Mora with the financial support of the Paul Getty Institute, started in 1988 and was completed in April 1992. After having been closed for about forty years, the tomb of Nefertari reopened to the public in 1955.

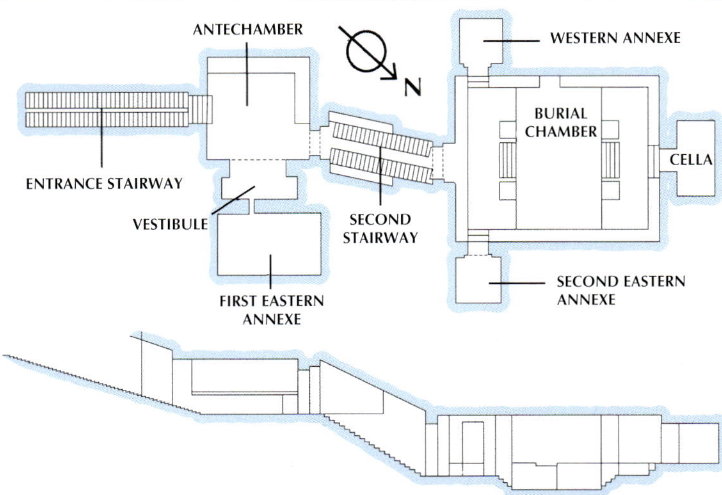

Theban region; besides, the handle of a box found in her tomb with the ornamental scroll of pharaoh Ay leads us to surmise a close relation with this king, who was a native of Akhmim, a town sacred to the god Min and located a little over a hundred kilometers to the north of Thebes. In the Ramesseum, Ramesses II's imposing funerary temple in Thebes, in the upper part of the second pylon at a height of over ten meters, there is an unusual representation of the Min festival, in which Nefertari dances in front of the sacred bull. Was this a tribute paid to the father of the bride, the pharaoh Ay of Akhmim, Tutankhamun's successor? Even though she had five or six sons by Ramesses, some of whom, like the beloved first-born Amun-hi-wenemef, died young, destiny willed that none of them would mount the throne: Ramesses II had his heir (prince Merneptah) by another Great Royal Bride, queen Isis-Nofret, whose tomb has not yet been discovered and which is probably located in the necropolis of Saqqara. The time and the cause of Nefertari's death are also unknown to us, but it happened before the celebration of the thirtieth anniversary of Ramesses' reign: the commemorative inscriptions of this period and the subsequent ones no longer carry the name of the beloved wife.

82-83 On the southern wall of the steps leading to the burial chamber, Nefertari stands facing a table of offerings and two braziers, in her customary elegant attire, and performs a wine offering as she holds out two nu*-pots to a group of deities (Hathor, Selkis and Maat, not visible in the photograph). The texts in vertical columns says: "The Great Royal Bride, Lady of the Two Lands, She Who Is Rich in Charm, Sweet of Love, Lady of Upper and Lower Egypt, the Nefertari Meri-en-Mut Osiris, Beside Osiris Who Is in the West".*

Eastern side of the tomb

A - Nefertari performs offerings to the god Osiris, Lord of the Afterlife and to Anubis.

B - The goddess Neith welcomes Nefertari.

C - Nefertari is led by Harsiesis in front of Re-Harakhty and Hathor-Imentit.

D - The goddess Isis brings Nefertari in front of the scarab-headed god Khepri.

E - Overall view of the eastern wall of the antechamber and of the vestibule: on the columns we distinguish Osiris to the left and Anubis to the right, while the architrave is decorated with a motif of alternating snakes and ostrich plumes, while at the centre there is a genius evoking the eternity of time. Inside we see the god Khepris to the left and Re-Harakhty with Hathor-Imentit to the right.

F - Nefertari with the sekhem-sceptre *consecrates two large tables of offerings in front of Osiris (to the left) and Atum (to the right), the Heliopolitan creator god considered as a manifestation of Re.*

G - Nefertari facing Thoth, the divine scribe, utters the magic formula prescribed in Chapter 94 of the Book of the Dead *in order to obtain the scribe's pot and palette of the god together with his magical powers.*

F

G

H

J

K

E

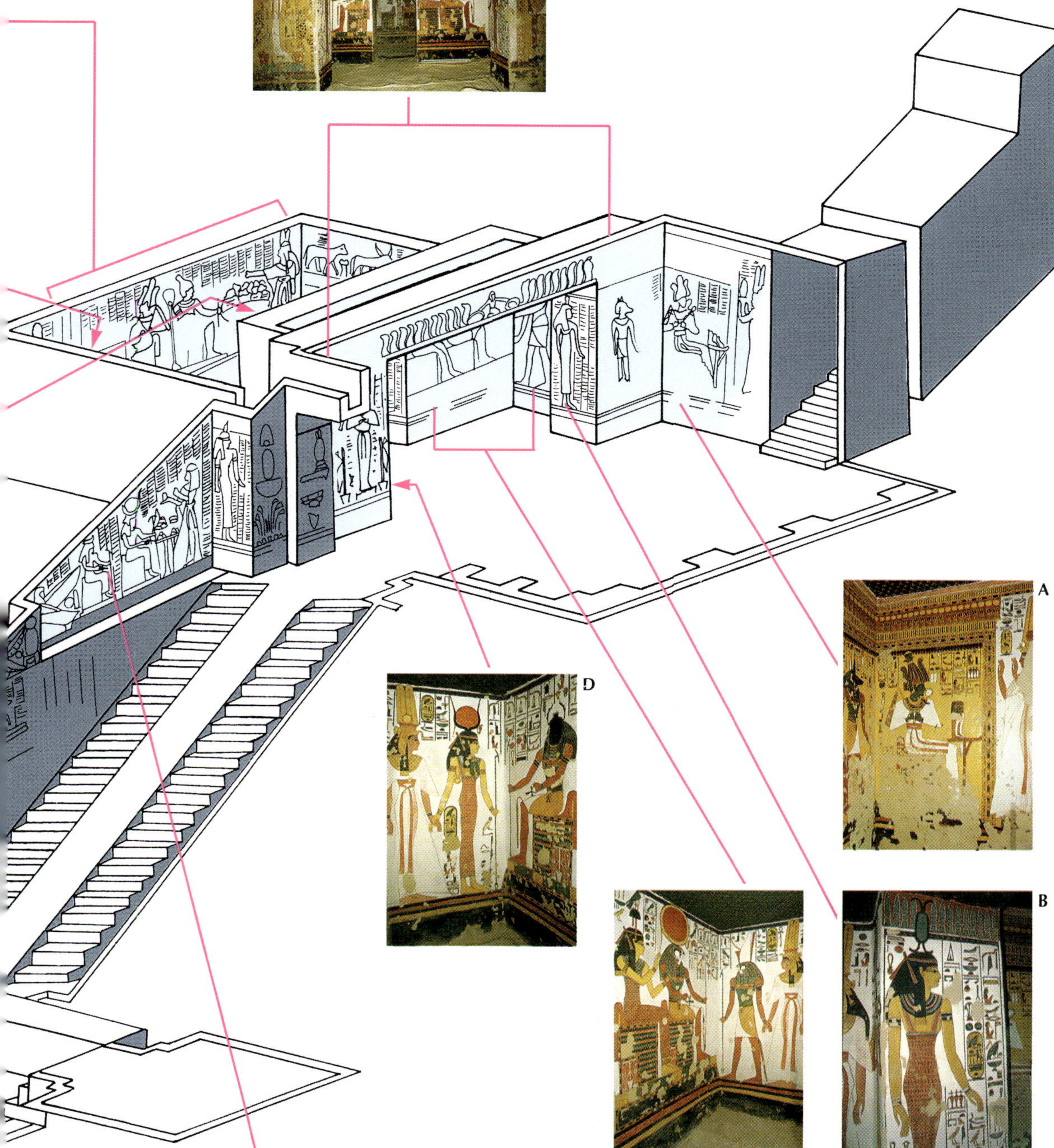

A

D

C

B

I

H - Nefertari makes an offering of linen material to the god Ptah, wrapped up in his classic white mummy-shaped sheath inside a chapel before a djed*-pillar. In the texts we read: "To give material to the Lord of the Truth, in the Sacred Land".*

I - Nefertari holds out ritual pots containing offerings to Hathor and Selkis while the goddess Maat spreads her wings in a protective attitude.

J - The genii watching the Third and Fourth gates of the kingdom of Osiris, respectively with heads of crocodile and bull, mentioned in Chapter 146 of the Book of the Dead.

K - Henty-reki, "He who drives the enemy far off", watchman of the Fifth gate of the kingdom of Osiris.

Western side of the tomb

B

A

C

D

E

F

A - Nefertari playing senet*; the royal* ba *representing Nefertari's soul in the shape of a bird; Nefertari kneeling as she prays.*

B - Texts from Chapter 17 of the Book of the Dead. *In the upper register from left: two lions beside the symbol of the* akhet*-horizon point to Ruty, one of the forms of Atum, the creator god, father of the god Shu and of the goddess Tefnut; the* benu-*bird, the ash-colored heron symbol of the soul of the sun god Re; the goddesses Isis and Nephthys in the shape of hawks protecting the queen's mummy; a deity painted in black with a mystic stick, related to eternity.*

C - Corbel with an "Egyptian throat"-style frame, probably meant for the funerary furniture, supported by pillars carrying the royal cartouche.

H

D - Nefertari, in front of a table of offerings, holds out wine to the goddesses Isis and Nephthys, behind whom we notice the goddess Maat with her wings spread out in a protective attitude.

E - A uraeus *with spread-out wings, between which a* shenu*-sign can be seen, protects the cartouche of Nefertari.*

F - The god Anubis welcomes Nefertari in the Kingdom of the Dead and addresses her at length, the speech being transcribed in the vertical columns of the text.

I

J

K

G

G - An image of Maat with her wings spread out in protective attitude decorates the architrave of the door leading inside the burial chamber.

H - The goddess Isis seated on a large nebu*-hieroglyph representing gold and with a* shenu*-sign in her hands, welcomes Nefertari.*

I - Nefertari referred to as "the Osiris, the Great Royal Bride, Lady of the Two Lands" turns to the three genii guards of the First gate of the kingdom of Osiris and recites the formula "in order to know the gates of the kingdom of Osiris in the West and of the gods dwelling in their recesses".

J - The three genii of the First gate of the kingdom of Osiris in Chapter 144 of the Book of the Dead.

K - The three genii of the Second gate of the kingdom of Osiris and in the foreground, one of the four pillars of the burial chamber.

88 top Nefertari playing senet, *a game not unlike draughts. In Chapter 17 of the* Book of the Dead, *this game symbolizes the trials and obstacles that the dead must overcome in order to enter the kingdom of Osiris.*

Entrance

A steep staircase leads into the first hall of the tomb, the square antechamber, extending eastward with a vestibule leading to a first lateral annexe, while in the eastern side of the northern wall begins the second flight of steps, descending to the burial chamber.

Antechamber

A first painting of great interest is visible on the ceiling of the door giving access to the ante-chamber: it is a representation of the solar disc in the eastern horizon of the sky, flanked by the goddesses Isis and Nephthys in the shape of falcons, evoking "the appearance in broad daylight" of Nefertari's soul at the end of its ritual journey inside the tomb. On the northern and western sides of the antechamber, whose blue astronomical ceiling spangled with yellow stars evokes the vault of heaven, we notice a corbel supported by little pillars, originally intended for the gathering of the offerings and of part of the funerary equipment. The paintings on the western wall and on the western side of the southern wall are related to Chapter 17 of the *Book of the Dead* and they show Nefertari under a canopy, engaged in playing at *senet*, which may be considered as an early forerunner of the modern game of draughts, followed by a representation of the queen worshipping an evocation of the god Atum, represented by the sign of the *akhet*-horizon supported by two lions. Next come an image of the *benu*-bird, the ash-colored heron evocation of the soul of Re, a representation of Nefertari's mummified body flanked by the goddesses Nephthys and Isis in the shape of falcons protecting the queen, two anonymous divinities in front of the necropolis door watched by a tutelary spirit and, finally, at the northern end of the wall, an *udjat*-eye, evocation of Horus's eye, a powerful protecting amulet. The images of the northern wall, partially ruined, are also related to Chapter 17 of the *Book of the Dead* and in the only portions now visible are two of Horus' Four Sons, originally standing by a chapel, inside which was found the god Anubis in the shape of a dog, a representation of Horus and Nefertari sitting on two thrones, and, on the easternmost side of the wall, above the beginning of the second flight of steps, we again see Horus with his Four Sons, all of them looking to the right.

The eastern wall of the ante-chamber is interrupted by a wide opening, flanked by the representations of Osiris (to the left) and of Anubis (to the right), that admits into the vestibule leading into the lateral annexe.

The vestibule

The paintings in the vestibule show Nefertari welcomed by the goddesses Selkis (to the left) and Neith (to the right), while she is shown into the presence of different divinities: to the left is the goddess Hathor introducing the queen to the god Khepri with the scarab beetle face, while to the right there is Harsiesis, falcon-headed with the double crown of Upper and Lower Egypt, who conducts Nefertari into the presence of Re-Harakhty and Hathor-Imentit.

88 bottom One of the most important images of the tomb from the theological and philosophical point of view, is found on the western wall of the first eastern lateral annexe: a ram-headed deity placed between Isis (to the right) and Nephthys (to the left) symbolizes the union of Re with Osiris and recalls the theme of the death and the daily rebirth of the sun. The hieroglyphic text commenting on the image says: "Here is Re resting inside Osiris, here is Osiris resting inside Re".

89 top The Seven Heavenly Cows, the Bull and the Four Helms of Heaven of Chapter 148 of the Book of the Dead *thanks to whose formulas the deceased was able to obtain the necessary food.*

89 bottom Nefertari facing Thoth, divine scribe "Lord of Hermopolis, Great God", recites the formulas prescribed in Chapter 94 of the Book of the Dead *so as to obtain the scribe's pot and palette and the related magical powers.*

The "Side room"

A narrow door in the vestibule is overlooked by a vulture with spread wings, representing the goddess Nekhbet. The jambs of the door are painted with the images of the goddess Maat, embodiment of the cosmic order, and it gives access to the lateral eastern annexe, which had been called the "Side room" by Schiaparelli's team when they discovered it. On the northern side of the western wall there is a splendid scene of Nefertari offering fabrics to Ptah, the god from Memphis. On the adjoining northern wall, Nefertari utters in front of the god Thoth, the divine scribe, the wordings foreseen by Chapter 94 of the *Book of the Dead*, that will permit her to obtain "the pot and the palette of scribe" of the god and his magic powers. The eastern wall of the annexe, which the visitor faces as soon as he has crossed the threshold, shows a double scene of offering made by Nefertari to Atum, the creator god in the Heliopolitan theology (to the right) and to Osiris "Who Presides over the West" (to the left), receiving in exchange, so say the texts, "eternity, the infinite and every joy". On the southern wall, on the other hand, a complex scene is represented, related to Chapter 148 of the *Book of the Dead*, by means of which the deceased was able to obtain food and nourishment in the Other World. The scene begins with the image of Nefertari, located at the end of the adjoining western wall, shown in the act of worshipping, and it includes, below, the Sky's Four Helmsmen, related to the four main directions of the universe and, above, the "Seven celestial cows" with the Bull, "the superior who dwells in the castle of the Red", evoking life's cyclic perpetuity. A last scene completing the decorative program of the western wall and coming right before the image of Nefertari, represents the sun god Re ram-headed united to Osiris, between the goddesses Isis (to the right) and Nephthys (to the left), while the accompanying text says "Here is Re resting inside Osiris, here is Osiris resting inside Re", a splendid evocation of the perpetuity of the daily cycle of the sun.

The second staircase

Two large symmetric scenes are painted in the upper part of the second staircase leading into the sarcophagus room. In them Nefertari, upright in front an offering table, proffers two ritual vases containing a liquid offering to two groups of divinities: to the left we see Hathor, Nephthys and Maat with her wings spread out on Nefertari's ornamental scroll, while to the right are represented Hathor, Selkis and Maat. Both these scenes are followed by a winged *uraeus*, the holy cobra symbol of royalty, protecting the queen's ornamental scroll with a posture similar to Maat's in the preceding scene. Under the *uraeus* we see to the left a large image of Anubis the Embalmer,

in the customary canine form, couched on top of a chapel and accompanied by Isis "the great, mother of the god, Lady of the sky". To the right, on the other hand, Anubis is represented together with Nephthys "Lady of the Sky, Lady of all the gods, She Who Dwells in the Western Desert". A long text transcribed in the vertical columns, in which Anubis speaks to Nefertari promising her a place in the "Holy Land" accompanies these last scenes. At this point the staircase ends in a great door leading into the burial chamber, on whose architrave the goddess Maat "daughter of Re" is represented with her wings spread out as she utters the following words: "I offer protection to my daughter, the King's Great Bride, Nefertari Meri-en-Mut, purified".

The burial chamber

The burial chamber, also called "golden hall", inside which the regeneration of the deceased magically took place, has a surface area of almost 90 square meters and is decorated with an astronomical ceiling supported by four large pillars painted on all sides. To the eastern and western sides of the hall open two small lateral annexes, while a third annexe called the "cella" is found at the center of the northern wall on the continuation of the tomb's main axis. At the center of the hall, between the four pillars, was originally located the queen's sarcophagus of red granite, of which no more than a part of the cover was found at the time of the discovery.

The scenes and the texts visible on the walls of the sepulchral chamber are related, in the western half of the hall, to Chapter 144 of the *Book of the Dead*, dealing with the doors of Osiris' kingdom, their watchers and the magic wordings that had to be uttered by the deceased in order to be able to cross them. Likewise, the wall decorations on the eastern half of the burial chamber illustrate Chapter 146 of the *Book of the Dead*, dealing with the gates of Osiris' kingdom in the Fields of Iaru. Each of the five gates of Osiris' kingdom in Chapter 144 of the *Book of the Dead* were originally shown in the western half of the hall (only the first three are visible at present). They were watched by three tutelary spirits referred to as "the Appointed", "the Guardian" and "the Announcer": to them Nefertari turns saying "I have paved the way, allow me to cross and to move off. May I always see Re". In the eastern half of the hall, which had been extensively looted, following a scene in which Nefertari makes offerings to the three main gods of the Afterworld - Osiris, Hathor-Imentit and Anubis - are represented the ten gates of Osiris' kingdom in the Fields of Iaru as described in Chapter 146 of the *Book of the Dead*, of which only the last five are still fairly intact today. Each of these gates was watched by a single guardian, generally with an animal face, to whom Nefertari turns, uttering his name, in order to surmount the obstacle and proceed on her way towards Osiris' kingdom.

90 bottom The north wall of the antechamber, with the door at the bottom of the second staircase leading into the sepulchral chamber.

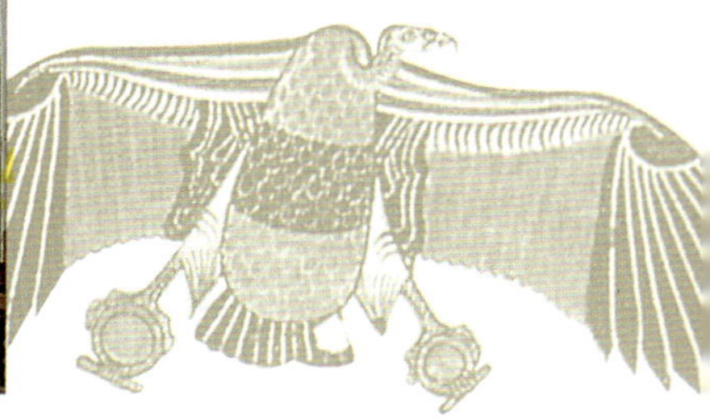

90-91 The burial chamber seen from the south. On the pillars two forms of Horus are shown related to ancient priestly functions: to the left Horus-iun-mutef ("Horus, Support of his Mother") and to the right Horus-nedj-itef ("Horus pillar of his father") while in the background can be seen two djed-pillars.

91 bottom On the lower part of the staircase are two large representations of Anubis "the Embalmer, the great god who dwells in the Sacred Earth". In one Anubis is depicted as a black jackal, crouched over a shrine with the nekhakha-*flail* between its back paws. The god receives Nefertari with a long speech beginning with the words: "Come unto me, oh worthy consort of the king".

The pillars

The decoration of the pillars in the burial chamber is not only of great interest, but is also perfectly preserved. When entering the hall the visitor is welcomed by two large figures of divinites wearing leopard skins, that constitute the decoration of the two southern pillars on the southern sides: these are Horus-iun-mutef, that is to say "Horus support of his mother" to the left, and Horus-nedj-itef "Horus protector of his father" to the right, two forms of Horus linked to ancient priestly functions. On the internal faces of all the pillars, along the longitudinal axis, there are four representations of Osiris "Who Presides over the West, Un-nefer, Lord of the Holy Land, the great god, the Lord of the Ennead" dressed in the same garment worn by Nefertari: a long white tunic tightened at the waist by a red band tied at the front with two pendants. On the pillars'external faces, along the transversal axis, there are four large *djed*-pillars, evoking Osiris' spine, which were originally turned towards the sarcophagus, whose main axis coincided with the transversal one of the burial chamber. On the six other sides of the pillars the decorations represent the queen in the presence of diverse divinities: Hathor, Hathor-Imentit, Anubis, Isis.

92 Painted on each of the four inner faces of the pillars is the djed*-pillar, which represents the spinal column of Osiris containing the bone-marrow of resurrection. At its side are the scrolls and titles of the queen.*

93 top left The god Osiris is portrayed no fewer than four times on the pillars of the sepulchral chamber. Erect inside a shrine, Osiris is shown dressed in the same tunic and red scarf worn by Nefertari, to indicate that assimilation between queen and god has taken place.

93 top right
The three genii of the Second gate of the kingdom of Osiris, referred to in Chapter 144 of the Book of the Dead: Un-hat-sen, Qed-her ("She who turns her head around") and Imsus. Each of these genii had a specific role and they are described as "the Doorkeeper", "the Guardian" and "the Annunciator". In the foreground is one of the four pillars, with Osiris and a djed*-pillar depicted on it.*

93 bottom right
Close-up the east pillar of the burial chamber, on which Horus-nedj-itef is shown wearing the characteristic leopard skin. Osiris, inside a shrine, can be seen on the other side.

The cell and the lateral annexes
The decoration of the cell is utterly lost today because of the complete detachment of the pictorial layer due to the superficial crystallization of salts coming from the underlying rock. The lateral annexe opening on the southern side of the western wall has preserved just a small portion of its decoration: among the scenes still visible we see the representation of a building with a façade of pillars evoking Osiris' tomb at Abydos, inside which two of Horus' Four Sons, Imsety and Duamutef, appear between two ibis-headed tutelary spirits, evocation of the Four Winds. The opposite western lateral annexe too is today almost empty and the only scene still entirely readable shows Nefertari praying in the presence of Anubis and Isis.

The meaning of the tomb
The whole complex decorative program of Nefertari's tomb evokes a ritual journey of the soul of the deceased descending into the subterranean world. This is Osiris' kingdom symbolised by the sarcophagus hall or "golden hall", to which Nefertari accedes after having crossed the doors and the gates of Chapters 144 and 146 of the *Book of the Dead*. Here takes place the gestation and the revival of the queen's soul which, coming back to the antechamber, is transfigured and shines bright according to Chapter 17 of the *Book of the Dead*, illustrated by the wall decoration of this portion of the tomb. Finally, Nefertari "appears in broad daylight" assimilated to Re rising on the eastern horizon of the sky, following an image evoked on the ceiling of the entrance door of the tomb itself.

THE TEMPLES OF MILLIONS OF YEARS

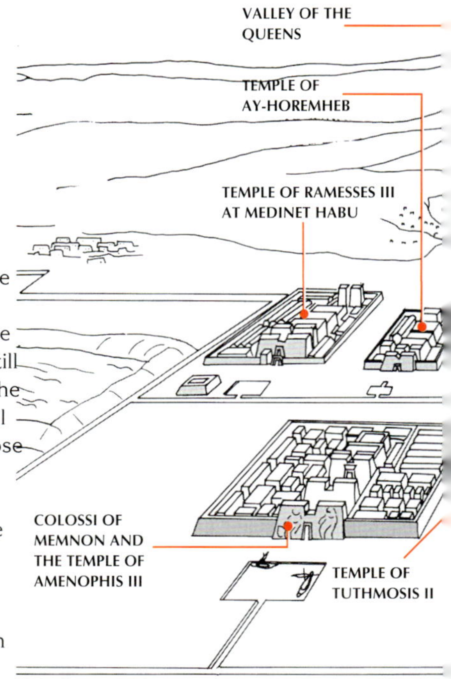

Built on the boundary between the tilled lands which were yearly flooded by the Nile's overflow and the spurs of the Theban mountain, and connected with the river by a network of canals, the temples of the Theban pharaohs of the New Kingdom extended, lined up parallel to the Nile and roughly oriented in an east-west direction according to the solar axis. These buildings, the majority of which have practically disappeared or survive in such a state as to be hardly interpretable for the tourists, like the temples of Amenophis III, Merneptah, Tuthmosis IV, Tuthmosis III and Ramesses IV, were referred to as "Funerary Temples", but the studies made on the structures and above all on the decorations of the few still well preserved temples, suggest that they should rather be defined as "Temples of the Royal Worship" or "Memorial Temples". Indeed, these temples, called by the ancient Egyptians "Temples of Millions of Years", were used for the worship of the king while he was still alive, deified and associated with the worship of the god Amun, principal deity of the Theban pantheon, whose son on earth was the pharaoh. By virtue of this ritual union, taking place yearly on the occasion of the Beautiful Feast of the Valley, the royal power was renewed and strenghtened. Also, during the thirtieth year of the pharaoh's reign the celebration of the *sed*-festival took place in the temples of millions of years.

This was a ceremony of very old origin whose aim was to regenerate the king's strength and, through him, that of all Egypt, whose supreme guarantor he was.

94-95 bottom General view of the necropolis, with the mountain of Thebes behind. Visible in the foreground, behind the two huge statues known as the Colossi of Memnon, is the site where the mortuary temple of Amenophis III once stood. The mortuary temples or temples of royal cult, which the ancient Egyptians called "Million year castles" were built on the lower slopes of the mountain. They were connected by a system of canals to the Nile which reached this level when in flood.

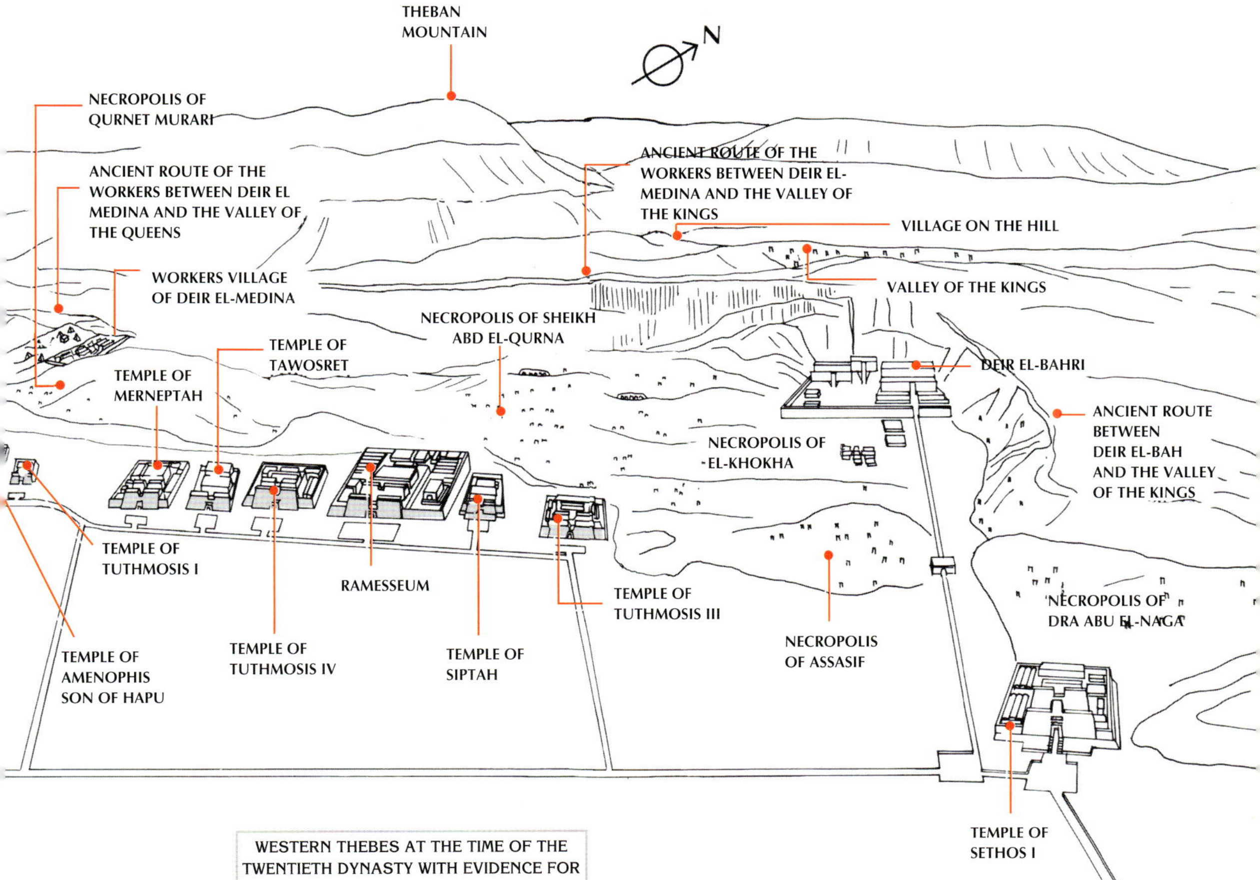

WESTERN THEBES AT THE TIME OF THE TWENTIETH DYNASTY WITH EVIDENCE FOR THE TEMPLES OF MILLIONS OF YEARS

95 bottom The Ramesseum complex with its adjoining buildings and the barely visible remains of the temples of Siptah and Tuthmosis III.

96 bottom The site of Deir el-Bahri, which owes its name to the presence of a monastery constructed in the Coptic age, is at the bottom of an imposing rock amphitheater at the foot of an impressive cliff. The site, considered sacred to the goddess Hathor, was selected during the Eleventh Dynasty by king Nebhepetre Mentuhotep for the construction of his burial temple. A few centuries later, during the Eighteenth Dynasty, the burial temples of Hatshepsut and Tuthmosis III were built on the same site.

DEIR EL-BAHRI

96-97 The site of Deir el-Bahri is dominated by the grandiose terraced temple of Hatshepsut: at the side can be seen the remains of the two other temples constructed by her grandson and successor Tuthmosis III and by the pharaoh Nebhepetre Montuhotep, founder of the Eleventh Dynasty.

The most famous and the most visited among the temples of Western Thebes is certainly the one Queen Hatshepsut had built at Deir el-Bahri, a valley ending in an ample amphitheatre demarcated to the west by the rocky face of the Theban mountain, which separates it from the adjoining Valley of the Kings, to the north by the hill of Dra Abu el-Naga and to the south by that of Sheikh Abd el-Qurna. The Egyptians held that this valley, anciently called *geser* "sacred", was sacred to the goddess Hathor, deity of the multiple attributes, but linked to the funerary worship in the Theban necropolis. At Deir el-Bahri (an Arabic name meaning "Monastery of the North"), since as in the Coptic era there was a monastery there, nowadays destroyed no less than three temples were built, arranged one at the side of the other and belonging respectively to the pharaohs Nebhepetre Mentuhotep, Hatshepsut and Tuthmosis III.

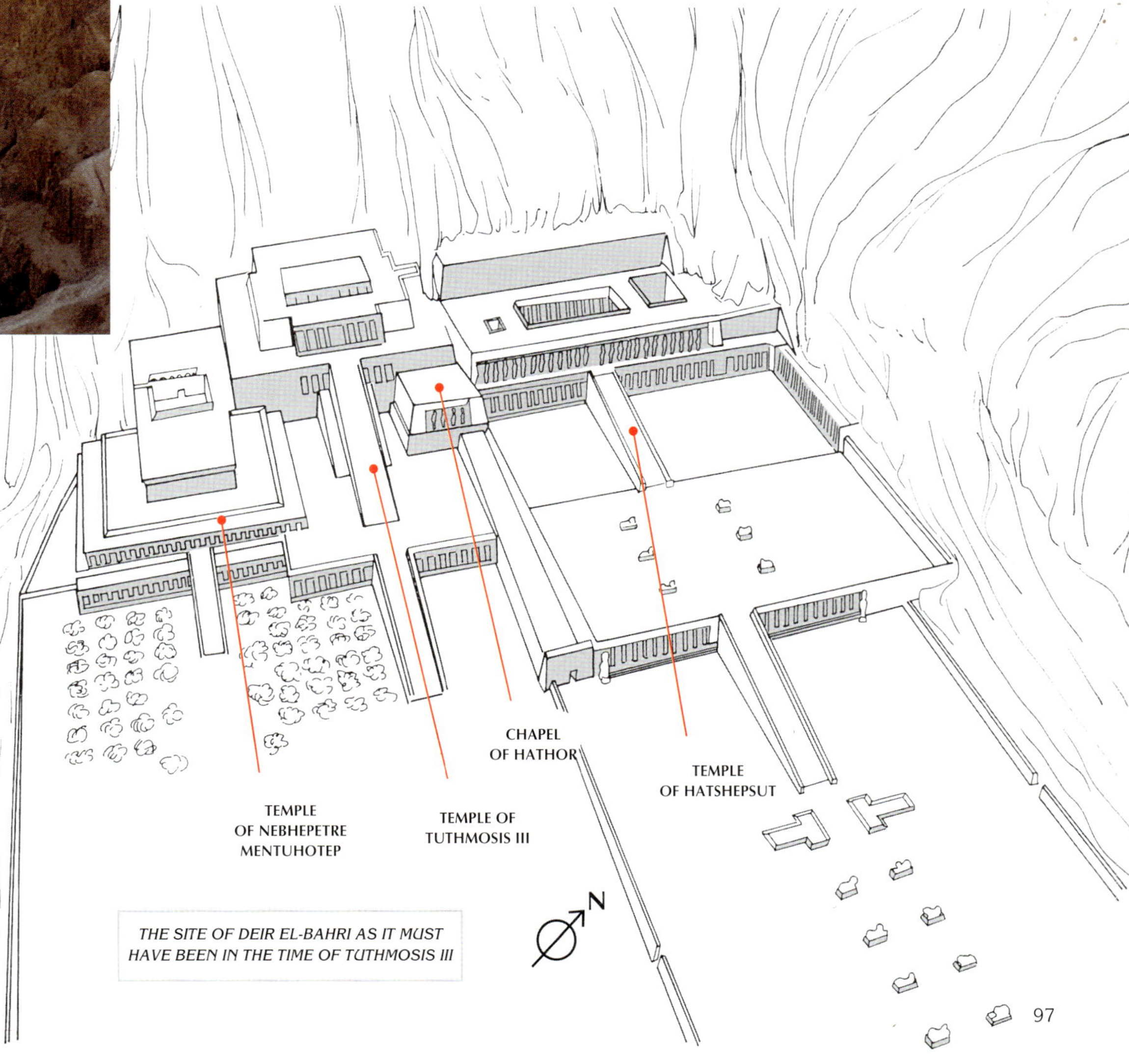

THE SITE OF DEIR EL-BAHRI AS IT MUST HAVE BEEN IN THE TIME OF TUTHMOSIS III

THE TEMPLE OF MENTUHOTEP

King Nebhepetre Mentuhotep was the first to build a temple to the goddess Hathor in the sacred valley. Unlike the other temples of Thebes West, Mentuhotep's was a real funerary temple where the deceased king, deified and revered together with Amun-Re, was worshipped according to a new theological concept which subsequently spread to the New Kingdom's "Temples of Millions of Years". Mentuhotep, the first ruler of the Eleventh Dynasty, who is credited with the reunification of Egypt, wanted to have a temple built for himself close to his tomb, following a tradition that went back to the Old Kingdom, a period in which the funerary temples were built next to the royal tombs, on the eastern side of the pyramids. The great architectural novelty of the temple of Mentuhotep is represented by its multi-level layout: a processional road started from the valley temple and led to a vast yard shaded by trees arranged in parallel lines. From the yard started a ramp leading through a colonnade to a terrace, in the center of which a mastaba was found. From the yard also opened an underground passage, marked on its surface by a cavity called by the Arabs *Bab el-Hosan*, leading, after a distance of 150 meters, to a cenotaph located exactly under the *mastaba*, where in 1900 Howard Carter, the future discoverer of Tutankhamun's tomb, found a beautiful statue of Mentuhotep in painted sandstone, now kept in the Cairo Museum.

To the west of the terrace and the *mastaba* a second yard was found, surrounded by pillars and leading to a rocky sanctuary intended for the royal cult and to a complex of six funerary chapels and six tombs intended for the royal brides and princesses. Still in the second yard was found the entrance to another long underground passage, leading to the funerary room dug inside the mountain, according to a concept which eventually found widespread application in the tombs of the Valley of the Kings. As in the royal necropolises of the Old Kingdom, the funerary complex of Mentuhotep was surrounded by the tombs of princes, princesses and royal brides (from this sector come the magnificent sarcophagi of the royal brides Kawit and Ashait, discovered at the beginning of the century and exhibited at the Cairo Museum), while the leading citizens and the dignitaries had rock tombs built for themselves on the northern side of the valley. The temple of Mentuhotep, discovered by accident by Lord Dufferin about the middle of the nineteenth century (1859-1869), was subsequently excavated on the initiative of the Egyptian Exploration Society between 1903 and 1907 by Edouard Naville and Charles Currely and, from 1920 to 1931 by Herbert Winlock on behalf of the New York Metropolitan Museum of Art.

The archaeological surveys of the temple were only carried out many years later, between 1968 and 1970 by the German Archaeological Institute at Cairo.

98 This statue of Nebhepetre Mentuhotep in painted sandstone, was discovered at Deir el-Bahri in 1900 by Howard Carter. It was found in the royal cenotaph, under the central mastaba, *which is reached through an opening called Bab el-Hosan. The king, who was responsible for the reunification of Egypt after the internal wars that had characterized the First Intermediate Period, is represented in Osiris form with the red crown of Lower Egypt.*

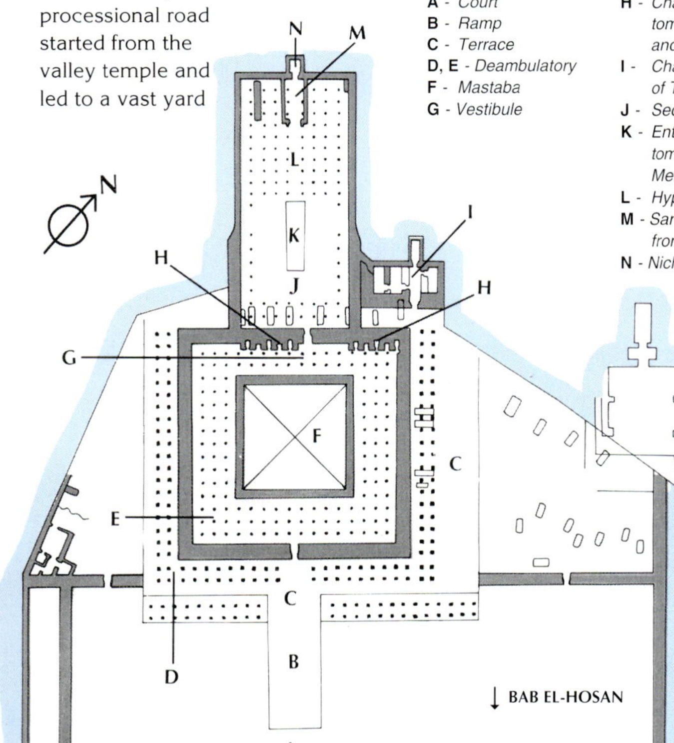

- **A** - *Court*
- **B** - *Ramp*
- **C** - *Terrace*
- **D, E** - *Deambulatory*
- **F** - *Mastaba*
- **G** - *Vestibule*
- **H** - *Chapels of the tombs of queens and princesses*
- **I** - *Chapel to Hathor of Tuthmosis III*
- **J** - *Second court*
- **K** - *Entrance to the tomb of Nebhepetre Mentuhotep*
- **L** - *Hypostyle hall*
- **M** - *Sanctuary carved from rock*
- **N** - *Niche*

THE TEMPLE OF TUTHMOSIS III

In the course of the restoration and cleaning work carried out in 1961, a small temple was discovered whose construction had been ordered by Tuthmosis III; it was found directly to the north of that of Mentuhotep and is situated between it and the Temple of Hatshepsut: this building was dedicated to the god Amun, and there was a chapel nearby dedicated to the goddess Hathor. The Temple of Tuthmosis III, built towards the end of his reign and dedicated to Amun-Re and Hathor, was abandoned by the end of the Twentieth Dynasty, probably due to a landslide which seriously damaged the buildings; it was used later as a quarry, and many centuries later, at the time of the Coptic occupation of the valley, it was transformed into a cemetery. The Temple was discovered in the course of the excavations carried out by the Polish Center of Mediterranean Archeology during the 1961-1962 campaign; excavations at the site continued up to 1967 and revealed magnificent polychrome bas-reliefs; two of them, the most beautiful, are now on exhibition at the Museum of Luxor. The building constructed under the guidance of vizier Rekhmire (whose tomb no. 100 is situated on the hill of Sheikh Abd el-Qurna) occupies the central position relative to the axis of the Valley; its architectural style was evidently inspired by that of the Temple of Hatshepsut. It included a system of ramps and terraces and had a large hypostyle hall sustained by 76 polygonal columns around the perimeter and 12 larger columns closer to the center; it was followed by a hall for Amun's boat and the sanctuary proper. The Temple played an important role during the Beautiful Feast of the Valley and probably replaced the Temple of Hatshepsut as the final destination of the holy procession. Studies of the structures of the Temple of Tuthmosis , as well as conservation and restoration works, are being carried out at present by the Polish-Egyptian Archeological Mission.

99 top In 1961 the archeologists discovered the remains of a temple placed alongside that of Hatshepsut and built by Tuthmosis III. The temple was dedicated to the god Amun and to the goddess Hathor.

99 centre During the excavations of the temple of Tuthmosis III a splendid high-relief was brought to light, depicting the pharaoh with the atef-*crown. This high-relief is on display at the Museum of Luxor.*

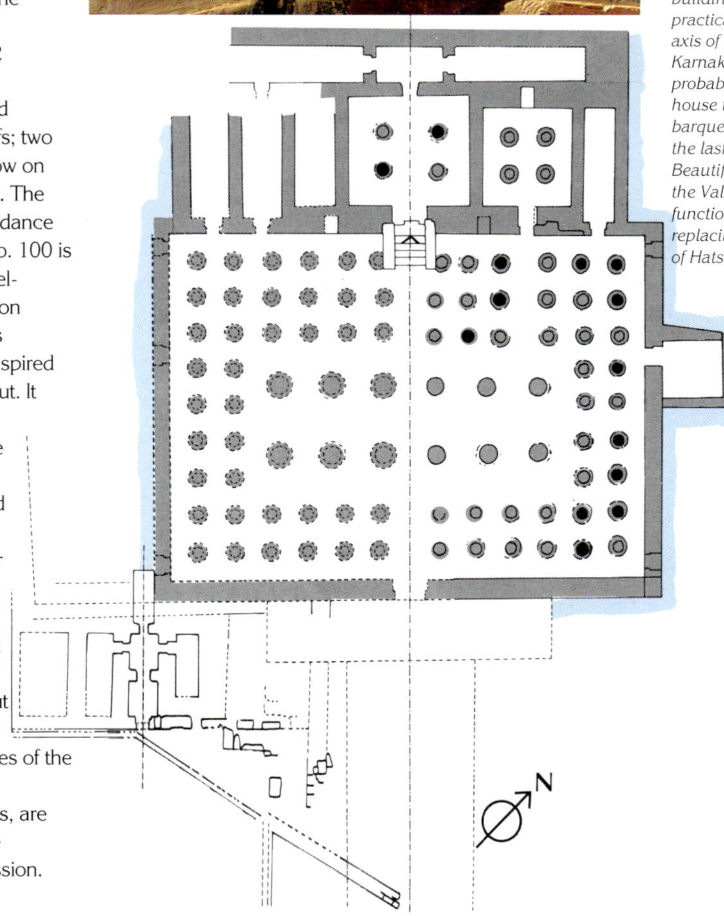

99 bottom Reconstructed plan of the votive temple of Thutmosis III, based on studies by S. Medeksza of Poland's Mediterranean Archaeology Research Centre. Erected at the centre of the Deir al-Bahri complex, this building is situated practically on the axis of the temple of Karnak. It was probably intended to house the sacred barque of Amun in the last phase of the Beautiful Festival of the Valley, thus functionally replacing the temple of Hatshepsut.

THE TEMPLE OF HATSHEPSUT

100 Painted limestone head representing Hatshepsut, belonging to one of the Osiris colossi of the upper portico of Deir el-Bahri. Hatshepsut was the daughter of Tuthmosis I. On the death of her brother Tuthmosis II, she assumed the regency for her grandson, Tuthmosis III, and subsequently had herself proclaimed queen.

The Temple of Hatshepsut which carried the name *djeser-djeseru*, or "the sublime of the sublimes", is undoubtedly the most impressive building of Western Thebes: in general, the design of this architectural masterpiece is attributed to Senenmut, "Chief Steward of Amun", who had his own tomb built right under the first terrace of the Temple, but it is known that, nearby, there was certainly another tomb, that of Djeut, "Overseer of the Treasury, Overseer of Works", whose tomb no. 11 can be found in the Dra Abu el-Naga necropolis. Senenmut wanted the building to appear integrated into the surrounding scenery; in this respect, he was certainly inspired by the innovative concepts already realized by the builders of the Temple of Mentuhotep, but he developed these concepts in ways that were indeed original. The Temple, reduced by now to a state of ruin, was excavated in 1891 by Egyptologist Naville, who was the first to make an attempt at its reconstruction, later continued by Winlock and by Baraize, and - many

years later - by the Polish Center of Mediterranean Archeology, which is still carrying out works at the site since 1961. This well-documented reconstruction work has once again given to the monument the grandiose appearance that characterized it in ancient times.
The construction of the Temple of Hatshepsut took fifteen years between the 7th and the 22nd years of her reign, but studies of the monument carried out up to the present have revealed that the original design underwent profound modifications in the course of the construction works: it is possible that the builders came across the site of an earlier, uncompleted building, but we have no definite information about this.
The site chosen by Hatshepsut for her Temple was the product of precise strategical calculations: it was situated not only in a valley considered sacred for over 500 years to the principal feminine goddess connected with the funeral world, but also on the axis of the Temple of Amun of Karnak and, finally, it stood at a distance of only a few hundred meters in a straight line from the tomb that the Queen had ordered excavated for herself in the Valley of the Kings (KV no. 20), on the other side of the mountain. As with the Temple of Mentuhotep, that of Hatshepsut was preceded by a temple in the valley, now lost, built on the bank of a reservoir connected to the River Nile. From there began - flanked on

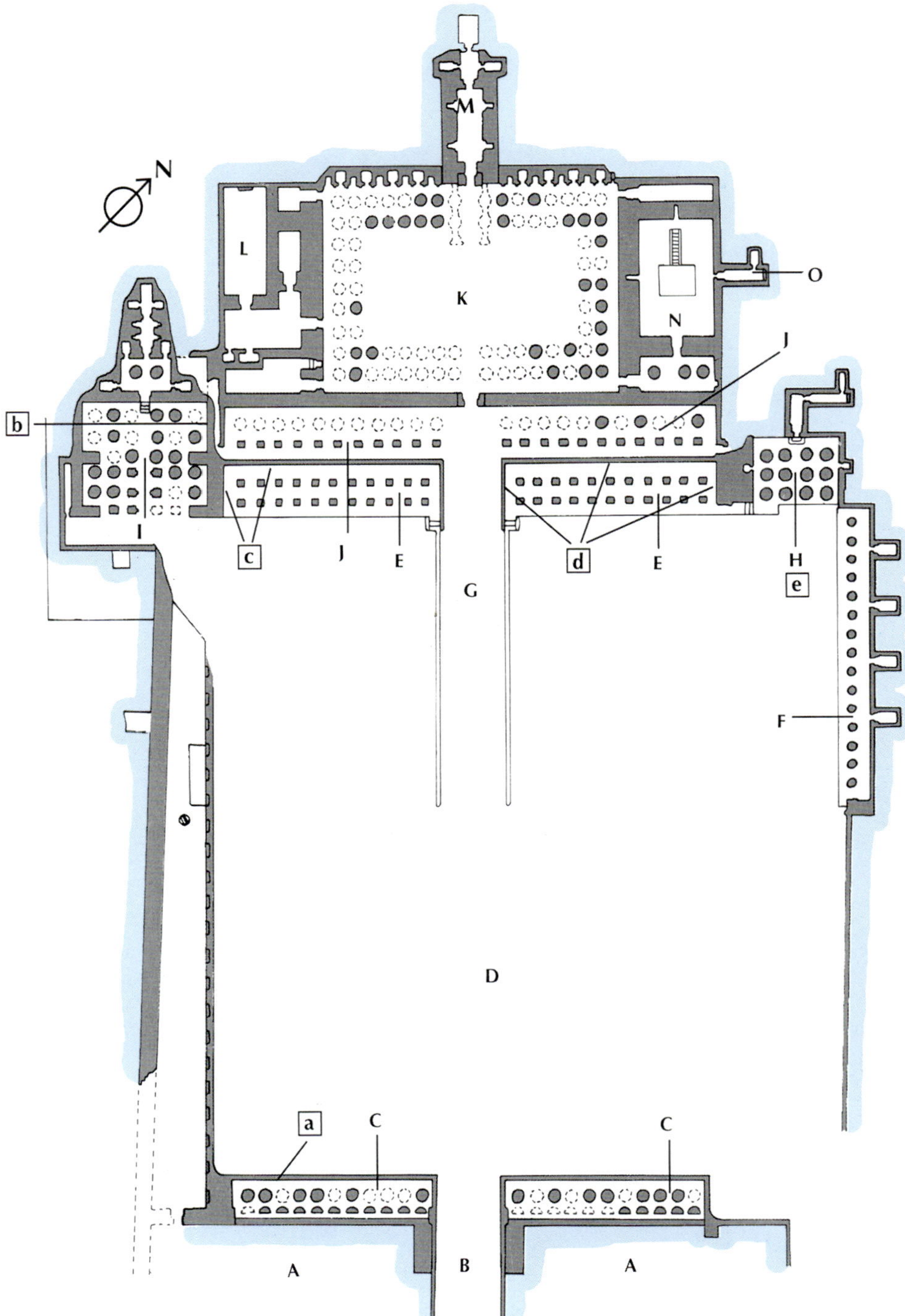

A - First courtyard
B - Ramp
C - Lower portico
D - Second courtyard
E - Middle portico
F - Northern portico
G - Second ramp
H - Lower chapel of Anubis
I - Chapel of Hathor
J - Upper portico
K - Upper terrace
L -. Chapels destined for the royal worship of Hatshepsut and Tuthmosis I
M - Amun's shrine
N - Courtyard dedicated to the sun worship of Re-Harakhty
O - Upper chapel of Anubis

Main scenes
a - Transport and offering of the obelisks to Amun; procession of soldiers
b - Boats and parade of soldiers
c - Punt expedition
d - Theogamy scenes: crowning of the queen
e - The queen in the presence of the deity

both sides by two rows of sphinxes - the avenue of processions which entered into the first courtyard limited in the west by a portico with 22 columns flanked on both sides by two Osirian colossi representing the Queen and adorned with bas-reliefs illustrating in the southern part (the obelisks portico) the transportation of two large granite obelisks from Aswan and their erection in the Temple of Karnak and, in the northern part (the hunting portico), ritual scenes of hunting and fishing. Two successive ramps lead from the first courtyard to the second courtyard and to the upper terrace, both delimited to the west by porticos. The intermediate portico is flanked by two chapels situated to the south and the north of it and dedicated respectively to Hathor and Anubis.
On the wall of this portico, two most important events of the Queen's reign are illustrated in polychrome bas-reliefs: in the southern part (the Punt portico) one can see illustrations of the expedition to Punt and, in the northern part (the birth portico), the divine birth of Hatshepsut is represented as if she were conceived by the god Amun in the image of her real father Tuthmosis I.

102 top left The capitals that reproduce the features of the goddess Hathor with cow's ears, thus called "Hathor-headed", adorn the top of the columns in the chapel of Hathor in the temple of Hatshepsut.

102 bottom left One of the bas-reliefs of the chapel represents a parade of the queen's soldiers in honor of the goddess Hathor.

102-103 The chapel of Hathor, which is reached today by the Punt portico is at the south-west end of the temple of Hatshepsut. Originally, it had its own independent access ramp.

The chapel of Hathor

The chapel of Hathor (in the southern part of the terrace), which originally had a separate entrance, includes a vestibule and a hypostyle hall followed by a sanctuary excavated in the rock which consists of a vestibule with two columns and two rooms. The vestibule, now accessible from the portico of Punt, consists of two square Hathor-headed columns in a central position adorned in their upper parts with masks representing Hathor with the characteristic cow's ears. These columns are flanked by two groups of four columns each while the hypostyle hall, which is situated at a clearly higher level, is supported by 12 columns. The perimeter walls of the vestibule and of the hypostyle hall are decorated with scenes of festivals celebrated in honor of the goddess and scenes of sacrifices to Hathor represented on her boat in the form of a cow. The part built in the rock consists of a vestibule with two columns from which there is access to the Sanctuary proper where the most secret parts of religious rituals were performed; it consists of the first narrow and long hall with a vaulted ceiling and four small niches on the northern and southern walls from where one can enter the last room. The walls are interrupted by two large niches, and in the corner of one of them, in a well-concealed position, there appears, quite unexpectedly, the portrait of Senenmut, as if the architect had wished to participate in a magic way, together with the Queen, in the most secret rituals of the cult of Hathor. The remaining part of the decorations of the Sanctuary is dominated by the motif of the goddess Hathor, always represented in the form of a cow nursing and protecting Hatsheput, and by the motif of the Queen offering sacrifices to her divine wet-nurse. And finally, on the back wall of the hall, the final scene of the cult of Hathor is represented: the consecration by Amun and Hathor of the Queen wearing the double crown and the ritual beard.

A - Vestibule
B - Hypostyle hall
C - Sanctuary carved from rock
D - Vestibule
E - Niche
F - First room
G - Second room

Main scenes:
a - *The goddess Hathor portrayed as a cow*
b - *Procession of the queen's soldiers and boats*
c - *Hathor in the form of a cow licks the hand of the queen*
d - *The queen moves towards Hathor*
e - *The queen between Amun and Hathor*
f - Senenmut

THE CHAPEL OF HATHOR

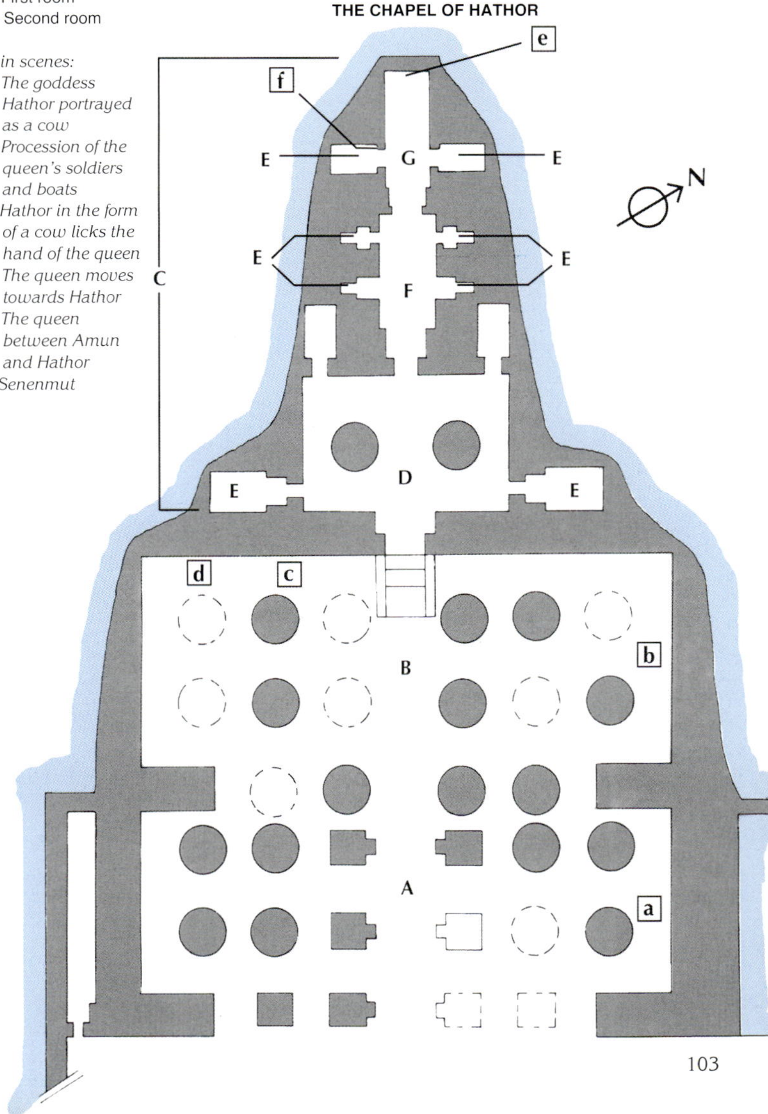

103 top right Bas-relief located in the chapel of Hathor, representing the goddess in the form of a cow with two high plumes that enclose a solar disc.

103 bottom left The entrance door of the rock shrine in the chapel of Hathor.

The lower chapel of Anubis

The lower chapel of Anubis (on the northern side of the terrace) has a splendid hypostyle hall with 12 grooved columns and an astronomical ceiling followed by two small rooms in succession at right angles to each other, with vaulted ceilings; farther on, there is a niche, also at right angle to the second room.

104 top left
The northern part of the hypostyle hall of the chapel of Anubis, is decorated with scenes of offerings to Anubis and to Sokaris.

104 top right
The god Amun with the distinctive attributes of the deity, the was-*sceptre and the* ankh-*cross.*

104 bottom The god Thoth, divine scribe.

A - Hypostyle hall
B - Niche
C - First room
D - Second room
E - Niche

Main scenes
a - Anubis with the queen (chiselled out)
b - The queen (chiselled out) withOsiris, Re-Harakhty and Nekhbet
c - The queen (chiselled out) presents offerings to Amun-Re
d - The queen (chiselled out) presents offerings to Anubis
e - Tuthmosis III presents offerings to Sokaris

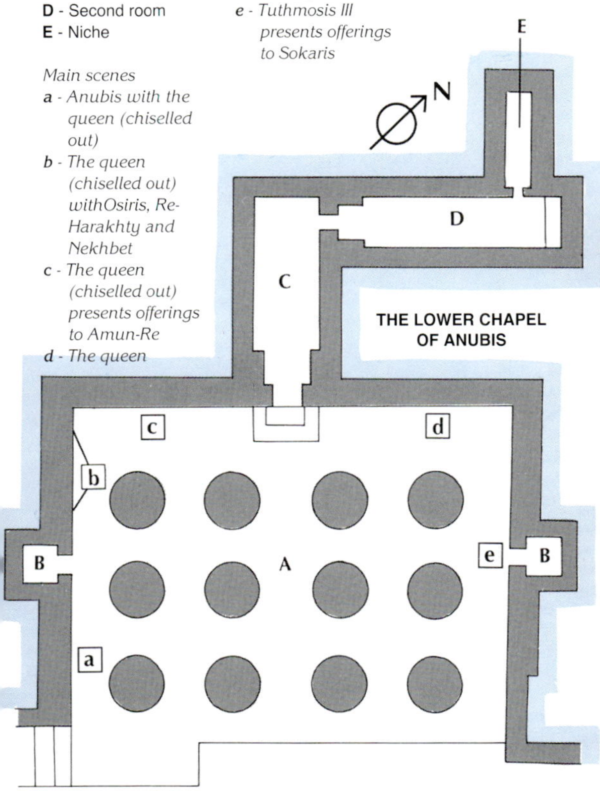

105 left The god Amun before a table of offerings.

105 top right In the bas-relief over the architrave that leads into the niche of the chapel of Anubis, Queen Hatshepsut is depicted, conventionally, with male features, in the act of ritual offering of wine to Re-Harakhty.

105 bottom right The goddess Nekhbet, guardian goddess of Upper Egypt, in the form of a vulture, stretches her wings in sign of protection: between her talons can be seen a shenu-*sign, a protective amulet.*

The upper terrace

A second ramp (at present closed to the public) leads from the center of the intermediate portico to the upper terrace whose portico consists of columns originally decorated with Osirian statues of the Queen, now mostly destroyed. Through a great doorway of pink granite, one enters a courtyard circled by columns. To the north and south of the courtyard, there are two areas dedicated respectively to the cult of the sun and that of the royalty. The northern part dedicated to the solar cult of Re-Harakhty includes a vestibule with columns leading into a courtyard with a solar altar in the center. In the northern part of the courtyard, there is another chapel dedicated to the cult of Anubis (the upper chapel of Anubis). There is no clear idea as to why there are two chapels dedicated to this divinity in the Temple, but numerous hypotheses have been advanced to explain this exceptional and unique fact; anyway, it appears clear that great importance was attached to this god in Deir el-Bahri, especially in comparison with other funeral gods, such as Osiris and Sokar, who acquired greater importance later, but always appear in a secondary role here. The southern part of the upper terrace dedicated to the royal cult consists of a vestibule from which one gains admittance to two chapels dedicated to the cult of Hatshepsut and that of Tuthmosis I. Moving towards the West along the axis of the Temple, one comes across the rock sanctuary of Amun excavated into the mountain slope and destined to receive the sacred boat during the Beautiful Feast of the Valley. This sanctuary, which also served as the place for celebrating the cults of Tuthmosis I and Tuthmosis II, was expanded during the Ptolemaic era and dedicated to the cult of two great deified architects: Amenophis, son of Hapu, the Overseer of Works of Amenophis III, and Imhotep, the designer of the stepped pyramid of Djoser in Saqqara, at a later date associated with Asclepius, the god of medicine; during that period, the third terrace became, in fact, a *sanatorium* frequented by sick people hoping to be cured. Other transformations were effected later, in the seventh century AD, when the place became the "Monastery of the North" from which the current name of the site originated. The Temple of Hatshepsut in Deir el-Bahri suffered much damage and mutilation during the reign of Tuthmosis III, who at great expense had her name very carefully cut out and who usurped the images of his aunt without, however, seriously damaging the bas-reliefs; this process went on with even greater frenzy during the reign of Amenophis IV / Akhenaten. In the course of that period dominated by heresy, numerous images of gods in the old Egyptian pantheon were destroyed, especially those connected with Amun, the main god in Thebes and great adversary of the unique god Aten. Other destructions were added during the Nineteenth Dynasty, particularly during the reign of Ramesses II who ordered the destruction of the Osirian colossi which decorated the portico of the upper terrace. And finally, the Copts, after they came into possession of the place to build their monastery, completed the destruction by cutting out the faces of the surviving pagan gods.

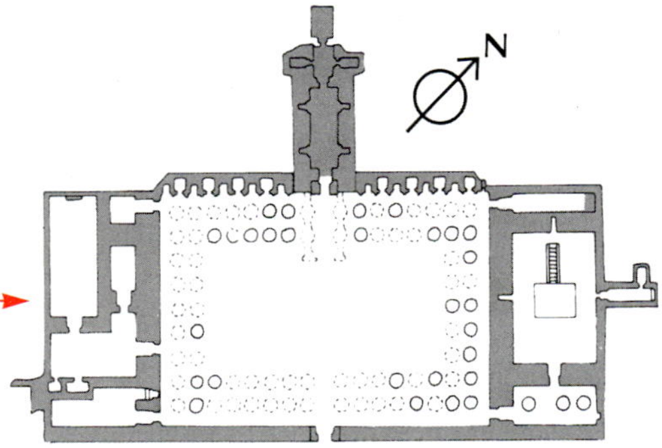

107 top Plan of the upper terrace.

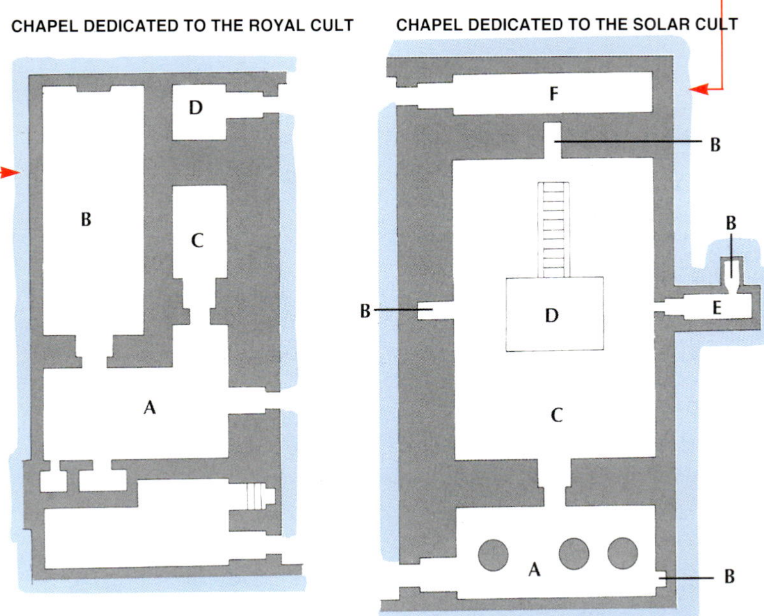

106 left One of the Osiris colossi of Queen Hatshepsut that adorn the upper portico.

106-107 General view of the upper terrace delimited by the portico to the east and by the rock wall of the mountain to the west; in the centre is the entrance to Amun's shrine, that opens into the mountain.

107 bottom General view of the monumental ramp leading to the upper portico and terrace.

Chapel dedicated to the royal cult

A - Vestibule
B - Chapel of Hatshepsut
C - Chapel of Tuthmosis I
D - Chapel of Amun-min

Chapel dedicated to the solar cult

A - Vestibule
B - Niche
C - Court
D - Solar altar
E - Upper chapel of Anubis
F - Chapel of Amun-Min

EXPEDITION TO THE LAND OF PUNT

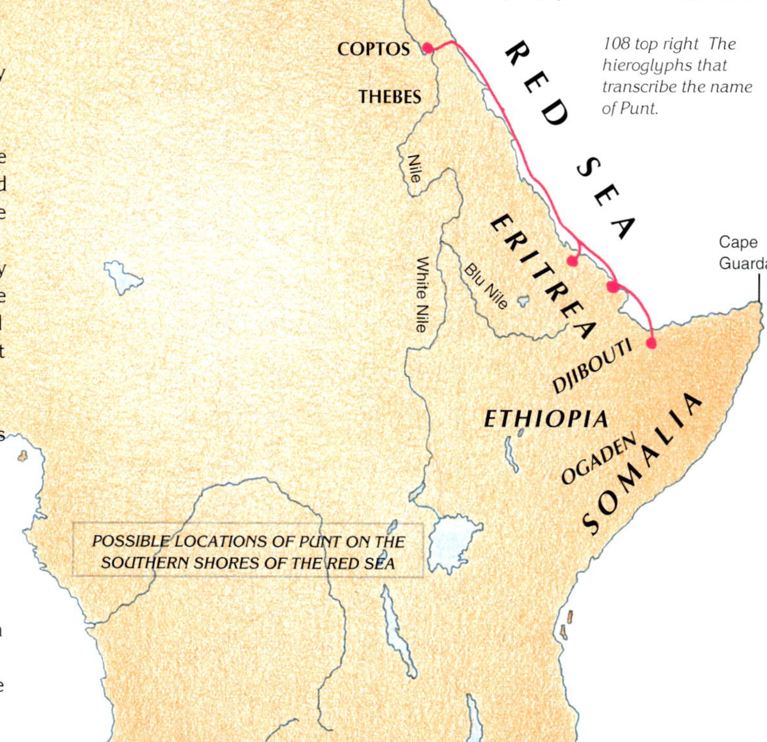

The most admirable bas-reliefs of the temple of Hatshepsut are undoubtedly those that illustrate the famous naval expedition to the mysterious Land of Punt sent by the Queen, probably in the 8th year of her reign; they are situated in the southern part of the portico of the second (intermediate) terrace. These polychrome bas-reliefs accompanied by a long text describe in detail the voyage along the shores of the Red Sea (called "Great Green" in the text), the arrival at Punt of the Egyptian vessels, the indigenous pile dwellings, the plants and animals of the region, the sacrifices and presents offered to the King and Queen of Punt, the loading on board the vessels of important raw materials much needed by the Egyptians: cinnamon, aromatic wood, gold, resin, furs, but first of all *antyu* and *senetjer*, two products identified as myrrh and incense, as mentioned in the text describing the scene: "The vessels were loaded with large quantities of the

108 top right The hieroglyphs that transcribe the name of Punt.

108 top The exact position of the land of Punt remains a mystery. At present, however, it is considered that the most plausible locations correspond to the coasts of Eritrea, Djibouti or Ethiopia.

108 bottom left View of the middle portico, also called the "Punt portico", supported by a row of square columns and decorated in the north part with scenes associated with Hatshepsut's divine birth, and in the south part with the scene of the famous expedition to the land of Punt.

108 bottom right The king of Punt, Parakhu, with Queen Aty, receives the Egyptian embassy. The queen is represented with a pathological obesity that could be the manifestation of a form of elephantiasis. This fragment of bas-relief is currently on display at the Cairo Museum and has been replaced on site by a copy.

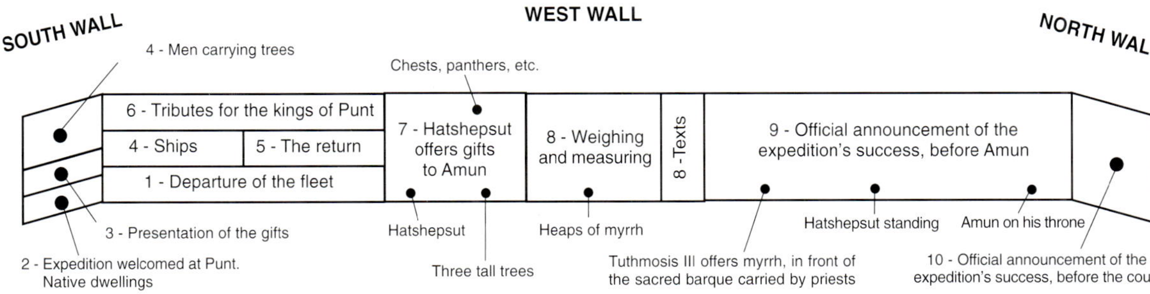

109 top Key to the interpretation of the portico of Punt, according to J.H. Breasted (1962).

wonders of the Land of Punt, with all the precious woods of the Land of God, heaps of gum of myrrh and living myrrh trees, with ebony wood and pure ivory, with the green gold of Amu, with aromatic wood called *tyshepses* and *khesyt*, with fragrances, incense, antimony, with baboons, monkeys and dogs, with skins of panthers of the South, with the natives and their sons..." After showing the return of the expedition to Thebes and the weighing of the imported goods, the bas-reliefs come to an end on the northern part of the portico by representing the arrival of the god Amun at Deir el-Bahri on the occasion of the Beautiful Feast of the Valley, to whom the Queen delivers a long speech stressing the valor of her enterprise that had made it possible to find the way to Punt in order to comply with the god's wish; they further feature the speech by Amun, the Lord of Karnak, who, having praised the Queen for all her actions and for the success of the expedition goes on to say that he was glad, since the precious goods from Punt confirmed he had created that land "to amuse his heart" and that he had provided for the final success of the difficult expedition, so that he could benefit from "all the good and beautiful things from the Land of God", satisfied that Hatshepsut had thus respected his will and honored her divine father. It is known that 31 myrrh trees arrived in Egypt in good condition and were planted in Amun's garden at the Temple of Karnak, although different climatic conditions probably prevented them from taking root, which later induced Tuthmosis III and still later Ramesses III to organize new expeditions to Punt.

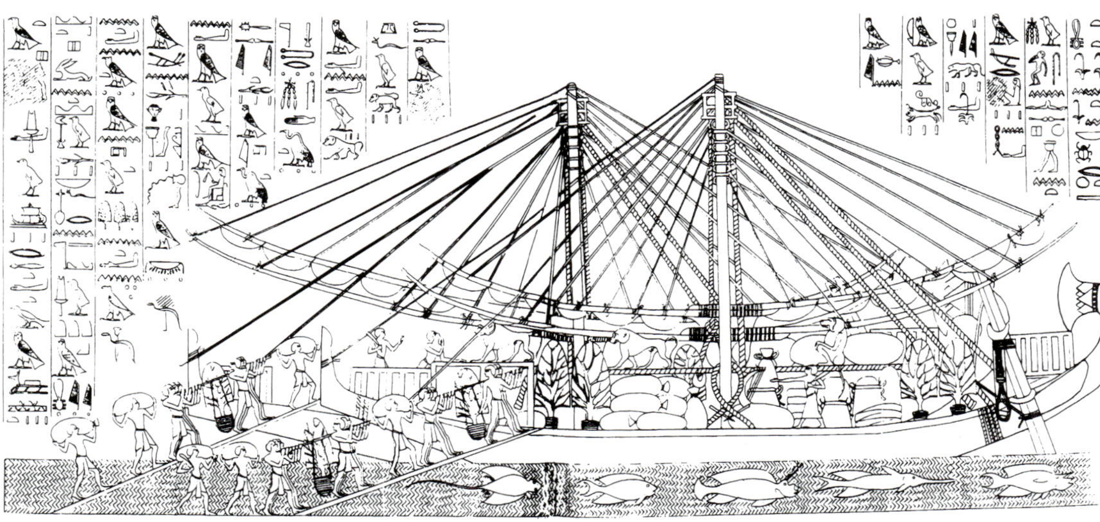

109 centre The Egyptian ships are loaded with products of the land of Punt. The Egyptian expedition had five ships, each about twenty meters long, with a crew of thirty oarsmen.

109 bottom The precious antyu *trees (a word that apparently denotes incense) with their roots, are placed in baskets and carried on board the ships.*

But where was the mysterious Land of Punt? The texts with the comments on various depicted scenes do not contain a hint about this; in any case, it is known that ever since the time of the Old Kingdom the Egyptians organized more or less regular expeditions to the Land of Punt, primarily with a view to importing incense and myrrh, the raw materials that could not be found elsewhere and were required for celebrating religious cults, in the course of which these substances were burnt in honor of the gods; they also found various use in the field of medicine, as evidenced by various papyri, such as Ebers or Harris 716.

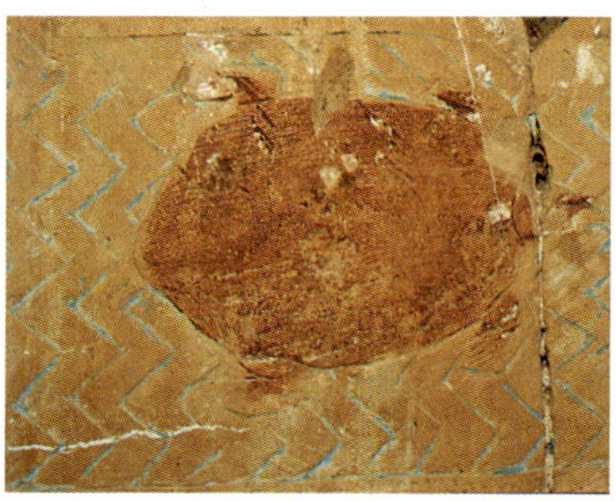

110 left The bas-reliefs show many specimens of the tropical marine fauna typical of the Red Sea, together with freshwater and saltwater fish that would suggest that the land of Punt was located at the mouth of a river.

110 top right The captain of the Egyptian expedition to the land of Punt, followed by his soldiers, offers, according to the hieroglyphic texts, "bread, wine, beer, meat and fruit" from Egypt: how these perishables could have been conserved during the voyage remains a mystery.

In particular, myrrh was principally used as a balsam, while incense, besides being burnt in special burners for its characteristic fragrance, was used in combination with other substances, such as honey, myrrh, wax, beer or fruit, for the treatment of numerous disorders from rheumatic pains to stomachache, and from liver disorders to problems of blood circulation and headaches. As to the real geographical location of the Land of Punt, numerous hypotheses have been advanced and, although there is no reliable proof, it is logical to assume that Punt, which the ancient Egyptians called the "Land of God" was situated on the shores of the Red Sea. And indeed, knowing the relatively modest navigational skills of the ancient Egyptians, who were engaged in river navigation much more than in sea voyages, and comparing the average speed of the ships in that age which amounted to

110 bottom right The inhabitants of Punt lived in dwellings with conical roofs, built on piles and reached by ladders. Huts of a fairly similar shape can still be seen today in some regions of Eastern Africa.

about 3-4 knots) to the time required for completing the expedition (about 30 to 40 days for the voyage along the coast using the dominant northerly winds and about three months for the return voyage on oars against the wind), it appears evident that the Land of Punt could not lie farther than Cape Guardafui, the southernmost point of the Red Sea. Besides, at these latitudes, on both the African and the Arabian coasts, the plants from which both myrrh and incense are produced, the *Boswellia* and the *Commiphora*, indeed grow. These were the two most important products of the Land of Punt; also, the examination of various archeological objects brought from Punt demonstrates their African origin without the shadow of a doubt. Thus, it would be logical to assert that the Land of Punt was situated in the area of the Horn of Africa, more precisely, on the coasts of Ethiopia and northern Somalia.

THE BEAUTIFUL FEAST OF THE VALLEY

In the time of Hatshepsut, the chapel of Amun situated on the upper terrace of the Temple of Deir el-Bahri was the final destination of the holy procession in the course of the Beautiful Feast of the Valley which, together with the Festival of Opet, was the main event in the liturgical calendar of Thebes. The Festival of the Valley described in the bas-reliefs of the upper terrace was the most ancient of all the various religious celebrations and took place during the second month of the *shemu* season, that is, during the tenth month of the solar year which, in the age of the New Kingdom, coincided with the beginning of summer. This recurrent festivity called *pa heb nefer* en painet, or the "Beautiful Feast of the Desert Valley" originated in the time of Nebhepetre Mentuhotep, and

111 Transport of the sacred boat of Amun containing the shrine with the image of the god, during the Beautiful Festival of the Valley. On this occasion Amun went to the western bank and halted in the different temples of the royal worship rendering homage to the deceased deified kings.

its name is an allusion to the Temple that this King had ordered built for himself in a valley situated to the south of Deir el-Bahri and known until this day as Nebhepetre Valley. The Beautiful Feast of the Valley was, in essence, a "celebration of the dead" in the course of which, as happens today, family members of the deceased visited the tombs of their buried relatives, spent some time there, ate, and received friends who paid their respects. On these occasions, the god Amun accompanied by leading inhabitants of Thebes took part in a large procession on the west bank to visit the gods of the West and the deified dead Kings: the priests of the Temple of Karnak then put up a tabernacle containing the holy image of the god on an imitation boat which was carried on their shoulders by the participants up to the jetty where it was placed on board the magnificent ship *Userhet*, or the "Powerful Prow", which was towed by the King's boat and was followed by the boats of Mut and Khonsu, the other two gods that, together with Amun, formed the Theban Triad. This squadron of boats crossed the Nile and, reaching the west bank, the procession marched towards the Temple of Millions of Years of the King, making its way through the acclaiming crowd of people offering ritual sacrifices of food and bunches of flowers which, on contact with the divine image, became impregnated with the very essence of the deity and were later deposited on the tombs in the necropolis where they ensured the spiritual revival of the deceased. The imitation boat of Amun was first carried to the interior of the Temple, to its hypostyle hall, then the priests carried the god's tabernacle to a nearby chapel containing also the ritual image of the Pharaoh, which magically transformed itself into the sacred image of the god, and left it there for the whole night. On the next day, the procession around the sacred image began anew and included the entire necropolis, making stops in the Temples of Millions of Years of the Deceased Kings, to guarantee in this way, through assimilation, the eternal nature of this royal cult. The final destination of the procession was the Temple of Hatsheput in Deir el-Bahri, in the sacred Valley of Hathor. Here Amun's tabernacle was deposited in the most sacred part of the Temple, the Chapel of Amun, situated on the upper terrace, where it stayed amidst bunches of flowers before it was transported back to Karnak at the end of the celebrations.

THE CACHE OF DEIR EL-BAHRI

Crossing the mountain range that is the southern limit of the valley of Deir el-Bahri, one would find oneself near a rocky precipice, practically invisible from afar, which originally housed the tomb, made in the form of a shaft, of the royal bride Inhapis (no. 320); it became famous under the name of the "cache of Deir el-Bahri". In the year 1881, Gaston Maspero, Director of the Egyptian Service of Antiquities, alarmed by the appearance on the market of objects originating from the royal tombs, after conducting investigations that led to the identification of a band of robbers operating in the Thebes area and to their confession, found at that site the remains of the most famous Egyptian Pharaohs, including those of Ramesses II and his father Sethos I. In fact, the Thebean priests of the Twenty-first Dynasty - around the reign of Pharaoh Siamun (978-959 BC) and of Chief Priest Pinudjem II (990-969 BC) - in their attempt to save the royal remains of the most important pharaohs from profanation which, they thought, was becoming ever more probable, since cases of robbery of the royal tombs by expert thieves had occurred already by the end of the Twentieth Dynasty and could become more frequent, decided to hide the remains in this rocky precipice of the mountains of Thebes which was justly considered more secure than the tombs situated in the Valley of the Kings.

112 top In 1881, Gaston Maspero discovered a hiding-place in a small valley located south-west of Deir el-Bahri, concealed in a bend of the rock wall and practically invisible from a distance. This famous "hiding-place of Deir el-Bahri" contained the mummies of some of the most famous pharaohs of Egypt, transported in secret by priests in order to preserve them from the profanations that were fairly widespread during the Twenty-first Dynasty.

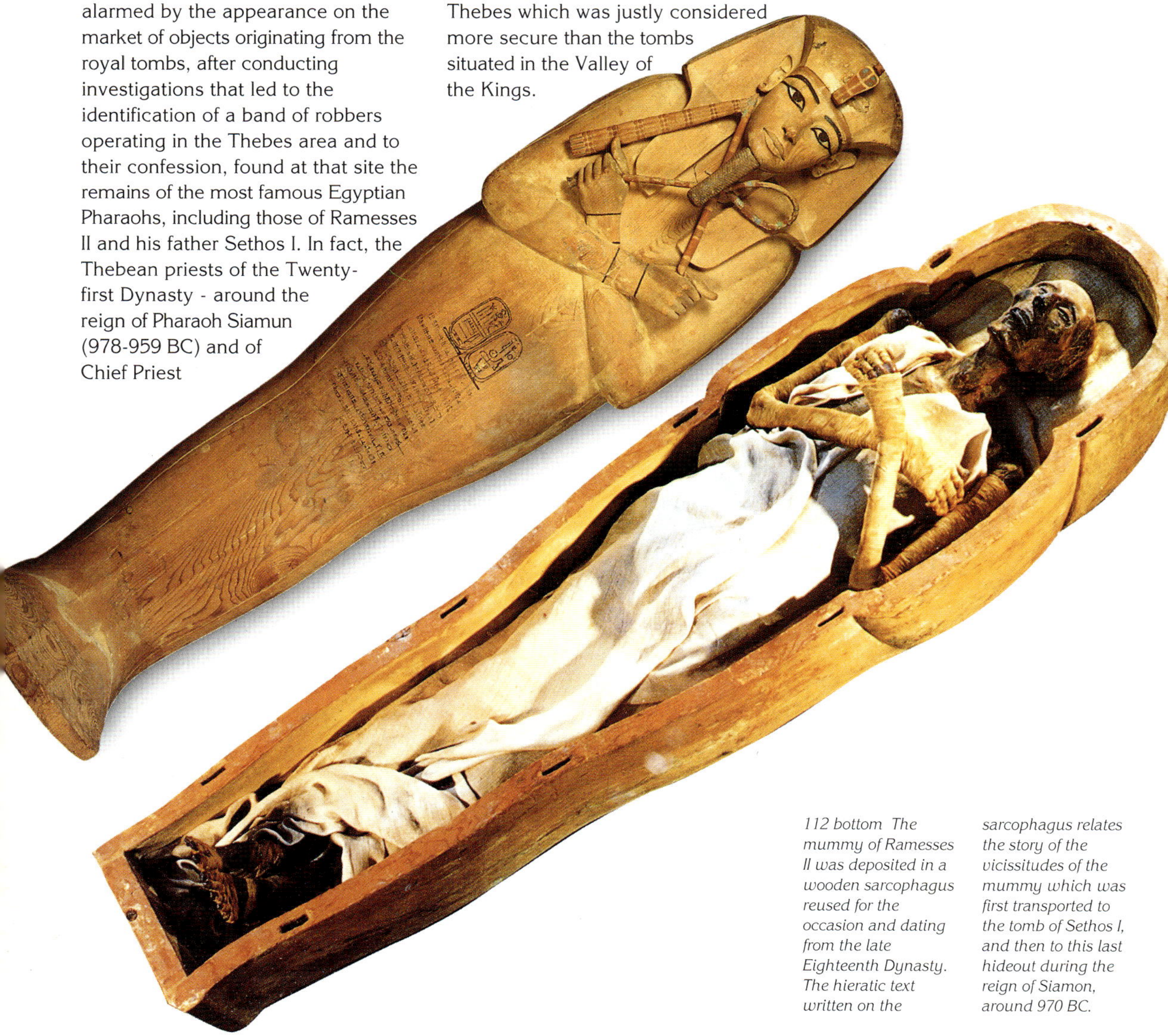

112 bottom The mummy of Ramesses II was deposited in a wooden sarcophagus reused for the occasion and dating from the late Eighteenth Dynasty. The hieratic text written on the sarcophagus relates the story of the vicissitudes of the mummy which was first transported to the tomb of Sethos I, and then to this last hideout during the reign of Siamon, around 970 BC.

THE SECRET TOMB OF SENENMUT
TT no. 353

Chief Steward of Amun
Eighteenth Dinasty

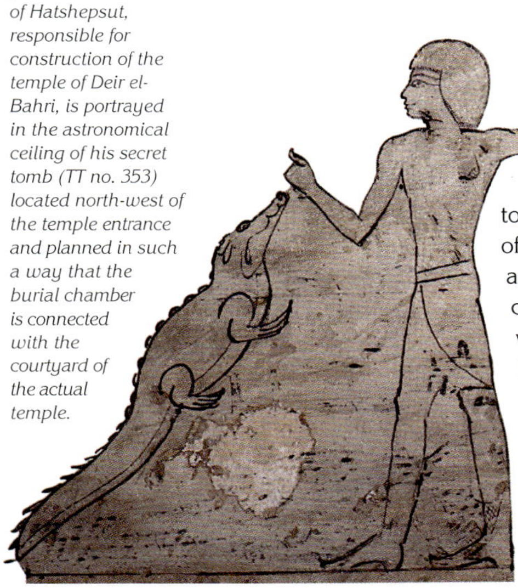

113 top The portrait of Senenmut, the famous architect of Hatshepsut, responsible for construction of the temple of Deir el-Bahri, is portrayed in the astronomical ceiling of his secret tomb (TT no. 353) located north-west of the temple entrance and planned in such a way that the burial chamber is connected with the courtyard of the actual temple.

Just before the entrance to the lower terrace of the Temple of Hatshepsut, at the northern side, there is a small but deep hollow opening, remnant of an ancient clay mine at the end of which is the entrance to the unfinished tomb of Senenmut, the "Chief Stewart of Amun", an extraordinary and enigmatic personality who played one of the most important roles during the period of Hatshepsut's co-regency, and primarily since the seventh year of her reign. Senenmut, who by that time had already had a great and impressive tomb built for himself in the necropolis of Sheikh Abd el-Qurna, near the hill top (TT no. 71), now in a state of complete ruin, later apparently wished to be buried closer to his beloved Queen, with whom, certain historians hypothesize, he might have had intimate relations, though they cannot point to any evidence in support of such an assumption. His tomb at Deir el-Bahri was excavated deeply into the rock in such a way that the whole complex was situated in exact correspondence with the first terrace. The long and steep descending corridor enters into a very small room on whose walls there are quotes from the *Book of the Dead*, and which is decorated with the most ancient astronomical ceiling known in Egypt, with the reproduction of the twelve months of the lunar calendar, as well as of the stars and constellations of the northern hemisphere. Starting from there, another descending corridor leads to another room and finally to the burial chamber. By studying the astronomical ceiling it was possible to fix the exact positions of Jupiter and Mars at the time, and by complex mathematical and astronomical calculations to arrive at the year 1463 BC, or the 17th year of Hatshepsut's reign. The date and circumstances of Senenmut's death remain a mystery; nor do we know anything about what happened to him after Hatshepsut's death which occurred in about the 21st year and the assumption by Tuthmosis III of full powers; nevertheless, it is known for certain that he fell into disgrace, and his secret tomb was probably abandoned precisely during this period.

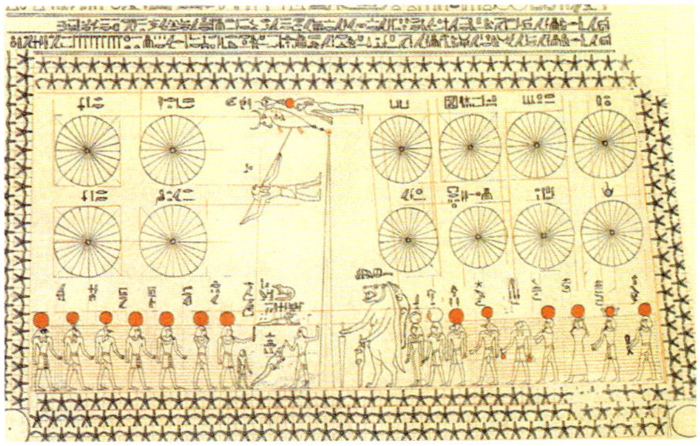

113 centre and bottom right The tomb's astronomical ceiling contains a very precise representation of the northern constellations and the twelve months of the year, symbolized by circles with radii. By study of the positions of the stars depicted, it has been possible to date this ceiling precisely to 1463 BC, corresponding to year 18 of the reign of Tuthmosis III.

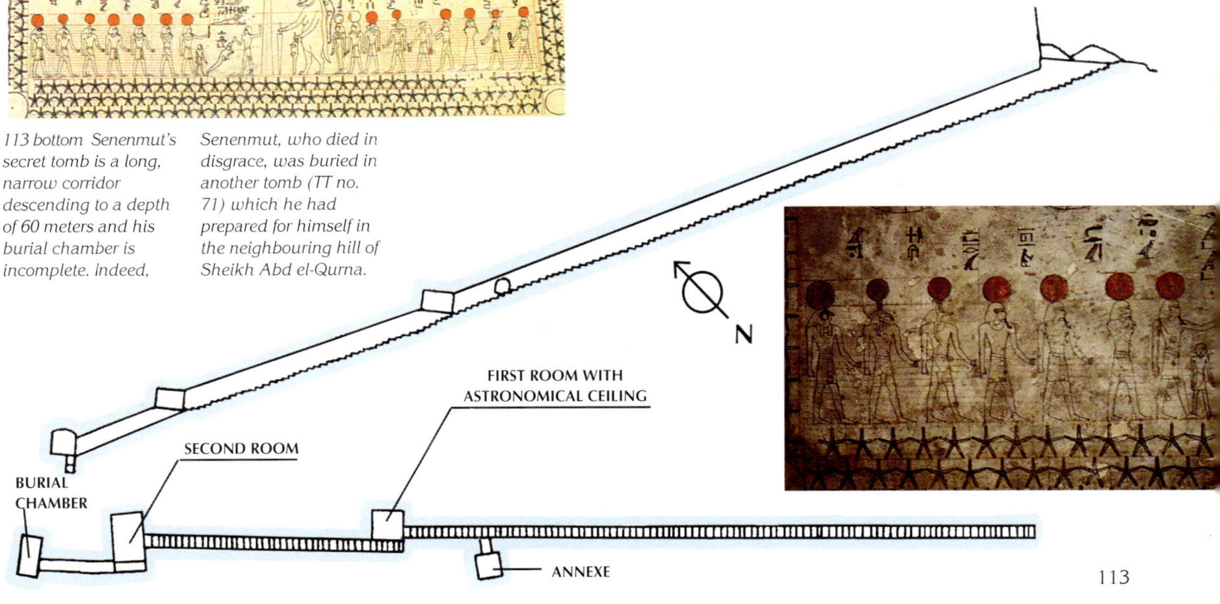

113 bottom Senenmut's secret tomb is a long, narrow corridor descending to a depth of 60 meters and his burial chamber is incomplete. Indeed, Senenmut, who died in disgrace, was buried in another tomb (TT no. 71) which he had prepared for himself in the neighbouring hill of Sheikh Abd el-Qurna.

THE TEMPLE OF SETHOS I

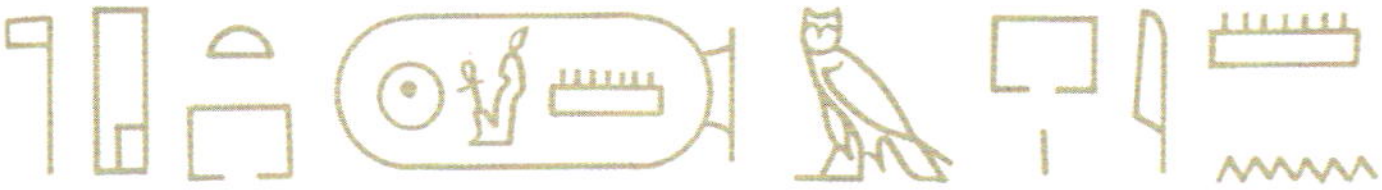

The Temple of Sethos I is the northernmost of all the temples of Thebes, near the western border of the village of Qurna. The nineteenth-century travellers called it the "Temple of Qurna" and the local people *Qasr el-Rubaiq*, but the ancient Egyptians called it "Glorious Sethos in the West of Thebes". It is probable that in those times the administrative center of Western Thebes was situated there, in the village known as *Heft-her-nebes*, or "City in front of its Master". Sethos I dedicated this Temple to Amun-Re and to the cult of his father Ramesses I who, in the course of his brief reign, did not have time to order the construction of his own memorial temple, as proven by the chapel dedicated to him and situated in the southern part of the Temple. This building, later completed by Ramesses II, included a powerful wall and two pylons made of unburnt brick that served as border between the two courtyards. From the great portal of the first pylon, a row of sphinxes crossed the courtyards up to the hypostyle hall. In the southern part of the first courtyard stood the royal palace - a structure whose function was primarily ritual, built at this place for the first time but copied repeatedly in the future. In other words, the royal palace made it possible for the deceased king to materialize during the great festivities in the Throne Hall where he was represented by a statue. Although the pylons of the Temple built of unstable materials like unburnt bricks have now disappeared completely, the Temple itself, constructed of sandstone, is perfectly well preserved and has a triple structure, in whose center is situated the hypostyle hall, decorated with elegant columns in the form of papyrus fascicles and, as

114 top View of the remains of buildings adjoining the temple of Sethos I, brought to light by excavations made by the German Institute of Archaeology. The ancient name of the temple was "Glorious is Sethos to the west of Thebes".

114 centre top View of the temple of Sethos I at Qurna, built by the "path on which Re lies down", as the ancient Egyptians called the roadway which led to the Valley of the Kings. Only the central part of the building, constructed from blocks of stone, is well preserved. Originally in front of it were two pylons made from air-dried bricks, of which few traces remain.

114 centre bottom The pharaoh presents offerings to the deified queen Ahmes Nefertari, wife of Amosis, founder of the Eighteenth Dynasty.

114 bottom Sethos I portrayed as he offers wine in two nu *ritual jars.*

in the Temple of Hatshepsut, there is, towards the south, an area dedicated to the cult of the king and, to the north, an area dedicated to the solar cult. The northern sector includes a courtyard with the central altar surrounded by niches housing statues of the king who could, in this way, take part in the sacrifices offered to Amun-Re. As to the decorative style, the bas-reliefs adorning the Temple walls are extremely elegant and resemble the style typical for the times of the Eighteenth Dynasty. And finally, the Temple also had warehouses, sometimes specially designed for the storage of agricultural products; these structures appeared then for the first time but were developed in the temples built later, particularly in the Ramesseum, the memorial Temple of Ramesses II. Due to its position, the Temple of Sethos marked the first stop of the processions organized in the course of the Beautiful Feast of the Valley and continued to perform this function until the Roman era, when the area was transformed into a sort of industrial zone where numerous artisans worked. And finally, during the Coptic era, the northern courtyard was transformed into a church, and private dwellings were built within the Temple perimeter; also during that period began the process of reusing the more easily transportable architectural elements, which were incorporated into new buildings. The German Archeological Institute undertook studies and restoration works of the Sethos I Temple in 1972, in the course of which some of the structures that had disappeared in the course of time were once again brought to light.

115 top Sethos I in the presence of Amun.

115 bottom A ram's head topped by the solar disc was the insignia of the great barque of Amun, whose shrine was situated in the central part of the temple.

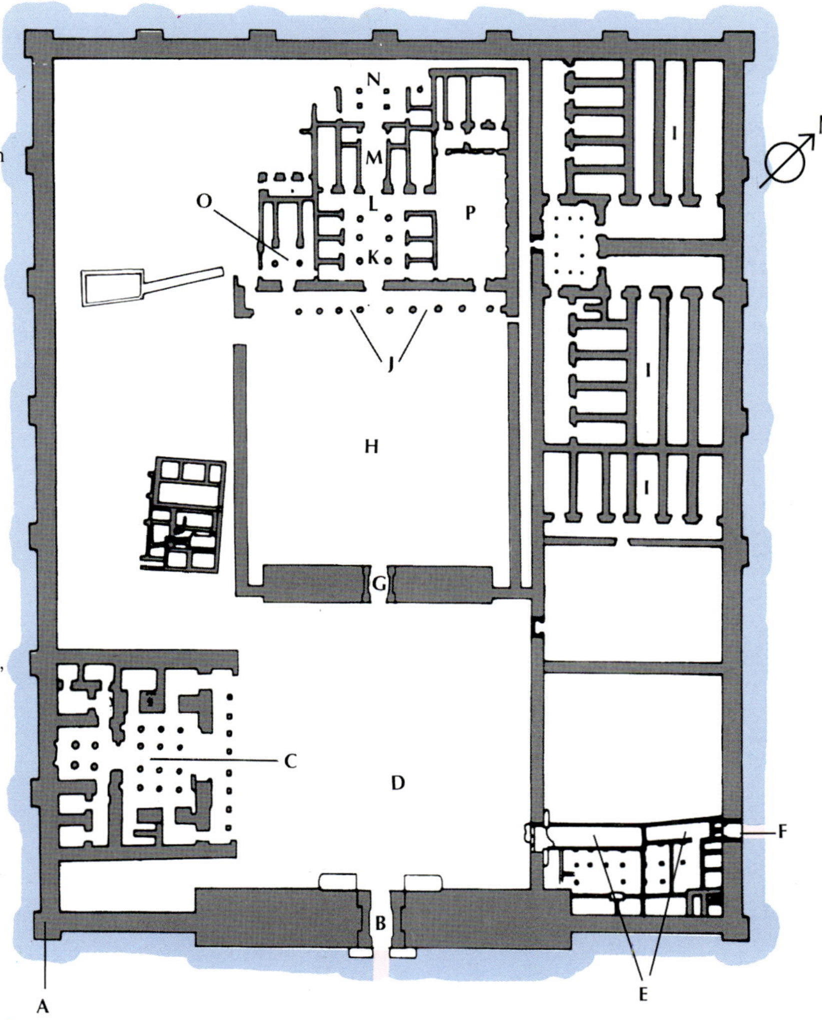

A - Enclosure wall
B - First pylon
C - Royal palace
D - First court
E - Processional route
F - Present entrance
G - Second pylon
H - Second court
I - Magazines
J - Portico
K - Hypostyle hall
L - Vestibule
M - Santuary
N - Room with four pillars
O - Chapel dedicated to the royal cult
P - Court for the solar cult

THE RAMESSEUM

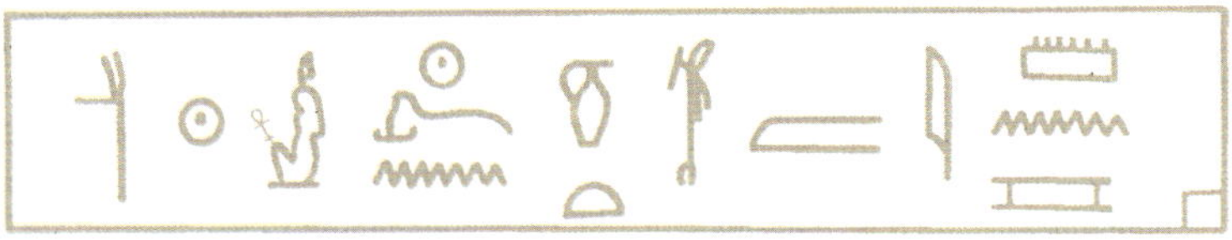

116 top Hieroglyphs stating the name used in ancient times for the Ramesseum. The transcription reads: "Temple of Usermaatre-Setepenre that is linked to Thebes in the estate of Amun to the west of Thebes".

It is widely believed that the Temple of Ramesses II is the most beautiful and elegant monument of Western Thebes. Champollion also held this opinion, and wrote in a letter: "The Ramesseum is perhaps something most noble and pure in Thebes as far as great monuments are concerned." The ancient Egyptians called the Ramesseum the "Temple of Millions of Years of King Usermaatre-Setepenre that is linked to Thebes in the estates of Amun, west of Thebes"; it was also mentioned by classical writers, such as Diodorus Siculus, who described it in detail under the name of "the tomb of Osymandias" (this was a corruption of the word *Usermaatre*, the first name of Ramesses II), and Strabo, who referred to it as *Memnonium*; however, it was Champollion who finally gave it the universally accepted name of the Ramesseum. The construction of the Ramesseum began soon after Ramesses accession to the throne under the guidance of architects Penre and Amenemonet who had introduced various architectural and stylistic innovations, such as the use of sandstone for the pylons and the construction of dromoi flanked by sphinxes in parallel to the three sides of the exterior belt. It was finished probably some time around the 22nd year of his reign and certainly before the 30th year when the great Royal Jubilee celebrations, or the *sed*-feast took place. The Ramesseum occupies an area of about 15,000 square meters, and the Temple is a structure of a classical type reproducing the fundamental motifs of the temple of Sethos I: an external belt, two pylons, and two courtyards which precede the complex of the hypostyle hall situated at a higher level relative to the plane of the courtyards. Outside the central structure of the Temple, there are other structures, represented

A - First pylon
B - First court
C - Royal palace
D - Colossal statue of Ramesses "Sun of princes", originally flanked by the statue of his mother, Tuya
E - Second pylon
F - Second court
G - Original position of the colossal statue of Ramesses II (the head was carried off to London by Belzoni)
H - Vestibule
I - Hypostyle hall
J - The "Room of barques" with its astronomical ceiling
K - The "Room of Litanies"
L - Sanctuary
M - Temple of Tuya and Nefertari

Description of the scenes:
a - Battle of Qadesh
b - Seige of the Syrian city in year 8 of the reign
c - Battle of Qadesh and Festival of Min
d - Seige and capture of the cities of Dapur and Tunip
e - Ramesses II is consecrated and crowned by Sekhmet, Amun-Re and Khonsu
f - Barques during the procession of the Beautiful Feast of the Valley
g - Litanies to Re-Harakhty and to Ptah

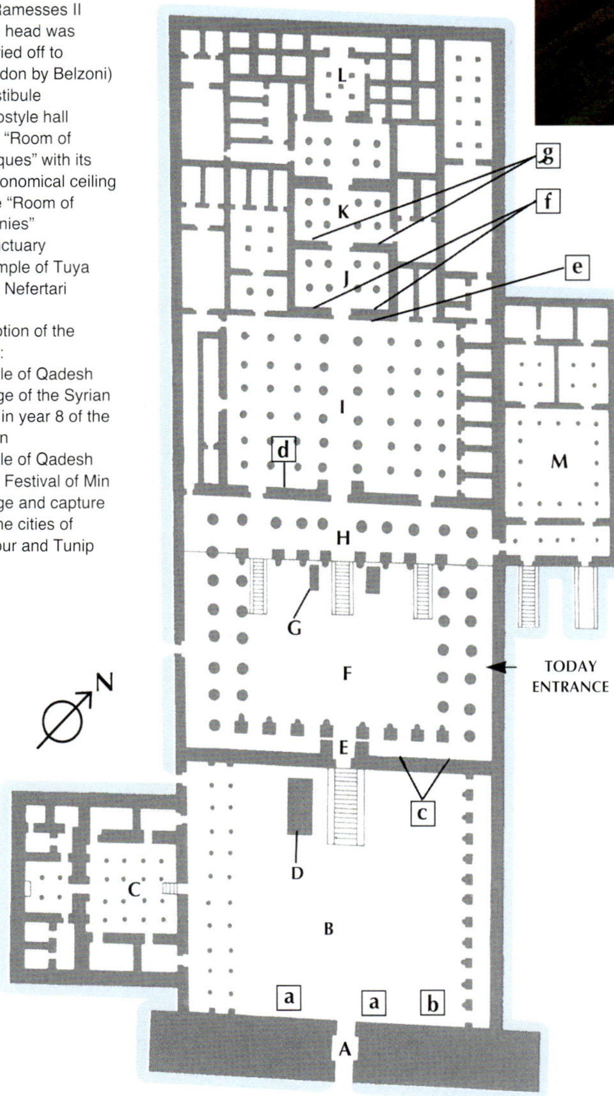

117 right The ancient name of the Ramesseum is inscribed on a block of stone.

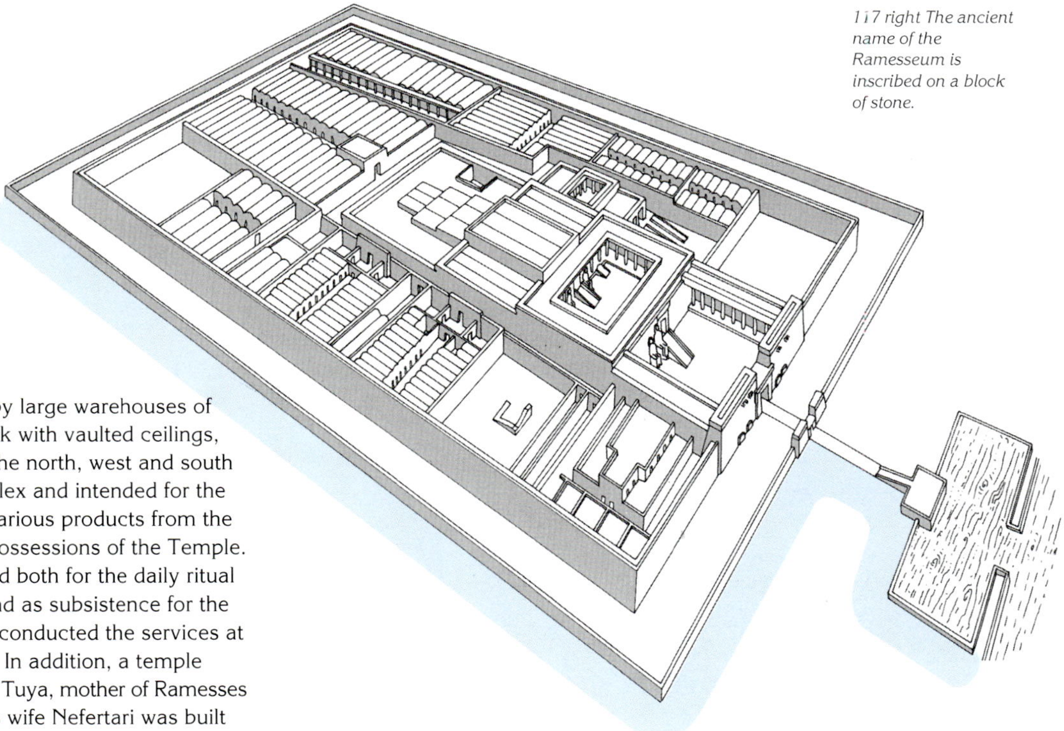

principally by large warehouses of unburnt brick with vaulted ceilings, situated to the north, west and south of the complex and intended for the storage of various products from the numerous possessions of the Temple. These served both for the daily ritual sacrifices and as subsistence for the priests who conducted the services at the Temple. In addition, a temple dedicated to Tuya, mother of Ramesses II, and to his wife Nefertari was built alongside the northern wall of the hypostyle hall, while near the north-western corner of the exterior belt, there was a chapel dedicated to Princess Meritamun and, along the southern belt, another chapel dedicated to Prince Wadjmes, son of Tuthmosis I, that was built during the time of Ramesses.

116-117 General view of the entire Ramesseum complex. Early in the 20th century the Ramesseum was surrounded on three sides by embankments. Until the construction of the Aswan Dam, when the Nile was in flood its waters reached the foot of the first pylon, on the edge of what are now cultivated fields.

118 top An originally colored relief, depicting the battle of Qadesh.

118-119 View of the second court and second pylon of the Ramesseum, with the colossus of Ramesses II, "Sun of Princes", lying on the ground.

118 bottom left An aerial view of the second court, vestibule and hypostyle hall of the Ramesseum. At the top of the photo it is possible to make out the foundations of the temple of Tuya and Nefertari and part of the magazines with their vaulted roofs.

118 bottom right The gigantic feet and other fragments of the colossus of Ramesses, "Re of Rulers", now lying on the ground in the first court

The first pylon, a greater part of whose northern tower collapsed due to terrain subsidence, was decorated with war scenes, some of which reflected the famous battle of Qadesh fought by the king against the Hittites near the Orontes river in Syria during the 5th year of his reign. Crossing its monumental door, now temporarily obstructed by a mass of unburnt brick supporting it to prevent collapse pending restoration, one enters the first courtyard, in whose southern part the royal palace once stood.
On the northern and southern sides of the first courtyard, there were two porticos, while on the western side stood a collossal statue of the king, side by side with that of his mother Tuya. This gigantic granite statue, which was originally some twenty meters high and represented Ramesses as the "Re of Rulers", is now lying on the ground face down, probably due to the excavation of blocks of rock from its base which evidently disturbed its balance.

119 top left Detail of the relief showing the capture of Dapur.

119 top Transportation of the barques of the deities during the Beautiful Feasts of the Valley.

119 centre The first pylon seen from the first court. The monumental gateway has been temporarily supported with air-dried bricks to increase its structural stability. Subsidence has already caused serious damage, in particular the collapse of part of the north tower.

119 bottom A statue of Merit-Amun, also known as the White Queen, daughter and "great royal wife" of Ramesses II. The statue previously stood in the north-west sector of the Ramesseum, where there was a shrine dedicated to the queen. (Cairo Museum)

This gigantic image of Ramesses II inspired the English poet Shelley who wrote the following poetic lines:
"My name is Ozymandias, King of Kings:
Look on my works, ye mighty, and despair!"
The second pylon, of which only the northern tower remains, opened the way to the second courtyard situated at a higher level that could be reached by the front staircase. This courtyard, which now houses the visitors' entrance, was completely surrounded by a portico whose eastern and western sides were decorated with gigantic statues often referred to as the "Osirian colossi" and representing Ramesses in the form of a mummy, his arms crossed, holding a flail *(nekhakha)* and a sceptre *(heqa)*, the characteristic attributes of Osiris. On the western side of the second pylon (the northern part), a large colored bas-relief continues the theme of the Battle of Qadesh reflected on the first pylon; descriptions of episodes in connection with the King's military activities in the Near East during the 8th year of his reign can be found on both sides of the bas-relief, while the upper parts illustrate episodes in connection with celebrations of the first harvest devoted to the god Min, the scenes of birds being set free to the four corners of the Universe, and the dance of Nefertari.

120 top left View of the west part of the Ramesseum and the Room of Litanies, with the Sanctuary.

120-121 The head of the young Memnon is transported from the Ramesseum to the Nile, in a water-color by G.B. Belzoni who himself organized this feat in November 1816.

120 bottom left The bust of the colossal statue of Ramesses II, called by Belzoni "Young Memnon", currently on display at the British Museum.

120 bottom right The lower part of the colossal statue of Ramesses II, that flanked, on the left side, the main stairway leading to the hypostyle room, is still in place; the bust is currently on display at the British Museum.

Three front staircases led from the second courtyard to the vestibule. The central staircase was flanked by two granite colossi representing the king, of which now remain only the very beautiful face of the northern statue and the pedestal of the southern one whose upper part, which was lying on the ground, evidently as a result of the earthquake that occurred in the second half of the 18th century, was taken to England in 1816 by Giovanni Battista Belzoni, the famous Italian traveller, and is now exhibited in the British Museum. A triple door led from the vestibule to the hypostyle hall, whose eastern side was bordered by a wall of which only the southern part is visible now. The hypostyle hall, supported by 48 extremely elegant columns in the form of papyrus fascicles, was

decorated with bas-reliefs representing, in their eastern part, episodes of the military activities of the king in the Orient, such as the capture of the city of Dapur (the south-eastern wall) in the 8th year of his reign, or the king's relatives, such as his mother Tuya, his royal bride Nefertari, as well as the royal princes and princesses (the north-eastern wall). The western part of the hypostyle, on the other hand, shows episodes in connection with various royal functions, such as the bestowal of the crown by the goddess Sekhmet, on either side of whom Amun-Re and Khonsu can be seen (the north-western wall), or the bestowal of the sceptre, symbol of royal power, by Amun accompanied by Mut (the south-western wall).

A large door leads from the western part of the hypostyle to a small room called the "Astronomical Hall" or the "Hall of the Barques" decorated with bas-reliefs illustrating episodes of the Beautiful Feast of the Valley, such as boarding the boats participating in the river procession that began at Karnak; this room of the Temple supported by eight columns is famous

for its splendid astronomical ceiling, a sort of celestial calendar where the constellations and the 36 Decans are clearly visible. It evidently served to determine the exact timing of religious functions and liturgical celebrations. The astronomical hall is followed by the "Hall of the Litanies" which has the same architectural structure with eight columns as the preceding; its bas-reliefs show Ramesses in the act of offering sacrifices as well as sacrificial libation and burnt offerings to Re-Harakhty (the south-eastern part) and to Ptah (the north-eastern part). Abandoned towards the end of the Twentieth Dynasty, the Ramesseum was successively used as burial ground for the priests of Thebes in the course of the Third Intermediate Period, as a quarry for building materials during the Twenty-Ninth Dynasty when, under Pharaoh Achoris, the Temple of Tuya and Nefertari was demolished with a view to re-using the blocks in Medinet Habu, and was finally transformed into a church by the Coptic communities who settled in Western Thebes in the 4th century AD.

121 top The magazines of the Ramesseum were housed in large vaulted buildings made from air-dried bricks.

121 centre The granite head of one of the two colossal statues of Ramesses II that flank the main stairs leading to the hypostyle room.

121 bottom The dedicatory inscription with the royal cartouche, carved later on the bottom part of the statue of Ramesses II, left on the site: here Belzoni inscribed his name and the date of his achievement.

THE COLOSSI OF MEMNON

These two enormous monolithic statues stood on both sides of the monumental door of the first pylon of the memorial Temple of Amenophis III, now completely destroyed, but thought to be the biggest of all Theban temples. This Temple, built on the farther side of the Nile's fluvial plain, was destroyed by annual floods and used as a quarry for extracting building materials. The two colossi representing the deified pharaoh serve as the most vivid testimony of that grandiose construction: the statues 16.6 meters high, cut from two blocks of quartzite, originated from the quarry of Gebel el-Ahmar near Cairo. As a result of the earthquake of the year of 27 BC, as recorded by Strabo (see Strabo, *Geography*, XVII, 1, 46), the northern colossus partly collapsed. After that time, an extraordinary phenomenon took place in the morning: due to heating by the solar rays and to the humidity of the night, the statue emitted sounds that resembled, according to Pausania, those of a zither.

The ancient Greeks looked for an explanation in the legendary story by Homer about Memnon, the son of Eos (Aurora) and Titon, who was killed by Achilles and reappeared in Thebes as a statue, and every morning sent lamentations at the sight of his mother rising in the skies. This phenomenon which acquired great fame in ancient times and attracted numerous visitors from every corner of the region (confirmed by numerous Greek and Roman signatures and inscriptions cut on the pedestal and on the feet of the statue) ceased after the restoration works ordered by Emperor Septimius Severus at the end of the 2nd century AD.

122 top left Detail of the top part of the northern colossus: this was the statue which in the early morning, in ancient times, emitted a curious lament-like note.

122 bottom left The southern colossus. Each of the two statues was hewn from a single block of stone and rested on a base. Altogether they stood about 16.6 meters high.

122-123 The Colossi of Memnon stood in front of the first pylon of the great mortuary temple of Amenophis III, now destroyed. The two colossi were flanked by two smaller statues of the royal wife Teye and the mother of Amenophis III, Mulemula.

122 bottom Detail of the southern colossus: queen Teye, wife of Amenophis III, is portrayed - as was customary - on a small scale, beside the leg of the king.

123 top On the back side of each statue is a column with a dedicatory inscription.

123 centre Aerial view of the Colossi of Memnon and the area beyond, where the temple of Amenophis III, the largest of all the Theban temples, once stood.

123 bottom Plan of the temple of Amenophis III, designed by the celebrated architect Amenhotep, son of Hapu (according to Haeny).

A - Colossi of Memnon
B - Enclosure wall
C - First pylon
D - Second pylon
E - Third pylon
F - Solar court

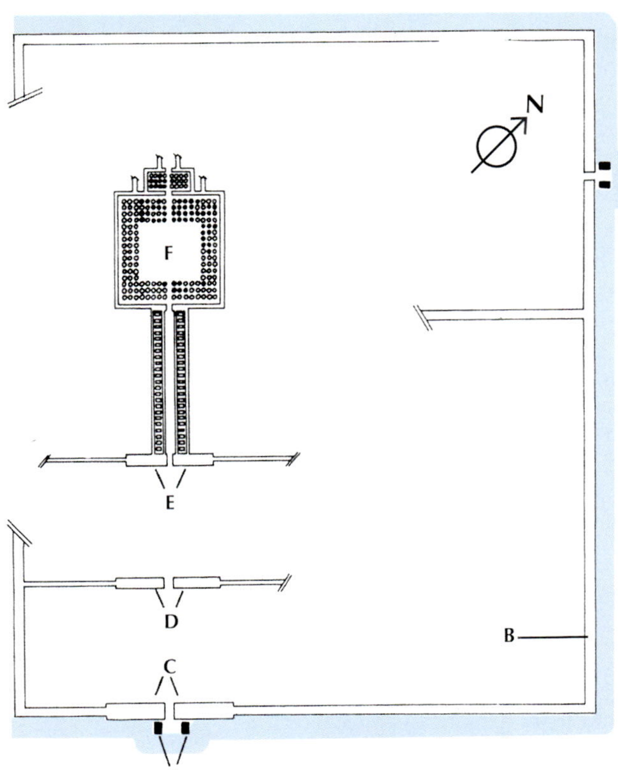

THE TEMPLE OF AMENOPHIS III AND THE COLOSSI OF MENNON

MEDINET HABU

Medinet Habu, a small village situated a little over two kilometers to the south of the Ramesseum, was called *Djanet* by the ancient Egyptians and, according to popular belief, it was the place where Amun appeared for the first time. This is why, from ancient times, it was the place of worship dedicated to this god, as evidenced by the existence in this place of a temple of the Eighteenth Dynasty dedicated to Amun of Djanet, built during the time of Hatshepsut and Tuthmosis III, probably on the ruins of a still more ancient temple; this was what later induced Ramesses III to order the construction there of his own memorial temple. The name Medinet Habu, or "the City of Habu", as the village is now called in Arabic, is of uncertain origin. According to one hypothesis, *habu* is connected with the word *hbw* which means ibis, the sacred bird of Thoth, because

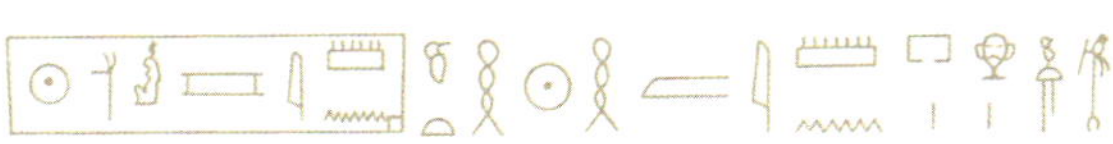

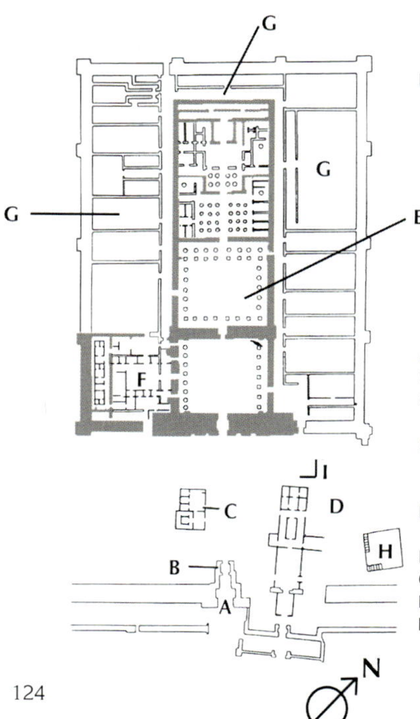

THE MEDINET HABU COMPLEX

- **A** - Entrance
- **B** - Migdol
- **C** - Chapel of the Divine Adoratrices
- **D** - Temple of the Eighteenth Dynasty
- **E** - Temple of Ramesses III
- **F** - Royal palace
- **G** - Magazines
- **H** - Sacred lake
- **I** - Nilometre

124 top Aerial view of the site of Medinet Habu, surrounded by a massive wall made from air-dried brick. Dominating the site is the huge temple of Ramesses III, flanked by the smaller temple of the Eighteenth Dynasty. Just visible to the right are the ruins of the mortuary temple of Ay and Horemheb, now totally destroyed.

124-125 The court and gigantic first pylon (with a length of 63 meters and average height of about 20 meters) of the mortuary temple of Ramesses III. Its general plan was modelled on that of the Ramesseum, of which it can be considered a larger version.

124 bottom left Hieroglyphs giving the name used in ancient times for the temple of Ramesses III. The transcription reads: "Temple of Usermaatre Meriamun that is linked to Thebes in the estate of Amun, west of Thebes".

124 bottom right The temple of Ramesses III differs from other mortuary temples: standing before it is a fortified migdol *tower, built along the same lines as Oriental fortresses*

125 top One of the best known bas-reliefs of the Medinet Habu Temple is on the external side of the north wall and depicts the battle against the Peoples of the Sea that Ramesses III fought in the 8th year of his reign.

nearby, in Qasr el-Aguz, there was a small Ptolemaic temple dedicated to Thoth. It is also possible that the word "habu" is derived from Hapu, since the funeral Temple of Amenophis, son of Hapu, the famous architect of Amenophis III, exists in the immediate vicinity. In the first millenium BC, Djanet was also thought to be the burial place of the Ogoad, the first four divine couples. At certain regular times, the so-called "Feast of the Tenth Day", the creator-god Amun-em-ipet ("Amun is in his harem") travelled to Djanet from his residence in the Temple of Luxor, the birthplace of the gods that comprised the Ogoad, to re-perform funeral rites for his ancestors, thereby giving them new life and, thus, renewing creation.

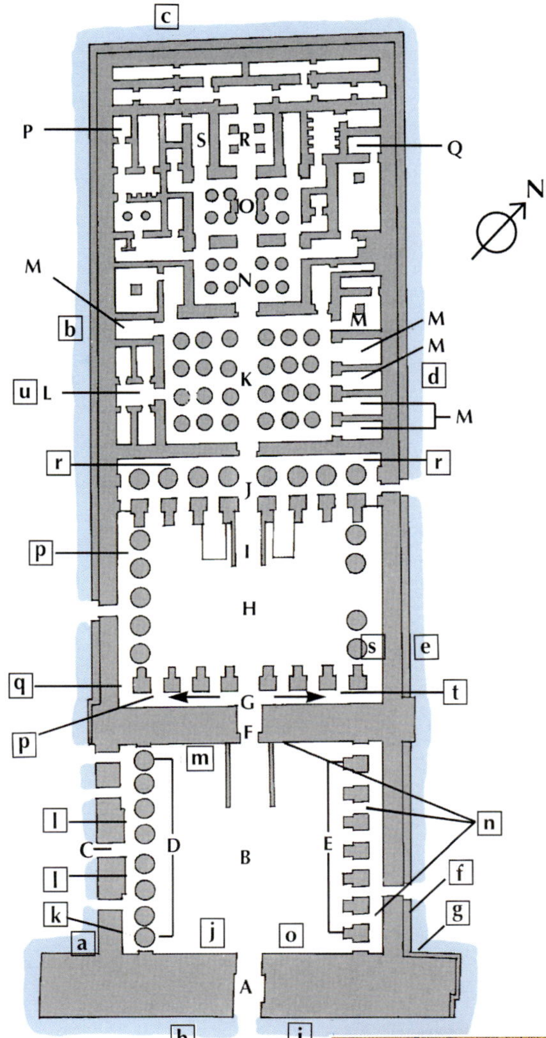

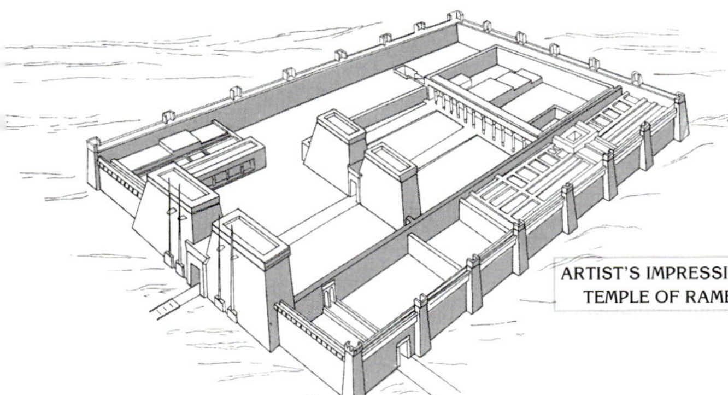

125 bottom right Decorating the post of a doorway on the south side of the temple are the elegant, linear forms of priests waving large fans.

A - First pylon
B - First courtyard
C - Window of the Appearances
D - Bell-shaped columns
E - Osirid pillars
F - Second pylon
G - Portico with Osirid pillars
H - Second courtyard
I - Ramp
J - Portico with Osirid pillars
K - Large hypostyle room
L - Royal treasure rooms
M - Chapels dedicated to various deities and to the deified Ramesses
N - Second hypostyle room
O - Third hypostyle room
P - Chapel of Ramesses III
Q - Chapel of Re-Harmakhis
R - Shrine of the sacred boarque of Amun
S - Chapels of Mut and Khonsu

Main scenes
a - Hunting the wild bull
b - Religious calendar; text of year 12
c - Ramesses' expedition in Upper Egypt
d - Naval battle against the Peoples of the Sea
e - The king with prisoners and Philistines
f - Libyan wars
g - Destruction of the Hittite strongholds
h - The pharaoh carries out the ritual sacrifice of the prisoners before Re-Harakhty and Amun-Re
i - The pharaoh carries out the ritual sacrifice of the prisoners before Amun-Re and Ptah
j - The pharaoh defeats the Libyans; text of year 2
k - The king goes to the Beautiful Feast of the Valley; military parade
l - Fight scenes and equestrian scenes.
m - The king sacrifices the prisoners to Amun and Mut
n - Upper register - the king makes an offering to various deities; lower register - battle scenes
o - Triumph of the pharaoh and parade of prisoners
p - Feast of Sokar
q - Counting of the hands and phalluses cut from the enemy
r - Upper register - the king makes an offering to various deities; lower register -representation of the sons of Ramesses III
s - Upper register - feast of Min; lower register - procession of the barques of Amun, Mut and Khonsu
t - The king before a deity
u - Ramesses III makes offerings to Amun and presents the treasure.

Column	◎
Osirid pillar	

During the Twentieth Dynasty, Djanet became the administrative center of Western Thebes and the meeting place of the striking workers and artisans of Deir el-Medina who stayed there waiting for their demands to be accepted. Later, by the end of the Twentieth Dynasty, this site became a place of refuge for the population during the war waged by the High Priest of Amun of Karnak against the viceroy of Kush, and still later, in the period of the Twenty-Fifth and Twenty-Sixth Dynasties, it was the place where the cult of the Divine Adoratrices of Amun was celebrated. The Medinet Habu complex was expanded during the Graeco-Roman period, and its long history still continued between the 1st and 9th centuries AD when the Coptic city of *Jeme* was built in the area and a church was constructed in the second courtyard of the Temple.

The excavations of Medinet Habu began in 1859 and, since 1924, studies at the site have been carried out by the Oriental Institute of the University of Chicago, which has published the complete epigraphical and architectural documentation of the Temple.

The Temple of Ramesses III

The Temple of Ramesses III is the best preserved among all temples of Thebes, and its decorated surfaces amount to 7,000 square meters. The structure of the Temple and its iconographic system are similar to those of the Ramesseum, although it can hardly equal the elegance of its forms and the balance of dimensions. A unique feature of this Temple, that used to be called in ancient times "the Temple of User-maat-Re Meriamun Who Joins Eternity in the Possession of Amun in the West of Thebes", is the presence on its eastern side, in front of the first pylon, of a tower built in the form of a *migdol* (a military fortress in Asia Minor) which gave the Temple the aspect of a fortress and had protective functions in the large wall surrounding the Temple. On passing through the *migdol*, one enters a vast space preceding the first pylon where, to the left, one can see the funeral chapels of the Divine Adoratrices of Amun and, to the right, the Temple of Amun of the Eighteenth Dynasty. The external lateral walls of the Temple are covered with important bas-reliefs; of particular interest among them are those of the northern wall illustrating the battles fought by Ramesses III against the Peoples of the Sea.

On the southern wall, numerous liturgical festivites are listed and reproduced, as well as the economic resources of the Temple necessary for its complex functioning and brought there from its numerous possessions donated to the Temple by the king at the time of its inauguration. The first pylon, on which one can see four large hollows intended to hold wooden poles from which flew the divine insignia, is decorated with bas-reliefs showing Ramesses III in the process of ritual massacre of Asian prisoners in front of Amun-Re (the southern tower) and Nubian and Libyan prisoners in front of Amun-Re-Harakhty (the northern tower). On the south-western side of the pylon, one can see a brilliantly illustrated scene of bull-hunting in the marshes; it is considered one of the artistic masterpieces of the Twentieth Dynasty. Having passed through the gigantic door of the first pylon, one enters the first courtyard, on whose northern and southern sides are two porticos; the southern portico has an opening, the so-called "Window of Appearances" connected to the royal palace situated outside. The dominant theme of the bas-reliefs in the first courtyard is represented by the king's troops annihilating the enemy (the Libyans and the Peoples of the Sea) whom Ramesses fought during the 8th year of his reign. On the walls are shown not only the vanquished enemies, who can be recognized by an

126 left This splendid relief, on the south-east part of the first pylon, shows the pharaoh on his war-chariot as he chases a wild bull in the marshes, followed by a procession of young princes. Thanks to its exceptional sense of movement, force of expression and general elegance, this work of art is considered one of the masterpieces of the Twentieh Dynasty.

126 top right On the north and south sides of the first court is a portico supported by square columns with Osirian pillars, delimiting the west side is the second pylon through which the second court is reached.

126 bottom right A relief on the left post of the gateway of the second pylon portrays the Sea Peoples, in particular Philistines with their distinctive headdresses.

127 top From the second court a wide ramp gives access to the portico, embellished with Osirian colossi, and from there to the hypostyle halls.

exhibition of parts of their bodies, but also the war booty, duly listed and quantified, together with the hands and sometimes the phalluses which the Pharaoh's soldiers used to cut off the dead bodies of the vanquished enemies to show their own valor.
The first courtyard is closed on the north by the second pylon, whose door leading to the second courtyard. The second courtyard which was also referred to as the "Courtyard of the Feasts" is surrounded by a peristyle: both porticos on the eastern and western sides are decorated with eight Osirian columns, while those to the north and south are supported by large columns in the form of papyrus scrolls. At first, the decoration motifs continue the military themes characteristic of the preceding courtyard (the eastern part of the southern portico) but, farther on, there are illustrations of great religious festivities dedicated to Sokar-Osiris (southern portico) and to Min (northern portico). The wall of the western portico, from which a staircase leads to the first hypostyle hall, is dedicated to the theme of royal power: in the northern part, the king is being purified by Thoth and Horus, and, in the southern part, one can see the scene representing the Pharaoh's accession to the throne where he is accompanied by Thoth in front of the Triad of Thebes. This wall also features the pictures of the sons of Ramesses III, the future Ramesses IV, VI, VII, and VIII, whose images were added in succession as these princes acceded to the throne. The first hypostyle hall, of which only the base of the 24 columns that supported the ceiling now remain, has in its south-western part a complex of four rooms, evidently intended to serve as treasury for the Temple, as is proved by bas-reliefs on the walls representing heaps of gold, silver and precious stones. Two more annexes situated in the corner between the first and the second hypostyle halls were intended to serve as sites for the cult of the god Montu (the first) and as an additional treasury (the second). The northern side of the hypostyle hall contained a group of five contiguous halls, perpendicular to the axis of the Temple and dedicated to various divinities. Moving towards the West, one enters the second hypostyle hall supported by eight columns, with two groups of lateral halls annexed: those situated in the southern part were dedicated to the Osiris cult of the deified king, while those in the north were dedicated to various solar gods, among whom the dominant role belonged to Re-Harakhty with whom the king was identified in his celestial resurrection.
Then follows the third hypostyle hall whose structure is identical to the previous one and whose lateral chapels are dedicated to various gods: Horus and Mut in the south, Amun-Re, the Ennead of Heliopolis, Min, Mut, and Khonsu in the north.

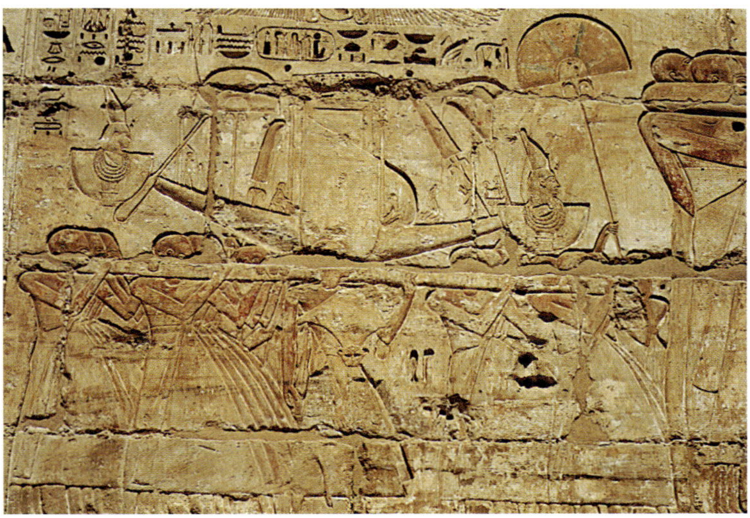

127 centre left On the north side of the second court bas-reliefs describe the procession of sacred barques.

127 centre right The square columns of the second court are decorated with scenes which show the pharaoh presenting offerings to the deities.

127 bottom General view of the hypostyle halls, of which only the bases of the columns remain.

The Royal palace

In the southern part of the Temple grounds, one can clearly see, within the space between the first and the second pylons, the foundation of the Royal Palace that was built in two successive construction stages. The Royal Palace was directly connected with the first courtyard of the Temple via the "Window of Appearances" through which the pharaoh made his public appearances. However, it is not known for certain whether the Royal Palace was in fact only a symbolic and ritual construction or whether it was indeed used by the Pharaoh when he travelled to the western bank to preside over the most important religious ceremonies.

The chapels of the Divine Adoratrices of Amun

The funeral chapels of the Divine Adoratrices of Amun are situated in a small building in the south-eastern part of the space preceding the first pylon. In the course of the Intermediate Period and in the period of the Twenty-Fifth and the Twenty-Sixth Dynasties (8th and 7th centuries BC), certain Divine Adoratrices of Amun were worshipped. These were royal princesses and priestesses enjoying great prestige and representing the pharaoh in the territory of Thebes, such as Amenirdis, the sister of King Shabaqo, Shepenwepet, the daughter of Osorkon III, and Nitocris, the daughter of Psammetichus I, all of them buried within the Ramesseum.

128 top Like the Ramesseum and the temple of Sethos I, the temple of Ramesses III also had an adjoining royal palace where the pharaoh took up residence during important religious festivities.

128 centre The royal palace communicated with the temple via a window in the south side of the first court: the pharaoh made public appearances from this window.

128 bottom During the excavation of the royal palace these colored faience tiles came to light. They show prisoners from different countries and relate to the king's military campaigns: from the left, a Libyan, a Nubian, a Syrian, a Shasu Bedouin from Syria and a Hittite. (Cairo Museum)

THE CHAPELS OF THE DIVINE ADORATRICES OF AMUN

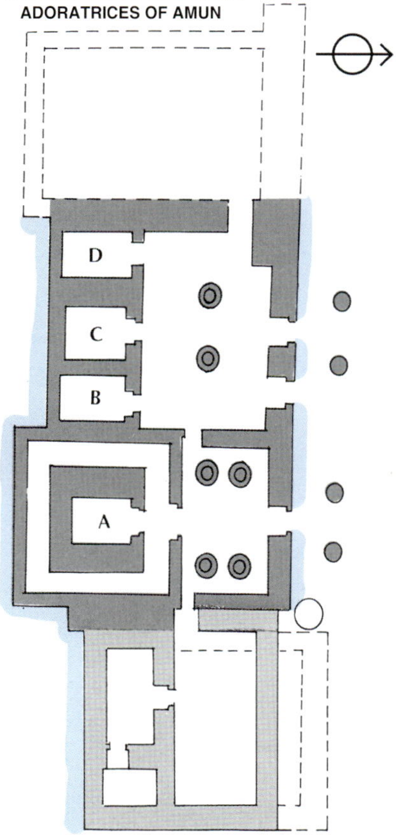

A - Chapel of Amenirdis
B - Chapel of Nitocris
C - Chapel of Shepenut
D - Chapel of Mehetnusekhet

The Temple of the Eighteenth Dynasty

To the north of the principal Temple of Ramesses III stands the Temple of the Eighteenth Dynasty dedicated to Amun by Hatshepsut and Tuthmosis III. This original building was repeatedly enlarged and modified up to the Ptolemaic and Roman periods. Numerous decorated blocks which originated from the Temple of Tuya and Nefertari, adjacent to the Ramesseum, were added to the building in the course of the Twenty-Ninth Dynasty, during the reign of Achoris; the eastern pylon, however, was added in the Ptolemaic period, while the courtyard and the structures preceding it were included during the Roman period. Directly to the north of the Temple there are the remnants of the Sacred Lake, a symbolic representation of the primordial waters, and further to the west, a Nilometre.

THE TEMPLE OF THE EIGHTEENTH DYNASTY

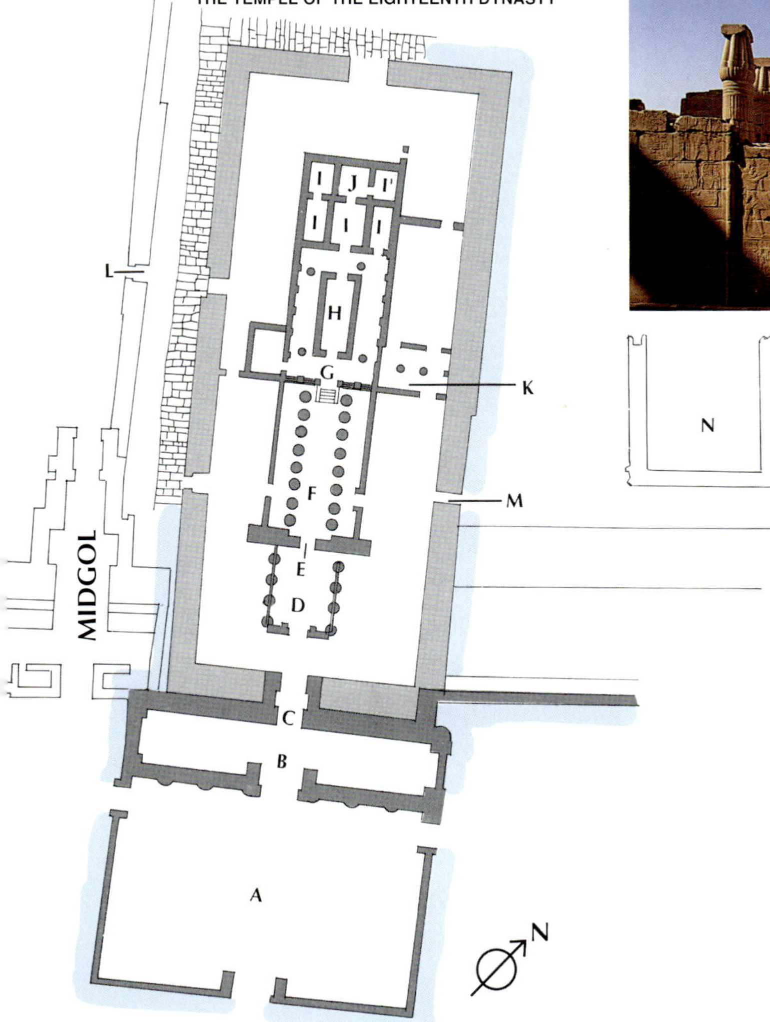

A - Roman courtyard
B - Roman portico
C - Ptolemaic pylon
D - Colonnace of Nectanebo
E - Pylon of Shabago
F - Courtyard with columns
G - Peristyle
H - Chapel of Hatshepsut and Tuthmos s III
I - Chapel
I' - Naos in pink granite
J - Shrine
K - Room of Achoris
L - Door of Nectanebo
M - Door of Taharqa
N - Sacred lake

129 left View of the enclosure wall of the Medinet Habu Temple with the two towers of the migdol and the Ptolemaic pylon of the small temple of the Eighteenth Dynasty.

129 right The small temple of the Eighteenth Dynasty, situated to the east of the first pylon of the temple of Ramesses III, was dedicated to the god Amun. In the Ptolemaic period it was enlarged with the addition of a pylon.

THE WORKERS' VILLAGE OF DEIR EL-MEDINA

The site of Deir el-Medina is situated in a small valley between the western slope of the Mountain of Thebes and the small hill of Qurnet Murai, not far from the Valley of the Queens, barely a kilometer to the south, and from the Valley of the Kings on the opposite side of the mountain. The name of Deir el-Medina, which in Arabic means the "City Monastery", was given to the site because of the presence there of a Ptolemaic temple dedicated to Hathor and transformed during the Coptic era into a monastery; a community of craftsmen and workers, who were engaged in the building and decoration of the royal tombs, lived in the village which was founded during the Eighteenth Dynasty, in the period of Tuthmosis I, and called *set maat* which could be translated as the "Place of Truth", or even better, the "Place of Order". The studies of the organization of this workers' village, one of the rare urban structures known today in Egypt, and of the tombs in the necropolis, as well as the epigraphic analysis of the elements found in the course of the excavations, among which there are numerous *ostraca* (pieces of pottery and limestone fragments containing sketches of ornaments or annotations and notes), have made possible a detailed reconstruction not only of the way of life in the settlement, but also of the social and industrial organization of these workers of pharaoh. The village, which occupied an area of about two hectares and, during the Ramessiad period, housed a population of about 400 persons, was enclosed in a wall belt of unburnt brick and included about 70 dwellings within the walls and about 50 more outside. The houses, of a more or less similar structure, were built of unburnt brick and covered with roofs made from planks of palm wood; they consisted of some contiguous small rooms, a terrace which could be reached via an internal staircase, and sometimes a cellar excavated in the ground. The internal walls were covered with a layer of stucco made of gypsum, limestone and crushed straw which was subsequently whitewashed and painted. A certain space was occupied by a small chapel with a stele intended for the domestic cult of the ancestors and of the goddess Meretseger, "She Who Loves Silence", who personified the Thebes Peak and was the protectress of the village. The floors were made of stone and sometimes they still preserve the traces and grooves left by the opening and closing of the wooden entrance doors. Wicker baskets served for the storage of various objects while foodstuffs and liquids were kept in ceramic vases. The relative abundance of small receptacles for cosmetic products and ointments, as well as of bronze mirrors, stress the importance attributed to the care of the body. The furniture consisted principally of chairs, stools, benches, and small chests. Various foods and remnants of foodstuffs found have made it possible to establish the principal elements of the workers' diet, that is, cereals and fish, which were

130 top General view of the site of Deir el-Medina with the workers' village that extends over an area of about 6,000 square meters, and the necropolis. Formerly this site, where the workers and the artisans appointed to prepare and decorate the royal tombs lived, was called set maat *"the Place of Truth" or, more exactly, "the Place of Order".*

130 centre The inhabited area of Deir el-Medina, founded at the beginning of the Eighteenth Dynasty, but developed above all during the Nineteenth and Twentieth Dynasties, allows an exact reconstruction of the plan and the arrangement of the houses, which all had a fairly similar structure.

130 bottom View of the burial chamber of the tomb of the architect Kha (TT no. 8) who lived in the time of Amenophis II - Amenophis III during the Eighteenth Dynasty, discovered by Schiaparelli's Italian Archeological Mission in 1906: the tomb was intact and contained a rich burial store that expanded our knowledge of the daily life of the workers who lived on the site.

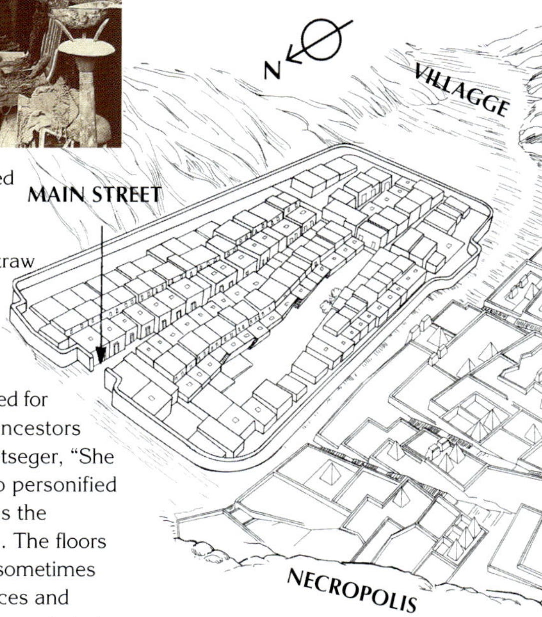

ARTIST'S IMPRESSION OF THE SITE OF DEIR EL-MEDINA DURING THE NINETEENTH DYNASTY

130 bottom right Reconstruction of the living area of Deir el-Medina during the Nineteenth Dynasty.

131 top The houses of Deir el-Medina in general had three or four rooms: an entrance with a door opening onto the street, a living room, a room with larder, a kitchen and one or more cellars dug into the ground. A ladder gave access to the roof.

131 centre left This ceramic vase, painted with floral motifs, was found in Sennedjem's tomb (TT no. 10). It dates back to the time of Ramesses II, and was discovered intact by Gaston Maspero in 1886. (Cairo Museum)

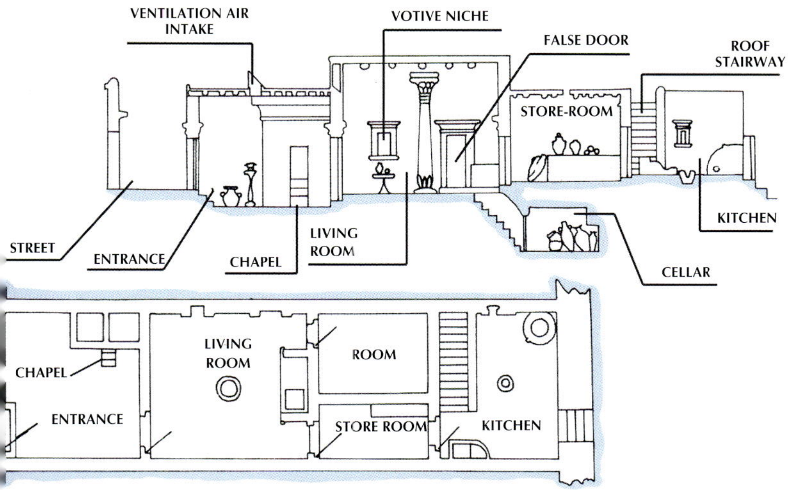

distributed to every worker in precise quantities by way of payment for the work done. This diet was supplemented by fruit, vegetables, honey, and sometimes by meat, generally poultry, which was considered luxury food. The traditional drink was beer made by the fermentation of grains. In cases when the distribution of foodstuff rations, which was the equivalent of wages, was delayed, the workers lodged regular protests to the Superintendent of Tombs who, in his turn, passed them to the vizier, as evidenced by a document written by such a superintendent in the 28th year of the reign of Ramesses III and addressed to vizier Tô: "... All the foodstuffs to be found in the treasury, the grain deposits, and in the warehouses have been exhausted. (...) That our patron should provide us with means of subsistence since we are dying; actually we are no longer living..." If such a situation was not corrected within a short time, the workers could organize a veritable strike. This workers' community of Deir el-Medina existed in isolation, without contact with the outside world, clearly due to considerations of discretion and secrecy imposed by the delicate character of their work of arranging the royal tombs. The community reported directly to the vizier, a functionary who played the role of the pharaoh's Prime Minister. In addition, it was controlled by a special corps of guards called *Medjay* which was stationed outside the village and whose general task was to guard the necropolis. The workers, who had the title of "Servants of the Seat of Order", were indeed a sort of a privileged corporation, and they went to work in the Valley of the Kings or the Valley of the Queens using two pathways that even now are passable; sometimes, when they had to do important and urgent work, they did not return daily to their lodgings but stayed during the whole working week, which lasted, in fact, nine days, in two small satellite villages situated, respectively, on the ridge separating the valley of Deir el-Medina from the Valley of the Kings (the so called "Village of the Hill") and within the Valley of the Queens. The workers' village of Deir el-Medina was active up to the end of the Twentieth Dynasty, but then it was abandoned, and the desert sands and fragments of the mountain covered it until it was recently found. The excavations at the site carried out early in this century by Ernesto Schiaparelli of the Egyptian Museum of Turin brought to light the entire village, perfectly preserved, as well as the adjacent necropolis where, among other finds, the tomb of the architect Kha was found intact. It is now reconstructed in the Museum of Turin. At present, excavations and studies of the site are carried out by the Institut Français d'Archeologie Orientale (IFAO) which replaced Schiaparelli's Missione Archeologica Italiana.

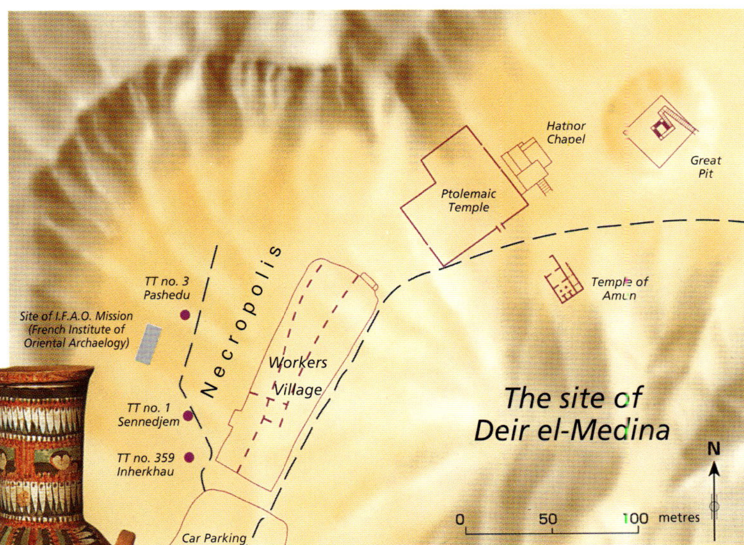

131 centre right Topographic map of the site of Deir el-Medina, showing the workers' village, the necropolis, a Ptolemaic temple flanked by a chapel dedicated to the goddess Hathor, a small temple dedicated to Amun and a deep cistern of the "Great Well".

131 bottom Also from Sennedjem's tomb, which was a kind of family tomb containing a score of mummies, comes the casket for shawabti *of Khons, one of Sennedjem's sons, decorated with pictures of the mummy. The* shawabti *were statuettes magically called down by the dead man through the magic formula provided in Chapter 6 of the* Book of the Dead, *to carry out the most difficult tasks in the Afterlife for him. (Cairo Museum)*

THE TEMPLE OF DEIR EL-MEDINA

Directly to the north of the workers' village, there is a small Ptolemaic Temple dedicated to Hathor and Maat, to Amenophis, son of Hapu, and to Imhotep; it was transformed into a monastery in the Coptic period, from which the site's present name originated. The Temple, built in the 3rd century BC at the time of Ptolemy IV Philopator and Ptolemy VI Philometor (3rd-2nd century BC), has been perfectly preserved, including a tall belt of walls made of unburnt brick, and the warehouses. Its architectural style, rather simple, includes a hypostyle hall with two columns and a vestibule decorated with scenes of Ptolemy VI worshipping various gods; in the left part, one can see the king burning incense in front of the goddess Hathor in the form of a cow. The bas-reliefs of the three chapels situated behind the vestibule, of which the central one has a door decorated with the seven heads of Hathor, and the sanctuary of the goddess, represent, in general, various scenes of sacrifices being offered to gods. In the left chapel, there is a representation of a trial by Osiris, a subject which, as a rule, never appears in the iconography of buildings dedicated to cults, but is represented in tombs or in funerary papyri. On the opposite wall of the same chapel, one can see Ptolemy VIII Euergetes II offering sacrifices to to Anubis wearing an unusual mantle. The Temple also contained objects pertaining to the cult of the deified rulers Amenophis I, founder of the Eighteenth Dynasty, and his wife Ahmosis-Nefertari, who enjoyed particular popularity among the village inhabitants.

132 top The walls of the temple's inside chapels are decorated with painted bas-reliefs that have conserved some of their original colors.

132 centre top The temple of Deir el-Medina was constructed in the third century during the reign of Ptolemy IV, enlarged under Ptolemy VI and Ptolemy XI between the 2nd and 1st century BC. Subsequently it was transformed into a Coptic monastery that is the source of the present name of the entire site, which means, in Arabic, "monastery of the city".

132 centre bottom A bas-relief representing the goddess Hathor, to whom the temple was dedicated.

132 bottom The goddess Hathor, seated on a throne, holds an ankh and a sceptre, in the form of a papyrus stem characteristic of the female deity.

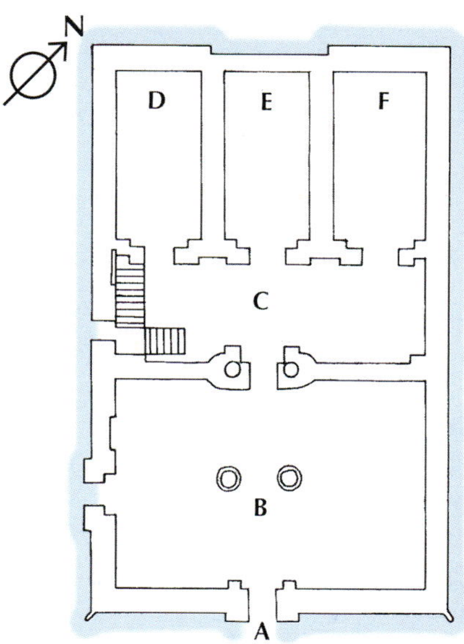

A - Entrance
B - Hypostyle hall
C - Vestibule
D - West chapel
E - Chapel of Hathor
F - East chapel

132 left The temple of Deir el-Medina is subdivided into three chapels: the central chapel was dedicated to Hathor-Maat, while the eastern chapel (right) was dedicated to Amun-Re-Osiris and the western chapel (left) to Amun-Sokar-Osiris.

THE NECROPOLIS

The artisans' tombs in Deir el-Medina were excavated on the mountain slopes, only a few dozen meters from the residential zone; their arrangement was one of the main occupations of the inhabitants during their leisure time. The structure of the tombs in the necropolis was rather uniform and included a small pylon, one or two courtyards in whose farthermost part there was a chapel with an entrance made of unburnt brick and surmounted by a small pyramid which, in certain cases, had a continuation of several rooms excavated in the rock. Inside, on the back wall, always oriented towards the east, there was a niche housing a statue of the deceased with a stele carrying the text of the hymn to the sun. The external chapel served as a place intended for practicing the cult of the dead who were buried together with a rich set of funerary objects in the burial chambers excavated deep into the mountain; these rooms were accessible by steep stairs that began from the exterior courtyard or, in the case of burial chambers excavated in the rock, from one of the internal rooms. The burial chambers had vaulted ceilings and, in contrast to the burial chambers of the civilian tombs of the Eighteenth and Nineteenth Dynasties which were almost never decorated, these were beautifully adorned with pictures on the walls where the deceased and his family were represented engaged in their everyday activities, or else the pictures reflected ritual motifs, such as the embalming of corpses or the rite of "Opening the Mouth", or religious rites.

133 left In this small tomb of Deir el-Medina, the entrance is through a door that opens into the unburnt brick pyramid, on whose top is the pyramidion.

133 right A classic tomb of Deir el-Medina as it appears after the restoration; the outside wall that encloses the courtyard and the chapel, is surmounted by the pyramid with the niche for the so-called "attic stele".

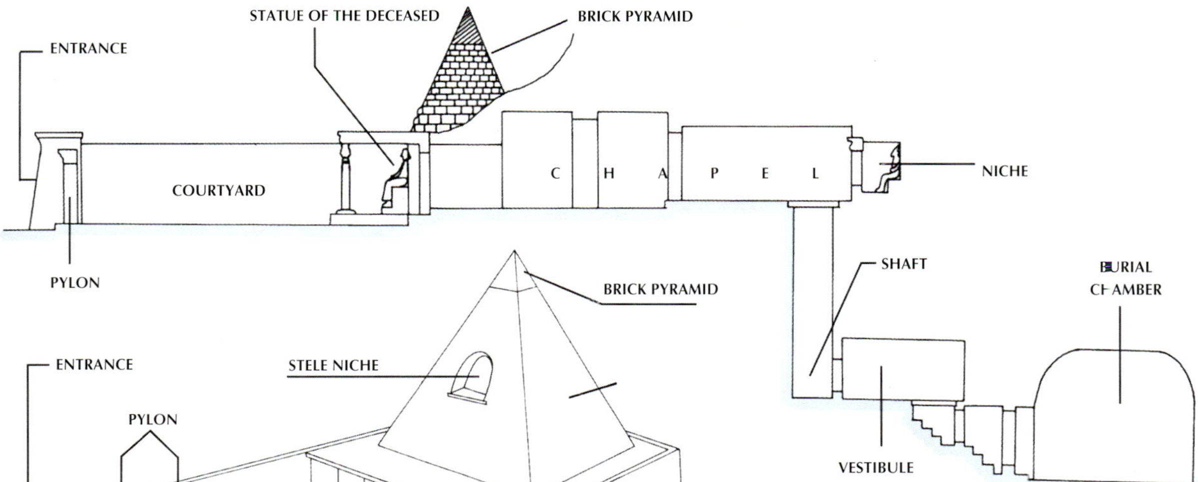

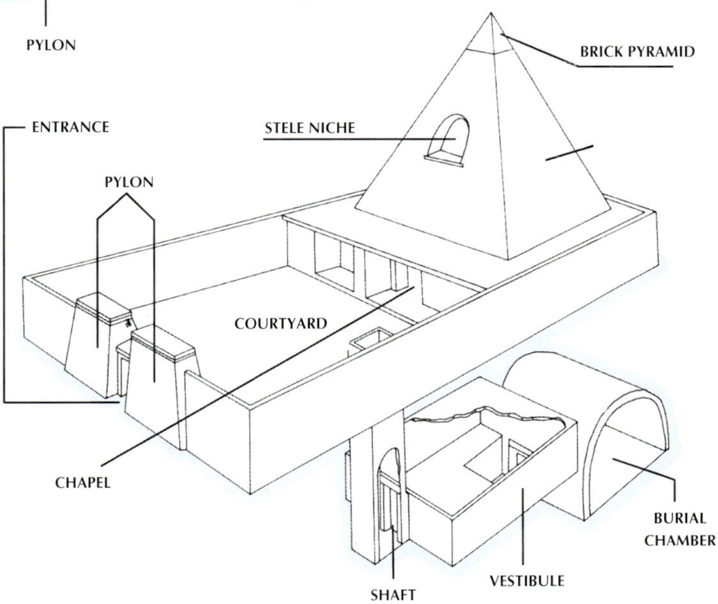

SENNEDJEM

TT no.1

"Servant in the Place of Truth"
Nineteenth Dynasty

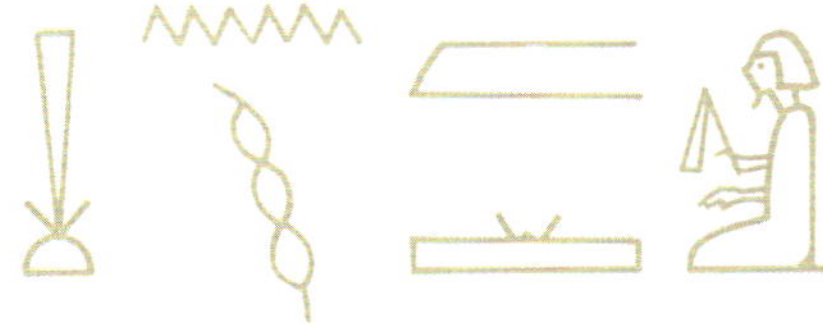

A

B

Sennedjem "Servant in the Place of Truth" lived in the time of Sethos I and Ramesses II (Nineteenth Dynasty) and his burial chamber was found intact in 1886 with outstandingly rich funerary equipment, now exhibited at the Cairo Museum, comparable to that found by Schiaparelli in the tomb of the architect Kha. The famous paintings decorating the walls of the burial chamber, whose background color is yellow ochre, are in a state of perfect preservation and may be considered among the most beautiful of the necropolis and, at all events, are the best known: their style is typical of the Ramessid era, even though it turns out to be spontaneous and fresh with lively and picturesque details, and the decorative program, exclusively related to the funerary world, is rather conventional. A narrow stairway leads directly inside the burial chamber, in the shape of a rectangle with the main axis directed westwards and with a vaulted ceiling, whose access is through a small room originally closed by a wooden door, also richly decorated and now exhibited at the Cairo Museum.

On the southern wall (on the left at the entrance), on two registers, the relatives of the deceased are shown, the sons performing libations in their father's honor, followed by the image of Sennedjem's mummy protected by Isis and Nephthys in the shape of falcons.

On the western wall Sennedjem and his wife Iyneferti worship different gods related to the funerary cult, overlooked by two images of Anubis in the form of a jackal, decorating the tympanum. On the great northern wall three scenes are arranged that evoke the entrance of the deceased into Osiris' kingdom:

in the first Anubis himself, shown in human form with a jackal head, introduces Sennedjem into the Afterworld, in the second the deceased is worshipping Osiris and in the third Anubis prepares Sennedjem's mummy, stretched out on the funerary bed while the accompanying texts reproduce

A - Detail of the wooden door that closed the burial room of Sennedjem's tomb. In the decorations Sennedjem can be seen with his wife Iyneferti , while playing senet, *an obvious reference to Chapter 17 of the* Book of the Dead; *the game in fact represents the judgment of Osiris and with the victory of the dead man, the entry into his kingdom. (Cairo Museum)*

B - The mummy of the dead man placed in the sarcophagus lying on the funeral bed and protected by Isis (left) and Nephthys (right) in the form of falcons. In the lower register the sons bring offerings and purify themselves before the parents.

C

D

C - Detail showing the dead man holding a sceptre- sekhem, *symbol of power, and his wife Iyneferti.*

D - Sennedjem and Iyneferti worship the gods of the Afterlife, while on the tympanum there is a dual representation of Anubis in the form of a jackal crouching on a shrine.

passages from the *Book of the Dead*. On the eastern wall the very famous scene is found, arranged on four registers, commenting on the 110th Chapter of the *Book of the Dead* in which Sennedjem and Iyneferti are busy carrying out agricultural labour in the Fields of Iaru, the magical Afterworld washed by the waters of a celestial river, an evocation of the earthly Nile, and shaded by manifold fruit trees, by sycamores and by palms loaded with dates. In the upper register Sennedjem and Iyneferti worship Re, Osiris and Ptah followed by a boy on a papyrus boat probably representing a son of Sennedjem who died young, and by a priest accomplishing the ceremony of the "Opening of the mouth". On the tympanum overlooking the scene two baboons are shown worshipping the barque of Re. On the adjoining southern wall, in the space between the entrance door and the eastern wall, the deceased and his wife worship the watchers of the gates of Osiris' kingdom. The ceiling too is entirely decorated with paintings: a white strip with texts divides the vault longitudinally, and it is also cut by three transversal strips, which thus divide the ceiling into two groups of four squares. In the first group the deceased worhips different divinities, including Thoth, Re-Harakhty and Atum, and several funerary tutelary spirits. In the second group the Sycamore Goddess is represented as she holds out food and beverages to the deceased and to his wife who, in the following scene, worship four stellar divinities; then comes the representation of the *benu*-bird, embodiment of the soul of Re, with Re-Harakhty and the members of the Heliopolitan Ennead, and that of Sennedjem opening the gates of the West, Osiris' kingdom.

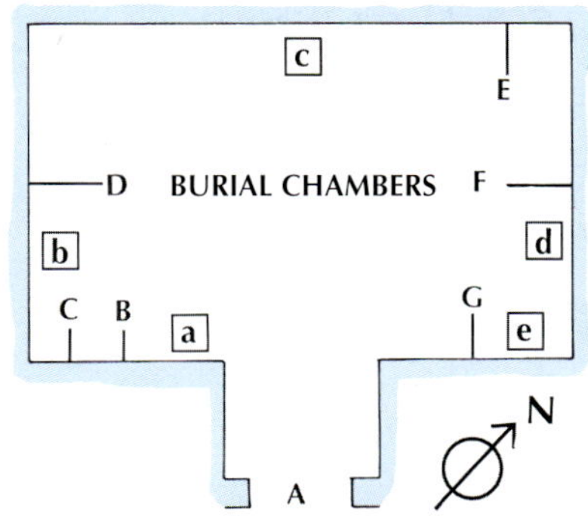

Description of the walls
a *- The mummy of the deceased with Isis and hawk-headed Nephthys; the family of the deceased*
b *- The deceased and his wife worship the afterlife gods*
c *- The mummy with Anubis and Osiris*
d *- Baboons worship the barque of Re; the deceased and his wife in the Fields of Iaru*
e *- The deceased and his wife facing the guards of the Gates of the kingdom of Osiris*

E

F

G

E - Sennedjem and his family.

F - The most famous of the scenes represented in Sennedjem's tomb portrays the fields of Iaru in the blessed Afterworld where the dead man and his wife sow, reap and plough. On the tympanum two baboons worship Re on his barque.

G - Sennedjem and Iyneferti receive offerings from the goddess of the sycamore, the celestial tree, manifestation of the goddess Nut in her role as protector of the dead.

135 bottom right
One of the most beautiful sarcophagi discovered in the burial chamber belonged to the lady Isis who may have been the wife of Khabekhenet, one of Sennedjem's sons. Isis is represented as a living person with a long white pleated tunic and with twigs of ivy in her hands.

INHERKHAU
TT no. 359

"Foreman of the Lord of the Two Lands in the Place of Truth"
Twentieth Dynasty

A

B

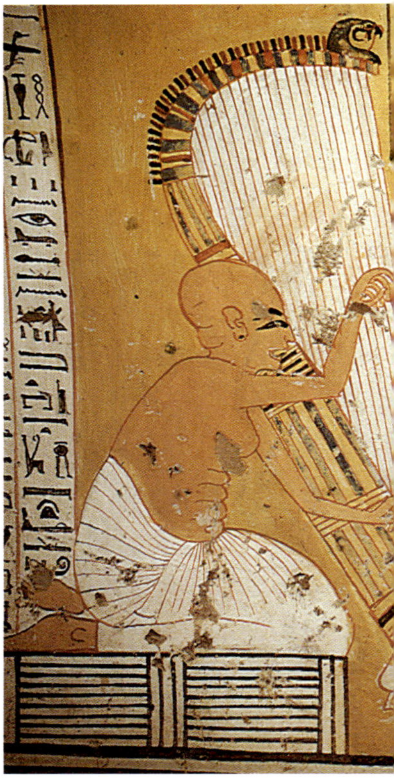

C

Inherkhau, who had the title of Foreman, lived several decades later than Sennedjem, during the Twentieth Dynasty, in the time of Ramesses III and Ramesses IV and, since he played a very important role, his tomb had extremely rich and refined decorations which undoubtedly constitute one of the best artistic examples of the Twentieth Dynasty, presenting scenes from the *Book of the Dead* and the *Book of the Doors*, as well as scenes from the Afterworld. The most beautiful pictures are those found in the deep burial chamber representing numerous scenes: 17 to the left and 14 to the right. Among them, the following are worthy of mention: to the left, the Cat of Heliopolis killing the serpent Apophis on the sacred tree, and the scene of sacrificial candles offered to the deceased and his wife. To the right: the deceased worshipping the sun disc and four spirits with heads of jackals, as well as a scene of the priests offering to the deceased - represented with his entire family - a statuette of Osiris, and a box for the *shawabti*. These *shawabti*, or "respondents" were small statuettes placed in the tombs to serve the deceased in the Afterworld by doing the most difficult kinds of work for him.

A - Thoth introduces Inherkhau into the presence of Osiris.

B - Detail of Inherkhau dressed as a sem-priest with the distinctive shaved head and the leopard skin.

C - The Souls of Pe and of Nekhen pay respect to the dead man.

D - A blind harpist plays before Inherkhau and his wife.

E - The "Cat of Heliopolis" kills the serpent Apophis under the ished *holy tree.*

F - Inherkhau with his two sons Kenna and Armin offers two torches to Ptah (left, fragmentary) and to Osiris (right).

G - A priest offers a box for shawabti *to Inherkhau and his wife, portrayed with their four sons, one of whom is headless due to a recent act of vandalism.*

H - In the top register Inherkhau worships the four jackals pulling the solar barque during its night trip, while in the bottom register five priests, the first holding a rod with a ram head, are in the presence of the seated dead man.

D

E

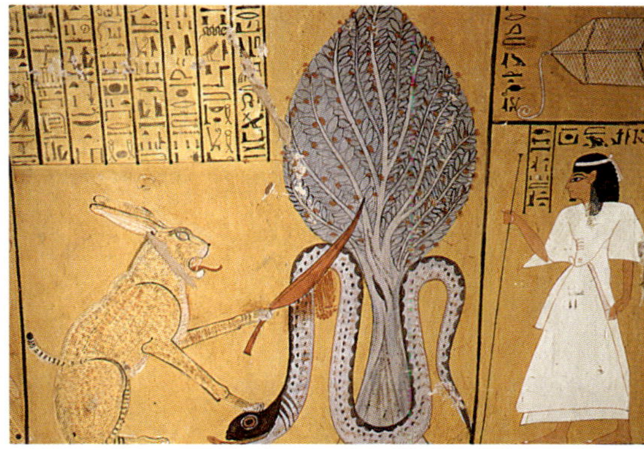

F

G

Description of the walls
a - *Scenes from the* Book of the Gates
b - *Texts from the* Book of the Dead *with a scene of* senet-*game*
c - *Inherkhau and his wife facing kings, queens and princes*
d - *Scenes from the world of Afterlife on three registers (17 scenes)*
e - *The deceased with children in the presence of Ptah and Osiris*
f - *The deceased in front of mythological creatures on three registers (14 scenes)*

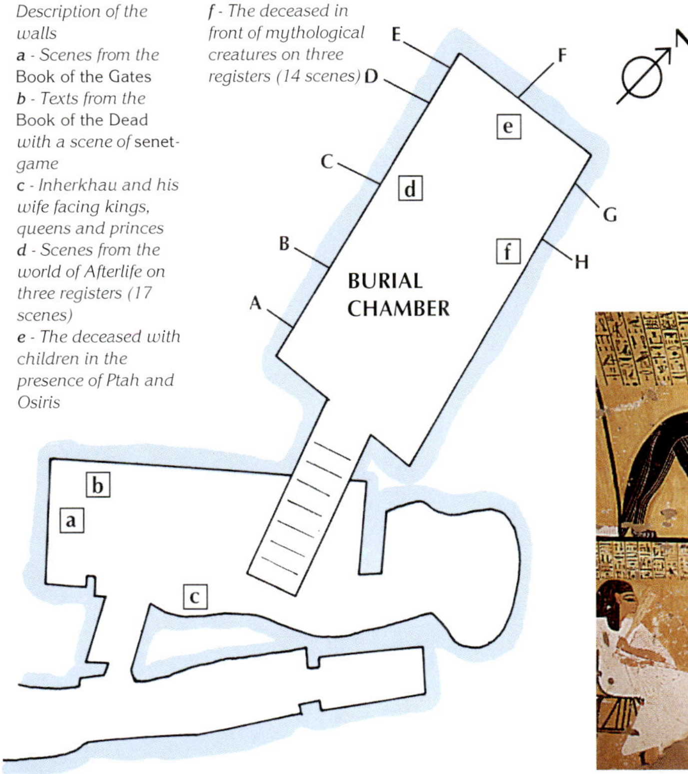

H

PASHEDU
TT no.3

"Servant in the Place of Truth on the West of Thebes"
Ramesside Period

The tomb of Pashedu, who held the title of "Servant in the Place of the Truth on the West of Thebes", which was only recently opened to the public, is known for the most famous scene shown on the eastern wall next to the entrance door and representing the deceased drinking from a small basin under a large palm tree. Only the burial chamber is decorated and is accessible through a small vaulted passage whose walls feature two images of Anubis in the form of a jackal. Other very beautiful scenes are those that adorn the tympanum of the back wall where one can see Osiris and Horus in the form of hawks in front of a large animated *udjat* eye supporting candles. In the tympanum of the opposing door (above the entrance door) one can see the god Ptah-Sokaris in the form of a hawk worshipped by Pashedu.

A - The narrow passage that leads into Pashedu's burial chamber is decorated with a dual image of Anubis in the form of a jackal crouching on a shrine and with the nekhakha*- flail between his hind paws.*

B - General view of the wall of the burial chamber: On the tympanum Pashedu and his son Menna respectively worship the god Ptah-Sokaris, in the form of a winged falcon on a boat, surmounted by an udjat*-eye, and a group of gods that appears on the north wall. Lower and to the left, Pashedu sits under a palm-tree, while to the right, arranged on three registers, are portrayed the dead man's attendants. In the left corner of the upper register there is also a representation of the sycamore goddess. Finally, in the picture we can see the initial scene of the lower register of the northern wall, made up of Pashedu, accompanied by a little girl, in the presence of Re-Harakhty and of a group of three other gods (Atum, Khepri and Ptah) not visible in the photograph.*

C - Pashedu, followed by his wife Nedjemtebehdet with two children, and by the attendants arranged on three registers, worships Horus (not visible), while on the walls are transcribed passages from the Book of the Dead. *In the vaulted passage is one of the two representations of Anubis in the form of a black jackal.*

D - Detail of the dead man's attendants.

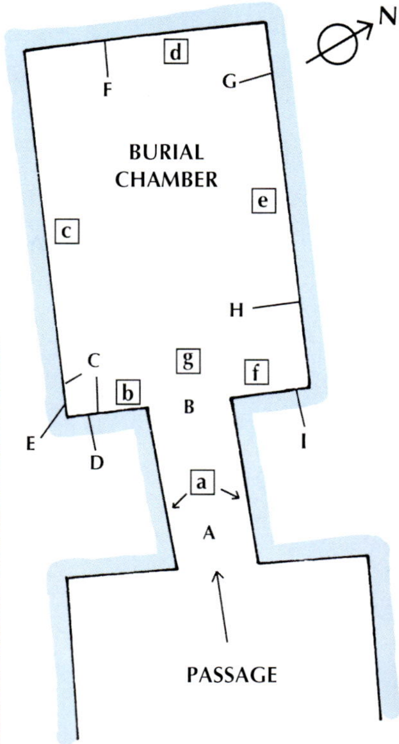

Description of the walls
a - Anubis in the form of a jackal
b - The relatives of Pashedu
c - The dead man and his family worship Horus in the form of a falcon, and Anubis
d - In the tympanum: the dead man worships Osiris, the udjat*-eye, and Horus*
e - Pashedu and a girl worship Re-Harakhty, Atum, Khepri and Ptah
f - The dead man quenches his thirst beneath a palm tree
g - In the tympanum: Ptah-Sokaris on a boat is worshipped by Pashedu.

E

G

H

F

I

E - Detail of Pashedu's wife, Nedjemtebehdet, portrayed in the typical style of the Ramessid period: the preparation of the wall is rough, but the style, although neglected in the details, is fresh and bright. Nedjemtebehdet wears her hair divided into many small black tresses and held on her brow by a cloth band that also supports the characteristic cone of scented oils.

F - Detail of the western wall tympanum. A large living udjat*-eye supports a torch while below Pashedu is portrayed in an act of worship.*

G - Pashedu with his wife and a daughter on a boat and before a table of offerings, make a pilgrimage to Abydos.

H - Details of the northern part of the vaulted ceiling with a procession of gods. From the right we observe Thoth, followed by Hathor, Re-Harakhty and Neith.

I - Pashedu is seated by a stream in the shade of a palm-tree laden with clusters of dates.

THE PRIVATE TOMBS

("TOMBS OF THE NOBLES")

The private tombs of the New Kingdom period in Thebes, usually referred to as "Tombs of the Nobles", have been excavated on the sides of the mountain in a rather large area extending between the Valley of the Kings and the Valley of the Queens; they are situated in various necropolises: Dra Abu el-Naga, el-Khokha, Assasif, Deir el-Bahri, Sheikh Abd el-Qurna, Qurnet Murai and Deir el-Medina. They constitute an extraordinary complex of more than 500 tombs decorated with paintings which, unlike those in the royal tombs, also show scenes and moments of daily life, thus enabling us to observe, as in a journey into the past, the daily routine of Egypt three thousand five hundred years ago. The tombs, whose structure obviously varies according to their date, generally include an outer yard, a funerary chapel intended for the offerings and the private worship of the deceased, preceded by an underground passage or a shaft leading to the burial chamber, usually not decorated. The classical Theban tomb has an overturned T - like plan with a first transversal room, or vestibule, and a second prolonged one with the main axis perpendicular to the previous, or a chapel ending in a niche in which the statue of the deceased was found. Above the entrance there was frequently a *pyramidion*, of the kind which adorned the Deir el-Medina tombs. On these necropolises numerous private dwelling-places have been built, incorporating in many cases part of the tombs, which are used as cellars or cowsheds. This phenomenon is not a recent one (it was extensively described by nineteenth-century's travellers, but today it is increasingly the cause of very serious problems and of damage to the very delicate wall paintings, both because of the increase in the number of houses and because of the enormous increase in water consumption: in the absence of a drainage and sewerage network, the waste water is absorbed by the limestone which forms the Theban mountain, thus increasing the moisture in the walls of the tombs and producing alterations and flaking of the wall paintings. Presently, only about fifteen tombs are equipped for touristic visits and are open to the public, about ten among them being the most beautiful and best preserved of the entire necropolis. They may be regarded as great masterpieces of the art of the New Kingdom.

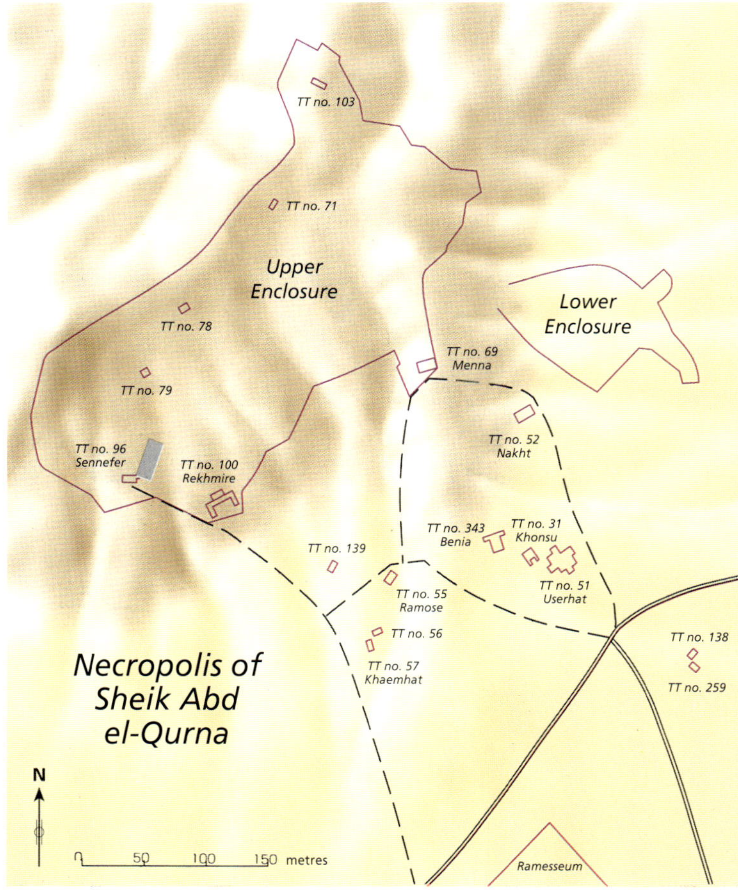

140 top General view of the Theban necropolis. On the right can be seen the necropolises of Assasif, el-Khokha and the hill of Sheikh Abd el-Qurna, which houses the greatest number of tombs.

140 bottom The entrance to the tomb of Ramose (TT no. 55, left) is at the foot of the hill of Sheikh Abd el-Qurna a few hundred meters from the asphalt road leading towards the Valley of the Kings. Further south, on the right, are the entrances to other tombs, including that of Khaemhat (TT no. 57).

KHAEMHAT
TT no. 57

"Royal Scribe, Overseer of the Granaries of Upper and Lower Egypt"
Eighteenth Dynasty

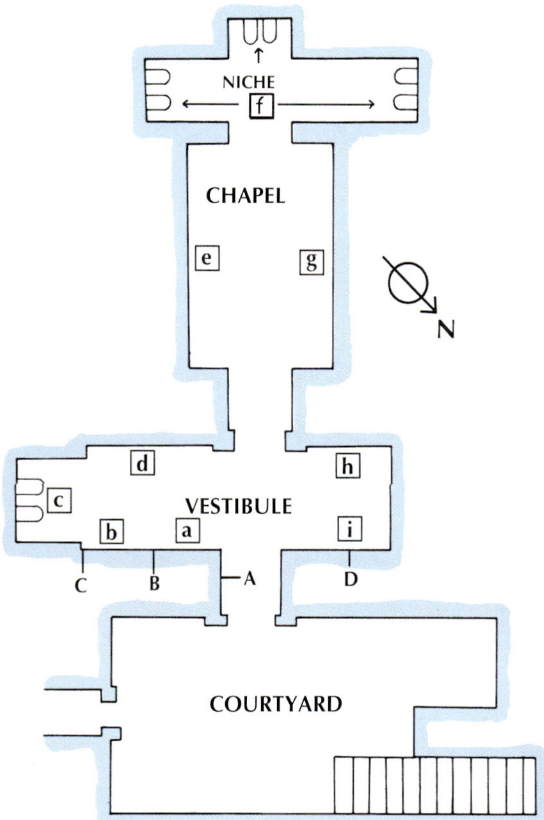

A

A - Bas-relief representing Khaemhat, "Royal Scribe, Overseer of the Granaries of Upper and Lower Egypt" in an act of worship. The columns of the text transcribe a hymn to Re.

B

B - Khaemhat, who is represented in high-relief, makes food offerings to the goddess Renenut, the "Lady of the fertile land", goddess of the crops and protector of the granaries. The rather refined and elegant style of the decorations of this tomb, which has clear stylistic similarities with that of Ramose (TT no. 55), is typical of the age of Amenophis III.

C

C - Detail of the masts of two armed transport boats with the shrouds and the halyards to hoist the sails.

D - A chariot drawn by four magnificent horses.

Khaemhat was a dignitary who lived in the reign of Amenophis III and carried the title "Royal Scribe, Overseer of the Granaries of Upper and Lower Egypt". His tomb is situated at the foot of the hill of Sheikh Abd el-Qurna, not far from the Ramesseum and the more famous tomb of Ramose.
The tomb is decorated in the "relief" style, in which the paintings are replaced, at least in part, with very fine uncolored sculptures with faintly accented reliefs.
The plan of the tomb is slightly different from the usual ones because the chapel has a vaulted ceiling and continues not with a simple niche, but with a proper transverse room with six large statues of the deceased, his bride Tyti and relatives. Even the decorative plan includes quite rare scenes and subjects like the adoration by the deceased of the sun, or the presentation of reports to King Amenophis III, complementing the usual representations of rural labors in the left part of the vestibule, where there are also two statues which represent Khaemhat and his father Imhotep.
In the chapel, whose decorations are partly destroyed, the themes are essentially mystic and religious, such as the funeral of the deceased and the pilgrimage to Abydos. There are also inscriptions of a cryptographic nature and passages from the *Book of the Dead* carved at the bottom of the walls next to the door which opens into the last room.

D

Description of the walls
a - *Agricultural scenes*
b - *Unloading of a ship; market*
c - *Niche with statues of the dead man and his family*
d - *A man leads the herd before the king.*
e - *Funeral scenes*
f - *Niches with statues of the dead man and his family*
g - *Fields of Iaru and pilgrimage to Abydos; sacrificial scenes*
h - *The dead man and notables of Upper and Lower Egypt rewarded by Amenophis III*
i - *Agricultural scenes*

SENNEFER

TT no. 96

"Mayor of the Southern City" Eighteenth Dynasty - Reign of Amenophis II

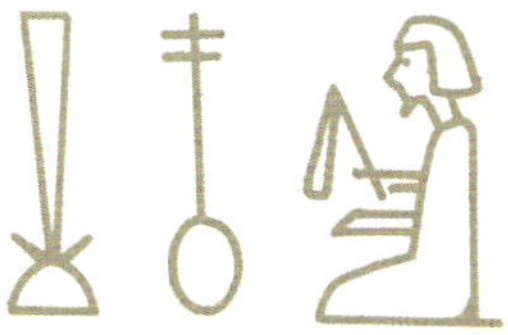

The tomb of Sennefer, "Mayor of the Southern City" and senior official who lived in the age of Amenophis II, is found on the upper side of the south-eastern slope of the Sheikh Abd-el Qurna hill, above that of the Vizier Rekhmire (TT no. 100), in a privileged position overlooking the Ramesseum - Ramesses II's great memorial temple - and the alluvial plain of the Nile.

This tomb (the upper chambers of which are inaccessible) is of outstanding beauty. It has a classical T plan, but differs from all the other tombs of the Eighteenth Dynasty both in the unusual amplitude of the four-pillar burial chamber and in the fact that these rooms are completely decorated, unlike all the other private tombs of the Eighteenth Dynasty (except that of an official who lived in the age of Tuthmosis III, the scribe Amenemhat, owner of tomb no. 82). It was normally the vestibule-chapel complex that was decorated, intended for the cult of the deceased performed by relatives and friends: nobody could penetrate into the burial chamber after the inhumation of the deceased. Only in later periods was the practice of decorating this part of the tomb started, but always with scenes of the religious kind and related to the underworld. The real uniqueness of the tomb of Sennefer is not in the fact that the burial chamber is decorated, but in its unusual decorative program: the real focus is not so much the underworld. as the deceased himself with his wife Merit (meaning "the Beloved"). The paintings constitute a real celebration of the noble couple united by a love that goes beyond earthly life and is assimilated to the divine one that unites Osiris to Isis, just as Sennefer and Merit themselves are assimilated to the two divinities. Finally, a further stylistic novelty is introduced in the decoration of the burial chamber and of the tomb's ante-chamber: the ancient artist decided to exploit the natural unevenness of the rock forming the ceiling of the two chambers, in order to confer a three-dimensional effect to the representation of a great pergola from which hang big bunches of grapes. This is an evocation of Osiris' vineyard, linked to the concept of vital strength, of revival and of regenerating power that constitutes one of the most typical prerogatives of the Lord of the Other World. The effect produced by the use of this innovative technique was of such beauty that nineteenth-century travellers, deeply impressed, called this hypogeum (considered today one of the highest expressions of the art of ancient Egypt), the "Tomb of the Vineyards".

Sennefer was one of the most influential officials in the court of Amenophis II, who lived in the second half of the fifteenth century BC, an age of great prosperity and wealth for Egypt: the country, after the victorious military campaigns of Tuthmosis III, Amenophis II's predecessor, was at the center of a large empire stretching from Asia Minor to the Nile's fourth cataract, in the southern part of present-day Sudan. Sennefer originated from a family of "civil servants", court officials and high ranking priests (his brother Amenemipet called Pairy, owner of tomb no. 29, was Vizier, equivalent to the pharaoh's prime minister) and enjoyed great prestige, beside having considerable personal wealth. Little is known of Sennefer's private life: the official documents tell us that he married a lady named Senetnay, of whom, however, there is no mention in the tomb, but who may probably be identified with lady Merit repeatedly appearing in the paintings. They had two daughters, Mut-Nofret and Tuya, the latter

142-143 View of the burial chamber, with the ceiling, (supported by four pillars), decorated partly with geometric motifs and partly with an extraordinary representation of a vine laden with bunches of grapes to which the artist has given a three-dimensional aspect using the unevenness of the rock surface, earning this tomb the nickname of the "Tomb of the Vineyards". On the pillar in the foreground Sennefer affectionately places his hand on the shoulder of his wife Merit, and on the back wall a priest (not visible) carries out a purification rite before the couple.

143 Sennefer and his wife, seated in the cabin of their boat, make the pilgrimage to Abydos and descend the Nile.
In the bow a priest dedicates a table of offerings.

mentioned in the tomb's antechamber together with another lady by the name of Setneferet, about whom we have no precise information.
The prerogatives of Sennefer, "Mayor of the Southern City", capital of the empire and center of religious life, granted him wide powers in the economic management not only of the city but also of the great temples and the huge properties annexed (and including, as far as the great temple of Amun at Karnak alone is concerned, more than four hundred gardens and over two hundred hectares of tilled soil).
The numerous titles with which Sennefer is referred to in his tomb not only testify to these manifold temporal powers, but also indicate that he must have enjoyed a peculiar and maybe preeminent position among all the court's high officials. It is also possible that Sennefer and his bride were never buried in the tomb on Sheikh Abd el-Qurna hill but in an even more privileged and exclusive spot: in the Valley of the Kings.
The discovery in tomb KV no. 42, intended, possibly, for Tuthmosis II but left unfinished, of numerous pots bearing the name of Sennefer and of his wife might support this hypothesis.

The antechamber

The wall decorations of the funerary chamber and of the antechamber of Sennefer's tomb are in a perfect state of preservation, even though the hypogeum has been open to visitors since the beginning of last century, probably because of its depth and the good quality of the rock in this section of the necropolis. A steep staircase opening off the yard facing the chapel leads into the antechamber located 12 meters down, after a sudden elbow bend. It is a small room adjoining the burial chamber, with which it communicates through a narrow door: the wall paintings of the antechamber show the deceased sitting under a pergola laden with bunches of grapes, that constitutes the decorative theme of the entire ceiling, as he attends the presentation of the funerary equipment and of the offerings composed of linen tissues, torches, a foreleg of beef and bread. The offerings are presented by a procession of priests led by Tuya, one of Sennefer's daughters, handing to her father an amulet with a little heart of lapis lazuli (western wall), while another procession of servants on the eastern wall carry on trays the ornaments of the mummy (collars, two *shawabti*, the sandals, a heart-shaped amulet and the funerary mask), the bed and Sennefer's personal belongings, locked up in two small boxes.
On the northern side, beside the door, the deceased and a lady by the name of Setneferet, "much beloved sister and singer of Amun" playing the sistrum, are shown in the act of worshipping Osiris and Anubis, the two major divinities of the Afterlife, no longer visible.

THE BURIAL CHAMBER

We penetrate into the splendid burial chamber, whose decorative program is particularly complex and reflects the life of the deceased and of his wife in the Afterworld. The ceiling, supported by four pillars painted on all sides, takes up again the motive of the pergola laden with bunches of grapes, already hinted at in the ceiling of the antechamber, while on the southern side it is replaced by geometrical decorations, typical of the ceilings of the Eighteenth Dynasty tombs. The decorations of the pillars are rather peculiar and always show on three sides Merit handing to Sennefer lotus flowers, perfumed ointments, food, myrrh, protecting amulets, linen bands, necklaces, and a sistrum; in one instance only, on the south-eastern pillar, we see Merit simply standing in front of her husband. The scenes figured on the fourth side of each pillar are different: on Pillar One (south-west) we see Sennefer and Merit under a sycamore, on Pillar Two (north-west) there is a representation of the "goddess of the sycamore" handing water to the couple, overlooked by a double representation of Anubis in canine form, while on Pillars Three (north-east) and Four (south-east) there are two evocations of moments in the rite of the "Opening of the mouth" (also illustrated in the paintings of the southern side of the eastern wall and on the eastern side of the southern wall), thanks to which the deceased magically recovers the use of his senses and speech. Sennefer is shown on top of an alabaster basin while being cleansed by four priests sprinkling water (Pillar Three) and finally, after his revival, again surrounded by four priests (Pillar Four). The wall decorations were not painted at random but in a quite precise order, following the ritual orientation of the tomb, according to which the east coincides with the door of the burial chamber. This ritual orientation reflects the journey in the Afterworld of the deceased's soul which, after going through different stages, ends with the transformation and regeneration of the deceased and his "appearing in broad daylight". The scenes start on the western (or more precisely on the north-western) wall, corresponding to the ritual south, with the representation of a scene of offering by Sennefer and Merit to Osiris-Unnefer "Lord of the Holy Land, Prince of Eternity" and to Hathor "Lady of the Western Necropolis", followed by Sennefer's funeral: the transportation into the necropolis of the deceased's sarcophagus hauled by four oxen, preceded by servants carrying the funerary equipment locked up in wooden coffers and the offerings, and accompanied by friends and by the highest-ranking officials. Next comes the representation of the details of the funerary rites: the washing and cleansing of the body, the transportation of the canopic jars containing the entrails of the deceased, etc. On the northern wall, or more precisely on the north-eastern, corresponding to the ritual west, we see, in the first portion, a double scene of food offerings to Osiris: Sennefer and his wife are shown facing rich tables of offerings, in front of which the priests carry torches and libations. The scenes are accompanied by texts transcribing the offering formulae. The text accompanying the first scene reads "Offering the king gives to Osiris, Lord of Eternity, so that he might provide bread and beer, meat and every good and pure thing for the *ka* of Sennefer purified".
The eastern side of the wall is dedicated to the representation of scenes of river-navigation, preceded by a scene in which Sennefer and Merit worship Anubis and the resurrected Osiris, whose face is painted with the reddish color traditionally used in depicting the living. The nautical scene that comes next (but which from a logical point of view precedes the worshipping) recalls the pilgrimage to Abydos, "holy" town where, according to tradition, was found the tomb of Osiris, Lord of the Afterworld, but at the same time

144 On the four pillars of the burial chamber, the Sennefer-Merit couple is represented no less than fourteen times: it is not known exactly who Merit is. As far as we know from official documents, Sennefer's wife was called Senetnay, but it may be supposed that the two are identical and that the "beloved" Merit is merely the idealization of Senetnay. In the photograph Merit hands to Sennefer, on a tray, a necklace made of gold petals, while with her other hand she supports on her husband's chest the pendant, which is made up of two hearts, one of gold and the other of silver, on which the cartouches of Amenophis II are etched.

145 top Merit offers Sennefer a goblet containing a beverage. In the upper part of the scene two udjat-*eyes are portrayed at the sides of a* shenu-*sign that has a protective role.*

embodiment of the regenerating power and of the concept of resurrection since he triumphed over death. In the myth of Osiris, the god, whose body had been dismembered by his evil brother Seth, was compassionately pieced together by Isis, his wife and a great magician, who succeeded in restoring him to life again and in having from her beloved husband a son: Horus.
At Abydos, where the kings of the First Dynasty had themselves buried and those of the following dynasties had cenotaphs built for themselves in order to take a symbolic part in the resurrection of Osiris, the deceased accomplished a ritual pilgrimage in order to assimilate themselves to the god. It was Osiris who presided over the divine court of justice and who "weighed" the soul of the deceased, comparing it to the feather of Maat, embodiment of the cosmic order and therefore of divine justice: only after having overcome this trial the deceased became *makheru*, that is to say "purified", identifying himself with Osiris. So we see Sennefer and his bride Merit aboard their funerary boat painted in green, a color symbolizing papyrus, but also metaphorically regeneration, sitting under a baldachin together with a priest performing a cleansing rite while they are about to accomplish the ritual pilgrimage. Sennefer's barque is hauled by a second, bigger craft in which are represented the helmsman, the rowers and the captain who steers downstream to Abydos.
In the bottom register the journey in the opposite direction and the return to the necropolis is described. The boat towing Sennefer's boat hoists a rectangular sail to help the rowers sailing upstream all the way to Thebes. On the eastern wall, the deceased and Merit are at first shown worshipping Osiris and Anubis, while at the center the scene illustrates Chapter 151 of the *Book of the Dead*: Anubis the divine Embalmer, flanked by Isis on his right and Nephthys on his left, attends to Sennefer's mummy, lying on the deathbed beneath which his *ba*, the soul of the deceased in the shape of a bird, is represented. At the corners of the rectangle in which

these scenes are found, we see the standing figures of Horus's Four Sons (clockwise Qebhsenuef, Duamutef, Imset and Hapu), protectors of the canopic jars and, in the lower part, two *shawabti* accompanied by a passage from Chapter 6 of the *Book of the Dead*, including the magic formula by which the deceased was able to call

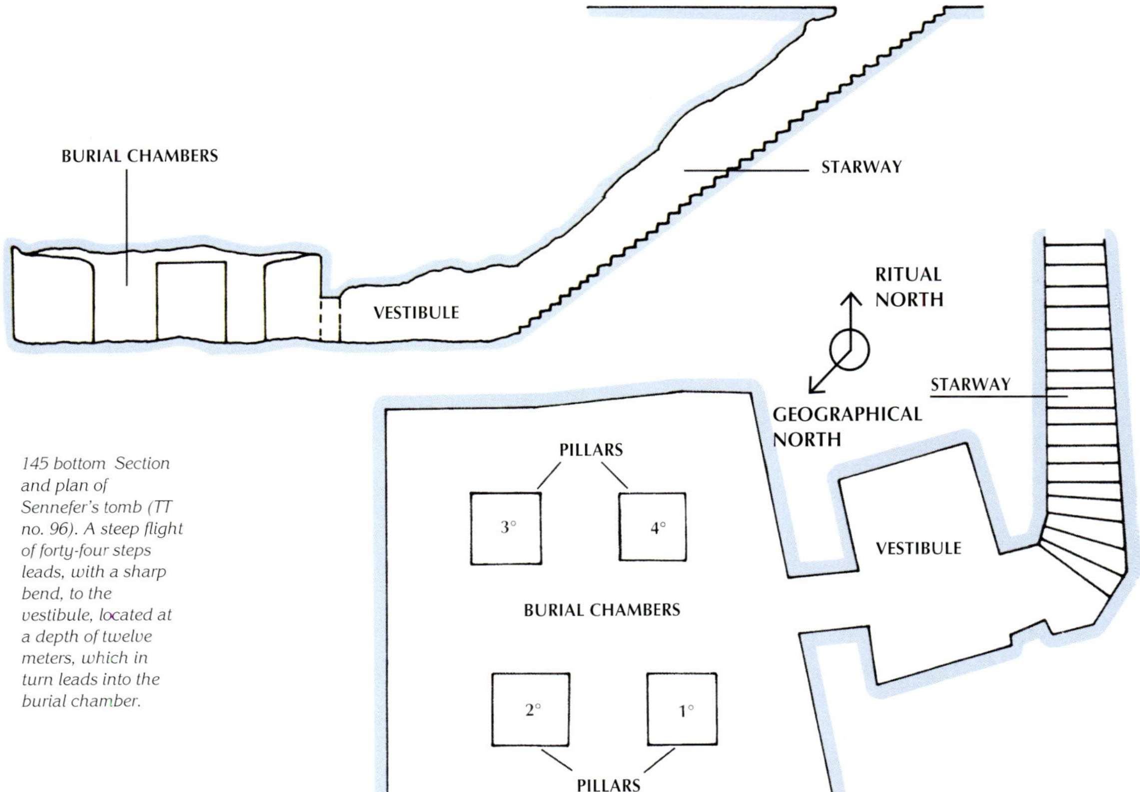

145 bottom Section and plan of Sennefer's tomb (TT no. 96). A steep flight of forty-four steps leads, with a sharp bend, to the vestibule, located at a depth of twelve meters, which in turn leads into the burial chamber.

A - In the vestibule, a representation of servants bearing the mummy's ornaments on trays: a large menat *collar, a second collar and leather sandals, two* shawabti, *the funeral mask and a heart-shaped amulet painted blue to symbolize lapis lazuli.*

B - The architrave of the small communication door between the burial chamber and the vestibule is decorated with a double representation of Anubis in the form of a black jackal crouching on a shrine, while the hieroglyphic texts transcribe an invocation to various deities, including Anubis, Mut, Amun-Re and Osiris.

A

J

B

I

H

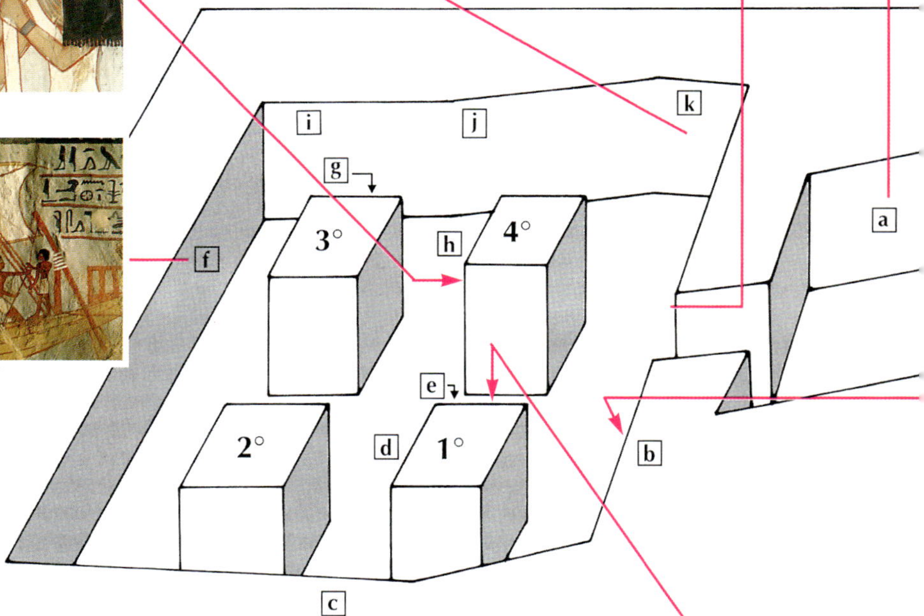

G

F

E

C - Sennefer and his wife Merit are portrayed seated in a conventional attitude. Merit has her hair tied with a band adorned with a large lotus flower, while under the high-backed chairs can be seen two alabaster vessels containing scented oils.

D - Detail of the ceiling of the burial chamber with a geometric decoration of zigzags interspersed with ornate squares.

E - Sennefer, seated under a sycamore with Merit at his feet, inhales the scent of a lotus flower and holds in his hand a sekhem*-sceptre, symbol of power and authority. In front, on a table, there are three vessels filled with ale around which lotus stems are twined.*

F - A different motif of geometric decoration of the ceiling, with simple colored zigzags.

G - The famous "bower decoration" with the bunches of grapes that seem to stand out from the ceiling.

H - Detail of the return journey form Abydos towards Thebes: the boat towing the craft carrying Sennefer and his wife has hoisted its sail to use the wind for its journey up the Nile.

I - Merit offers two white linen bands to Sennefer who is smelling a lotus flower.

J - A sem*-priest, holding in his hand a gold* nemset*-vessel, purifies Sennefer and his wife.*

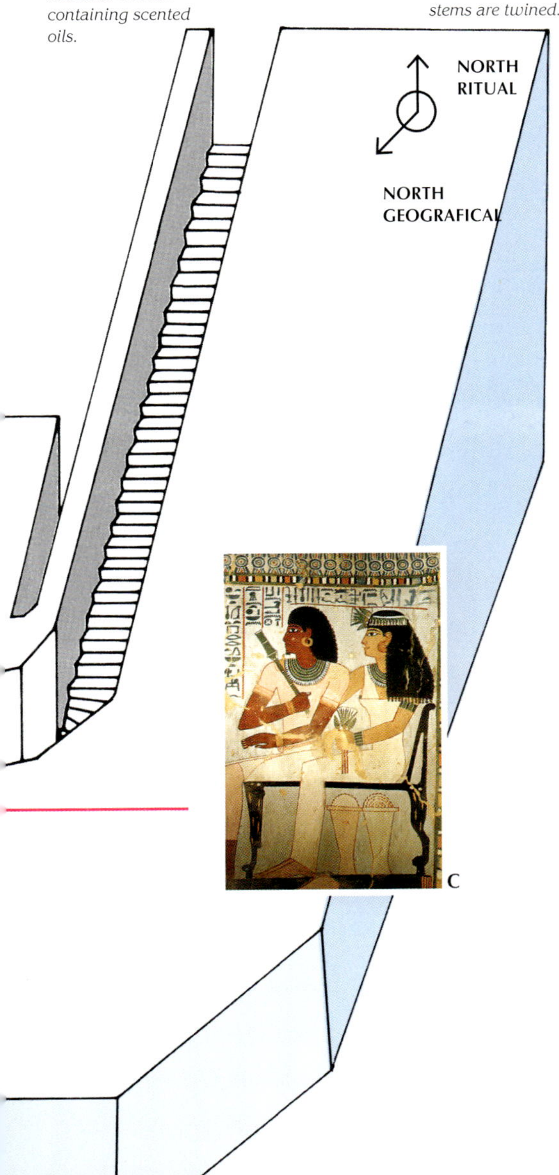

C

D

the *shawabti* (a word meaning "the responders") and order them to undertake in his stead the heaviest labours in the Afterworld. On the southern side of the wall there is a representation of a peculiar moment of the ceremony of the "Opening of the Mouth": Sennefer and Merit are being cleansed by a *sem*-priest, a very ancient priestly figure of the funerary rite wearing a characteristic leopard skin. The adjoining scene, with which the southern wall begins (corresponding to the eastern wall of the ritual orientation, at the centre of which the door opens), show a priest performing libations and burnt offerings in front of the couple. Finally, in the western half of this wall there is a double representation of Sennefer and Merit, first portrayed in a conventional way sitting on two high-backed chairs and then standing while they get ready to "appear in broad daylight" in order to "see the (solar) disc in its daily journey", and finally symbolically coming out again from the door of the burial chamber, whose architrave is overlooked by a double image of Anubis, "the Embalmer" and "Lord of the Holy Land" in the shape of a black dog smelling a bunch of lotus flowers on top of two chapels, ritual representations of the tomb itself.

Description of the walls
a *- Funeral procession*
b *- Sennefer and his wife Merit*
c *- Funeral procession; the deceased before Osiris and Hathor*
d *- Sennefer's wife offers him flowers*
e *- The dead man with his wife in the shade of a sycamore tree.*
f *- Pilgrimage to Abydos*
g *- The deceased is purified by four priests*
h *- Sennefer's wife offers him two white rolls of linen*
i *- Sennefer and his wife worship Osiris and Anubis*
j *- Ritual representation of the tomb as indicated in Chapter 151 of the* Book of the Dead
k *- Purification of the deceased and his wife. The mummy of the deceased and his soul with Anubis, Isis and Nephthys*

REKHMIRE

TT no. 100

"Governor of the Town and Vizier"
Eighteenth Dynasty
Reign of Tuthmosis III - Amenophis II

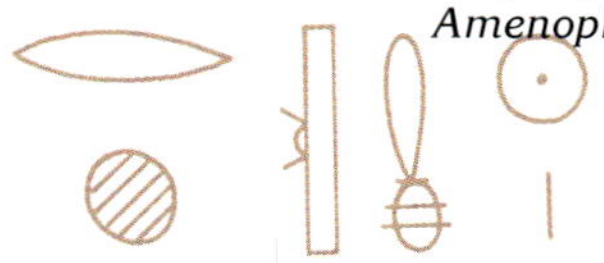

148 top Detail of a funeral banquet: a young maid-servant helps a lady adorn herself with her jewels.

148 centre During the funeral banquet three young musicians play the harp, the lute and the tambourine. The style of this scene, which is extraordinarily elegant, shows traces of archaism typical of the Eighteenth Dynasty.

148 bottom A procession of servants transports the deceased's burial riches.

149 top left Various stages of the work of the goldsmiths (upper register), the tanners and the furriers (lower register).

149 top right A portrait of Rekhmire, "Governor of the Town and Vizier", who lived in the age of Tuthmosis III and Amenophis II.

149 bottom Illustration of the various stages of the preparation and transport of mud bricks, the most widely used construction material, then as now.

The tomb of Rekhmire, located on the upper side of the south-eastern slope of the Sheikh Abd el-Qurna hill, a little more than a hundred meters beneath the tomb of Sennefer no. 96, is one of the most outstanding and interesting tombs of the whole Theban necropolis. Rekhmire lived in the time of Tuthmosis III and Amenophis II, acting as Vizier, the highest among the State's offices; considering the importance of the personage, it is not surprising that he had himself built an extraordinary tomb. The epigraphy of the tomb allows us to trace its construction back to the reign of Tuthmosis III but it also shows that Rekhmire was still living during the reign of Amenophis II. Even though the tomb of Rekhmire, who lived in an age of great expansion of the Empire, has a rather simple and conventional "T" structure, typical of the Eighteenth Dynasty tombs, it differs from all the others in its imposing dimensions, in the quality of the decoration and in the variety of the iconographical program.
A first transversal hall or vestibule, itself quite large, is followed by a longitudinal hall or chapel stretching out considerably not only in length along its main axis facing south, but above all in height: the ceiling starts from three meters, and climbs diagonally until it reaches nine meters. This elevation brings the total decorated surface to 300 square meters.
An architectural peculiarity of this tomb is the absence of a funerary shaft and this has led to the assumption that Rekhmire was never buried in this tomb but rather in the Valley of the Kings, in some tomb as yet unknown, a privilege granted to the highest-ranking officials who enjoyed the pharaoh's favor.
The paintings are of quite high quality, as is their state of preservation, very good in the first transversal hall but exceptional in the gigantic chapel. The pictorial style is sometimes the archaic style of the Middle Kingdom tombs, from which it appears to draw inspiration, even though it is more lively and richer in chromatic range, while in other instances the paintings possess a vivacity and a dynamism typical of the second half of the Eighteenth Dynasty. The multiple themes dealt with in the decorative program are also of enormous interest; beside some conventional scenes, many others are absolutely

unique, giving us a complete and detailed outline of many aspects of daily life and of the artisan activities of the time. There are also scenes of religious rites, such as the ceremony of the "Opening of the Mouth" or the description of the Beautiful Feast of the Valley, which are the most important among those that took place in the necropolis. Unfortunately, the incredible height of the scenes in the upper registers of the chapel makes their observation almost impossible and, in any case, the richness of the iconographical program is such that a thorough analysis would require a special treatment beyond the scope of an introductory guide to the Theban necropolis. For lack of space we shall therefore limit ourselves to the description of the main scenes outlined in the lower and middle registers, which the visitors can observe.

The vestibule

On the south-western wall of the vestibule, which the visitor finds on his left when entering, the products of Upper Egypt are illustrated in five registers while a text describes the goods of the Vizier, originally portrayed in the audience hall in the act of inspecting some subordinates (the image is now lost). On the adjoining small western wall there is a long autobiographical text, while on the north-western wall a scene of great interest shows the tributes from foreign countries, subdivided into five groups and duly registered by the scribes: the inhabitants of the mysterious land of Punt with incense trees, baboons, monkeys, animal hides; the inhabitants of Kefti, a territory probably to be identified with today's island of Crete, carrying pots and cups; the Kushites or Nubians, represented together with animals typical of equatorial Africa's fauna (giraffes, leopards, baboons, monkeys and dogs), offering ivory, animal hides and gold; the Retenus or Syrians bringing pots, carts, weapons, beside various animals (horses, a bear and an elephant) and a fifth group uniting diverse foreign populations from different countries, among whom can be seen women with negroid features leading their children by the hand. On the eastern side of the southern wall, Rekhmire (the image of the Vizier is now lost)inspects the tributes from Lower Egypt and the workshops of the craftsmen working in the temples, while on the eastern wall several among Rekhmire's relatives are shown; on the eastern side of the northern wall the products coming from the Mediterranean strip of Lower Egypt are shown with scenes of vintage, fishing and hunting.

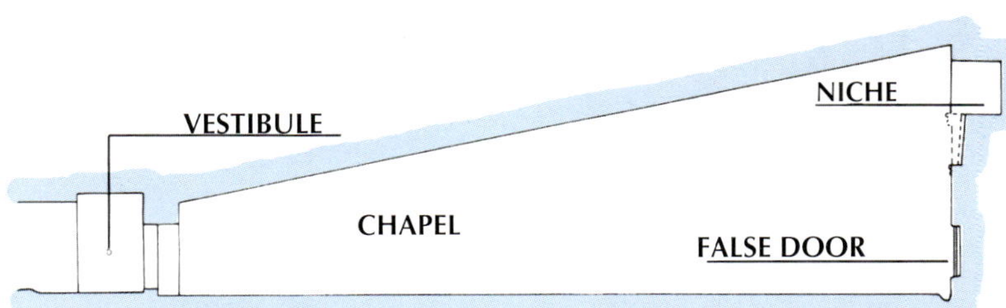

The chapel

The paintings of the chapel are undoubtedly the most interesting and the best preserved of the whole tomb. On the western wall the deceased is first shown supervising the gathering and the preparation of the food provisions allotted to the temple and their distribution in a series of scenes arranged in six registers, while in the

A - The chapel of Rekhmire's tomb is made up of a narrow corridor with walls rising to a height of nine meters; the surface, about three hundred square meters, is completely decorated.

B - Bearers of tributes from foreign countries offer elephant tusks, valuable skins, ostrich egg and feathers, a baboon and a monkey.

C - A splendid giraffe, portrayed with a monkey climbing its neck, was part of the tributes.

D - A stage of the weighing and recording of the gold and silver under the control of a scribe who records the amount weighed.

E - The different stages of working and decorating metal vessels.

C

D

E

B

A

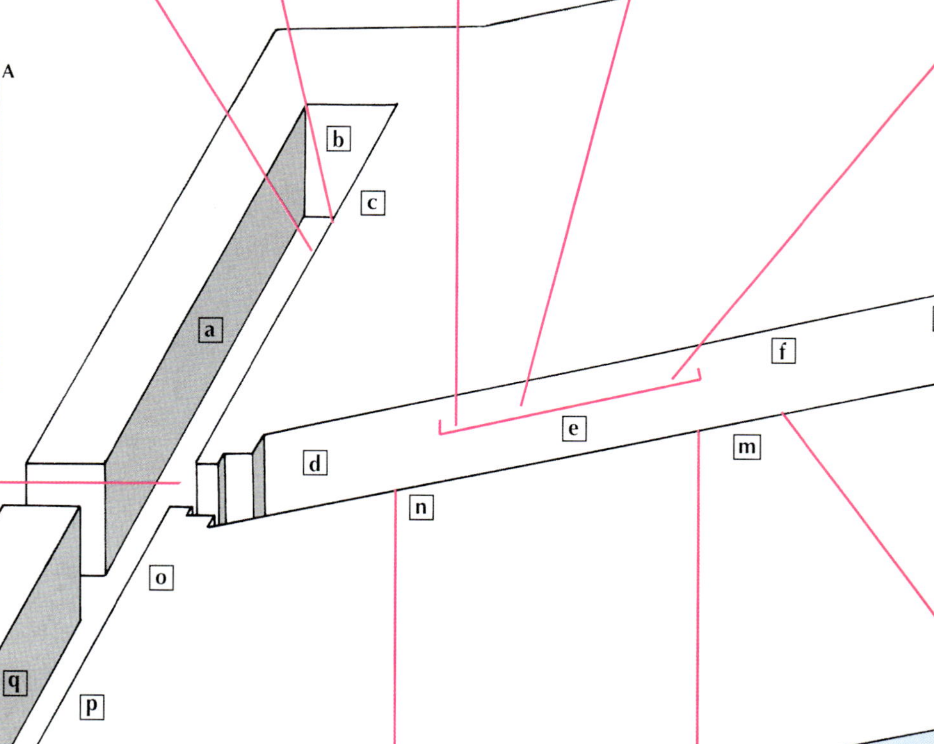

K

J

following series of scenes, arranged in eight registers, are represented all the labours carried out by the craftsmen who worked for Amun's temple: potters, carpenters, decorators, goldsmiths, sculptors and masons busy manufacturing bricks of unburned clay, making use of processes employed up to the present, and their transportation for the building of a great inclined plane, while some sculptors are busy constructing two colossal statues of red granite. The following scenes, arranged in ten registers, are of a funerary character and illustrate the funeral procession heading for the necropolis, the setting up of obelisks, the catafalque hauled by nine friends of the deceased, the pilgrimage to Abydos, the cleansing of the deceased and scenes of dance and of ritual slaughter of beasts.
On the narrow background wall we can see a niche in which a stele was found (now at the Louvre Museum) and, below, a false door, a decorative element dating back to the Old Kingdom, which symbolically led into the Afterworld, while the paintings, accompanied by columns of texts transcribing the formulae of the offerings, represent the deceased bowing down before Osiris while Menkeperreseneb, Rekhmire's son, gives offerings to the deceased father and to his wife Merit. Finally, on the eastern wall of the chapel we find two sons of Rekhmire, Amenophis and Senusert who, with Menkeperreseneb, are in the presence of their deceased father and mother. In the following scenes are shown, in ten registers, the rites carried out in front of the statue of the deceased with scenes of ritual slaughter of beasts, of cleansing, and of preparation of the food in front of the deceased sitting on a high-backed chair, with the representation of a magnificent garden, a pool and a boat. Then comes the beautiful scene, arranged in ten registers, of the funerary banquet during which the deceased's sons and daughters hand flower wreaths to Rekhmire and to his wife while musicians, both males and females, wearing bright clothes, play diverse instruments among which we notice lutes, tambourines, flutes, harps and castanets, while the guests eat sitting on mats and are waited on by numerous servants. Finally, in the last series of scenes, which complete the decorative program of the eastern wall of the chapel, we witness a journey undertaken in a boat by the deceased in order to receive a high decoration from Pharaoh Amenophis II, a further scene of offering of flowers to Rekhmire by his son and an audience granted by the Vizier to dignitaries and petitioners. Though brief and necessarily incomplete, this description of the paintings in the tomb of Rekhmire gives, nevertheless, an idea of the complexity and the completeness of the decorative program of this superb work of art from the first half of the Eighteenth Dynasty, in which the archaic and manneristic tendencies are often softened and transcended by the extraordinary talent of the artists who worked there.

F

G

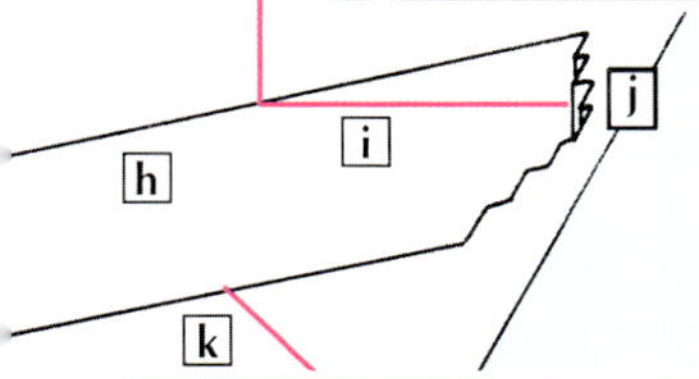

H

I

F - In a pond surrounded by trees, the workers draw the water used to make the earth into a paste and, with a mould (seen on the right), to make the green bricks.

G - The wall at the back of the chapel ends with a false door over which is a niche in which a stele was originally placed.

H - The vizier Rekhmire with the sekhem*-sceptre in his hand, and his wife Merit.*

I - A young musician plays the tambourine.

J - During the funeral banquet a maid-servant serves a goblet of drink to a lady.

K - A large cargo boat with unfurled sails and the oarsmen at work, goes up the Nile.

Description of the walls
a - *The deceased superintends the collecting of Upper Egypt's taxes; weighing of the gold.*
b - *Inscription*
c - *Tributes of the foreign populations*
d - *Preparation and storing of the food*
e - *Artisans, smiths and bricklayers at work*
f - *The deceased superintending the activities of craftsmen and workers*
g - *Funeral procession*
h - *Hathor-Imentit, Anubis and Osiris*
i - *The deceased and his wife before the table of the offerings*
j - *False door, inscriptions and niche*
k - *Scenes of offering and purification*
m- *Scenes of life and of cultivation in a garden*
m- *Funeral banquet; scenes of musicians*
n - *The deceased returns from a royal audience; ships*
o - *Hunting scenes in the desert*
p - *Grape harvest; preparation and storing of food*
q - *Scenes of country life (damaged); the deceased superintends collection of Lower Egypt's taxes*

NAKHT

TT no. 52

"Scribe, Astronomer of Amun"
Eighteenth Dynasty

A

B

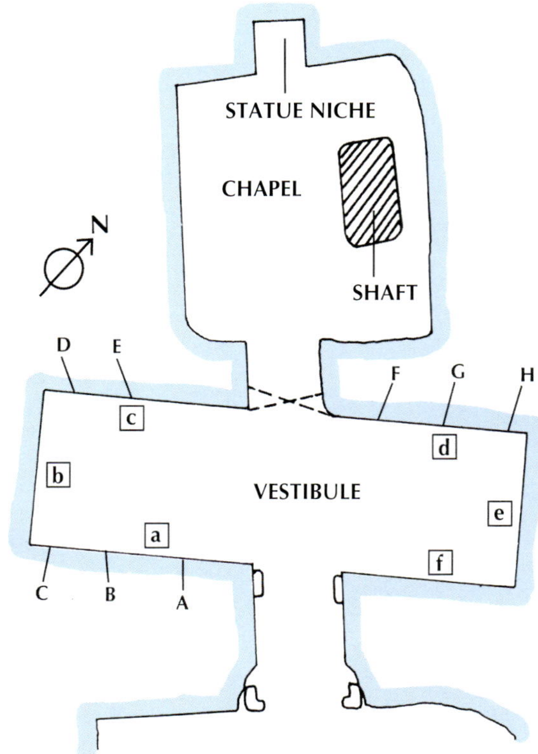

Description of the walls
a - Scenes of country life
b - False door; the goddess Nut gathers the offerings
c - Funeral banquet
d - Hunting and fishing scenes; grape harvest and preparation of the wine
e - Bearers of offerings and priests before Nakht and his wife
f - Purification of the offerings before the deceased

The Tomb of Nakht was the subject of an experimental restoration carried out at the end of the 1980s with the purpose of finding a technique to provide adequate protection to the tombs' paintings while also improving the condition of the tombs themselves. Unfortunately, the relatively sophisticated technology used in the tomb of Nakht, which requires complete insulation with sheets of glass of all the vestibule walls, the only painted part of the tomb, turned out to be too expensive and difficult for use on a large scale. Represented on the walls, besides scenes of offerings and funeral rites, are moments from rural life having to do with the cultivation of grain, digging of small canals for irrigation, harvest, fishing and hunting in the Nile Delta. On the left wall, there is a stele in which are

A - Sowing: a peasant strews seeds on the ground from a container. They are planted in the ground by a second farmer who assists with an appropriate wooden instrument.

B - Two farmers plough the fields with a wooden plough pulled by two oxen.

C - Two groups of peasants, using wooden implements, throw the threshed grain into the air to winnow it.

D - A maid-servant helps three ladies to adorn themselves with jewels.

C

D

E

E - By its charm and elegance, this has become one of the most famous scenes of all ancient Egyptian paintings: three young musicians accompany the funeral banquet, playing the harp, the lute and a wind instrument. The musician in the centre, who plays a kind of lute, is portrayed, for the first time in Egyptian painting, almost completely naked.

F

G

F - Splendid and fine detail of Nakht's wife holding a small bird.

G - A double scene of hunting birds in the marshes. Nakht is portrayed, with his wife and two small sons in a papyrus boat, grasping the hunting stick.

H - This group of scenes relates to the preparation of food and drink. In the upper register two peasants are gathering grapes, while others press them; the must produced in this way is then stored in conical jars. In the lower register servants drag a net that contains a great number of birds, the result of a day's hunt in the marshes. The birds are carefully plucked, cleaned and prepared for cooking.

depicted servants and two women presenting offerings. The theme of the offerings is repeated in the paintings lining the entrance, showing offering of food to the deceased and his bride, Tawi, who carried the title "Singer of Amun", while in the next scene the couple makes offerings to Amun. On the lower part of the wall, on the left side, is portrayed the funeral banquet with the famous image of the three singers, which for the first time in Theban painting features female nudity.

H

MENNA
TT no. 69

“Scribe of the Fields of the Lord of the Two Lands of Upper and Lower Egypt”
Eighteenth Dynasty

In the tomb of Menna, similar in form, style and dimensions to that of Nakht, all the classic themes of Theban painting of the period are represented, but the more notable paintings illustrate above all agricultural labors, spread across five levels which cover the entire left lateral wall of the vestibule (the

Description of the walls
- ***a*** *- Agricultural scenes*
- ***b*** *- The deceased and his wife in the presence of Osiris*
- ***c*** *- The deceased and his wife, funeral banquet (fragmentary)*
- ***d*** *- Bearers of offerings and funeral procession*
- ***e*** *- The deceased before the judgment of Osiris*
- ***f*** *- Niche with statues of the deceased and his wife*
- ***g*** *- Menna with his family hunting and fishing in the marshes*
- ***h*** *- Pilgrimage to Abydos*
- ***i*** *- The deceased and his wife receive offerings and list of the ritual offerings*
- ***j*** *- Steles in three registers: a) the deity of the West; b) seated couples; c) the deceased and his wife in an act of worship*
- ***k*** *- Offering scenes*

C

D

A

B

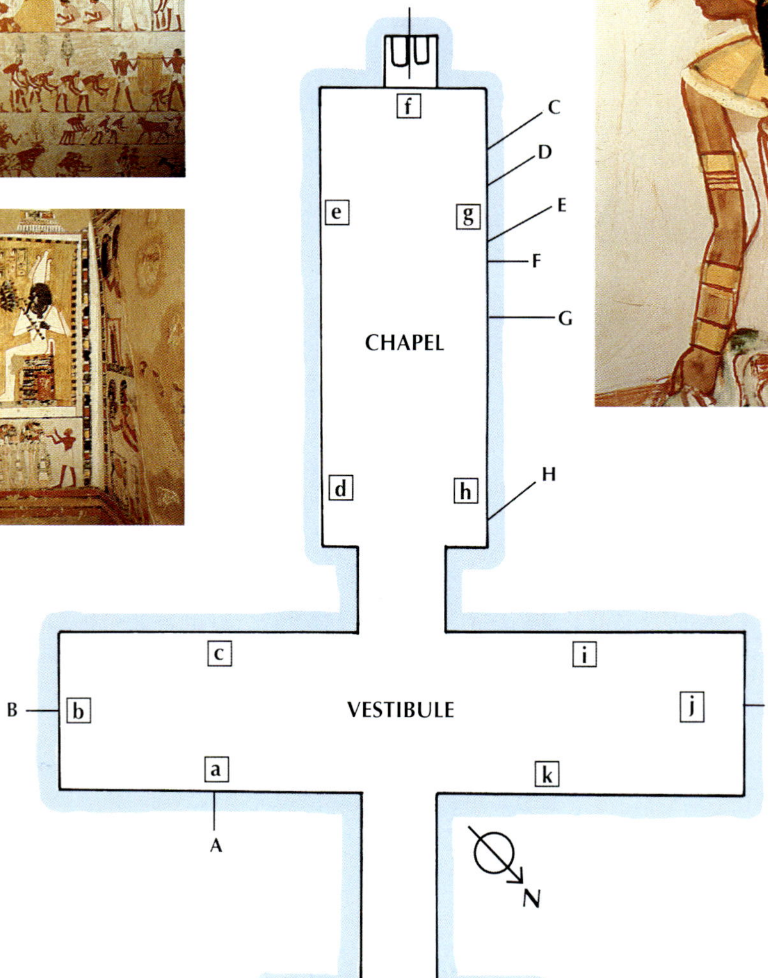

A - The tomb of Menna who bore the title of Scribe of the Fields of the Lords of the Two Lands of Upper and Lower Egypt contains many scenes relating to agricultural labours. On this wall, arranged on four registers, we see different stages of reaping and of the wheat harvest, an operation carried out under the supervision of the scribes who scrupulously record the amount.

B - The deceased and his wife, before a table of offerings, worship the god Osiris seated on a throne inside a chapel.

C, D - A young daughter of Menna picks the scented lotus flowers (C) while another carries lotus flowers and the birds that have been caught (D).

E - Magnificent naturalistic detail of life in the marshes among the papyrus and lotus plants, which swarm with life and where many types of birds lay their eggs. At right can be seen a rodent and a cat dangerously close to a nest and, up above, two butterflies.

F, G - A dual fishing and hunting scene in the marshes, similar to that portrayed in Nakht's tomb (TT no. 52). Menna stands on a papyrus boat accompanied by his wife and sons. On the right he fishes with a harpoon and is portrayed catching two fish (detail in F); on the left he brandishes a stick for hunting and catching birds, while the birds take off from a thicket of papyrus. Given the extraordinary stylistic similarities, it is probable that Menna's tomb and Nakht's tomb were the work of the same artist, who probably worked at the beginning of the reign of Amenophis III.

G

E

H

H - In the upper register there is a representation of the pilgrimage to Abydos with the fleet of boats returning to Thebes. The lower registers are dedicated to the rites carried out before the mummy and in particular to the ceremony of the "Opening of the Mouth".

F

same position as that of the same subject in the tomb of Nakht), in which are illustrated the harvest and gathering of grain closely supervised by the scribe, along with more intimate scenes of small details, like a little girl taking a thorn out of a friend's foot, or the mother cradling a newborn under a tree, which seem to be real renderings of everyday life. On the lower part of the wall of the vestibule (left side) the deceased, followed by his bride Henut-taui, is represented in the presence of Osiris, seated inside his shrine. On the right wall of the chapel a splendid scene can be admired, in which the deceased is depicted while hunting birds and fishing in the marshes on boats of papyrus accompanied by his bride, while on the opposite wall there is a complete representation of the funeral of the deceased.

I

I - On the western wall of the vestibule is a stele subdivided into three registers. Re-Harakhty is depicted in the upper register with the main gods of the funeral cult, while the middle register has a double representation of the deceased with his wife Henut-taui.

RAMOSE
TT no. 55

"Governor of the Town and Vizier"
Eighteenth Dynasty

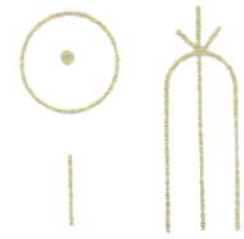

A - Portrait of a guest at Ramose's banquet. The large scenes of the funeral banquet are sculpted simply in relief on limestone slabs without use of colors except to show the eyes of the figures. Despite their rigid, conservative style, these scenes are distinguished by an elegance and an unequaled stylistic purity and constitute one of the highest manifestations of ancient art.

B - Detail of a large scene of Ramose's obsequies; this is the only painted scene in all the tomb: the servants carry the burial riches of the deceased, which will be placed subsequently in the burial chamber.

C - A group of women with their hair loose as a sign of mourning, lament the death of Ramose, lifting their arms at the passage of the sarcophagus, depicted in the upper register. This scene, considered a masterpiece of Eighteenth Dynasty art, is marked by a lively style that gives expression to the feeling of grief in face of death.

D - Detail of the scene of purification of Ramose, "Governor of the Town and Vizier", who lived in the age of Amenophis III and Amenophis IV.

A

The tomb of Ramose, a very high dignitary during the reigns of Amenophis III - Amenophis IV, is placed chronologically in a period after that of Khaemhat and, as in the latter's tomb, the decorations here are "in relief".
The tomb is situated at the foot of the hill of Sheikh Abd el-Qurna, not far from the tomb of Khaemhat, and is unfinished because its proprietor probably had to follow the pharaoh in the Amarnan adventure and have another tomb constructed at Akhetaten, the new capital founded by Amenophis IV/Akhenaten.
The architecture of the tomb, which has a traditional "T" plan, seems influenced by a form of gigantism, the dimensions of both the vestibule and the chapel greatly exceeding the customary dimensions. Some of the representations in relief are extremely refined and the details are particularly elaborate, but the style is clearly of a later date than that of the tomb of Khaemhat and introduces some motifs which were to be developed in the art of the succeeding Amarna period. The decorations in relief of the two walls which line the entrance to the vestibule, whose ceiling is sustained by thirty-two columns, have as their theme the funeral banquet, while the left wall is decorated with colored paintings illustrating the celebrated scene of the deceased's funeral, with crying women, the funeral court, and the funeral furniture which was supposed to be deposited in the tomb. The lower wall of the vestibule, onto which opens the entrance to the chapel (inaccessible), has two representations of Ramose in the company of Amenophis IV: the scene on the right in which Ramose offers flowers to the king and to the goddess Maat is inspired in the classic style, while in the scene on the left we can clearly distinguish the typical Amarna style. Here, the king and the queen take part in the ceremonies in honor of the deceased.

B

C

D

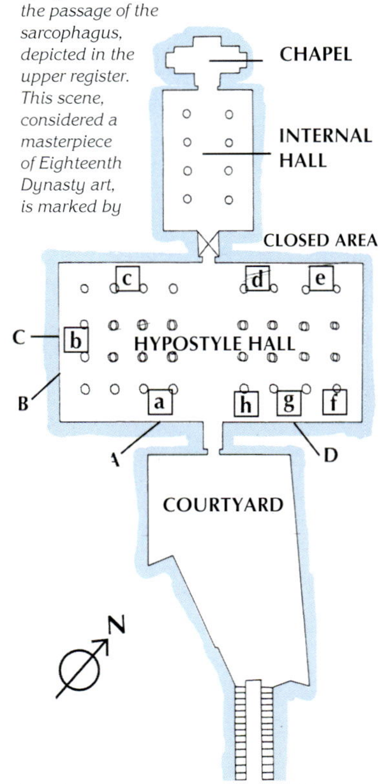

Description of the walls
a - Funeral banquet
b - Funeral procession
c - The deceased makes an offering to Amenophis IV and to the goddess Maat
d - The deceased before Amenophis IV and queen Nefertiti followed by dignitaries
e - Ramose is hailed and receives foreign delegations and garlands of flowers from the temple
f - Priests before the deceased and his family and ritual list of offerings
g - Three maidens with sistra before the deceased and his wife. Purification of the statue of Ramose
h - The deceased, with his wife and bearers of offerings, burn incense

KHONSU

TT no. 31

"First Prophet of Menkheperre"
Eighteenth Dynasty

This tomb, TT no. 31, was built for Khonsu, called To, "First Prophet of Menkheperre-Tuthmosis III" and is decorated with beautiful scenes of the feast of the god Montu; on one side the deceased (depicted as a priest) and his brother spread incense and make offerings to the boat of Montu. On the opposite side, in a kiosk, the deceased makes offerings to the boat of Tuthmosis III which arrives at Armant (a site located to the south of Thebes and the birthplace of the god Montu) and is then brought by the priests to the temple. Another wall shows scenes representing the deceased, his wife and Usermontu, the Vizier, brought by Harsiesis for trial by Osiris, Isis and Nephthys with the ritual weighing of the heart in the presence of Maat, goddess of justice and cosmic order, and the various divinities. At the bottom appears a funeral procession with crying people near the pyramidal tomb, a detail extremely important in giving us an idea of the original look of the chapel-tombs of Deir el-Medina. The northern wall of the tomb displays the feast of Tuthmosis III; the procession of the royal boat in front of the temple, received by the priests and priestesses; herdsmen and shepherds with dogs offering cows and goats with the property symbol of Tuthmosis III to the deceased and his wife and family. There is also a scene of two people on their knees, praying under the trees. The ceiling of the passage to the inner chamber, is decorated with grapes while that of the inner chamber shows a generous naturalistic decoration of ducks with their wings spread and three locusts. The niche is decorated with interesting scenes, of which one depicts the deceased offering a bouquet of flowers to Mentuhotep-Nebhepetre (Eleventh Dynasty) who wears the white crown of Upper Egypt and grips a sceptre, symbol of power.

A

B

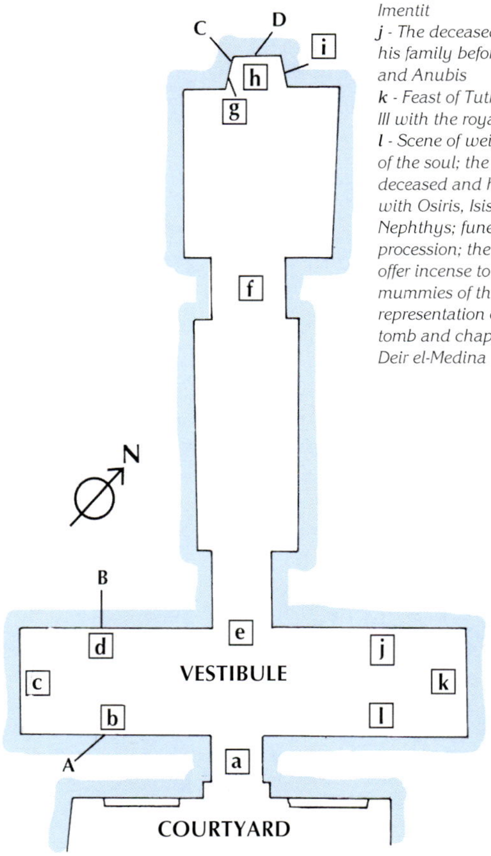

Description of the walls

a *- The deceased, his wife and children worship Re. Ceiling decorated with birds.*

b *- Representation of Montu's barque; priests in a sacrifice to Montu's barque; Montu's barque in the kiosk*

c *- Continuation of the procession of Montu's barque*

d *- Priests carry Montu's barque; pillar of the temple of Montu (partial)*

e *- Architrave: offerings of incense to Osiris, Hathor and Re-Harakhty*

f *- Ceiling decorated with birds and three locusts.*

g *- Khonsu in priestly dress offers lotus and papyrus to the pharaoh with the white crown (Upper Egypt)*

h *- The deceased in priestly dress makes offerings to Osiris and Anubis*

i *- Khonsu in priestly dress makes offerings to the goddess Hathor-Imentit*

j *- The deceased and his family before Osiris and Anubis*

k *- Feast of Tuthmosis III with the royal boat*

l *- Scene of weighing of the soul; the deceased and his wife with Osiris, Isis and Nephthys; funeral procession; the priests offer incense to the mummies of the dead; representation of a tomb and chapel of Deir el-Medina*

A - A boat propelled by five oarsmen sails on the lake of the temple of Montu, a war deity originating in ancient Per-Mont (the present-day Armant), a few kilometers south of Luxor.

B - A group of priests carry a simulacrum of the boat of Montu on their shoulders into the temple.

C - The deceased (not visible) offers flowers to the king Mentuhotep Nebhepetre.

D - The deceased carries out a fumigation before Osiris and Anubis.

C

D

USERHAT
TT no. 51

"First Prophet of the Royal Ka of Tuthmosis I"
Nineteenth Dynasty

A

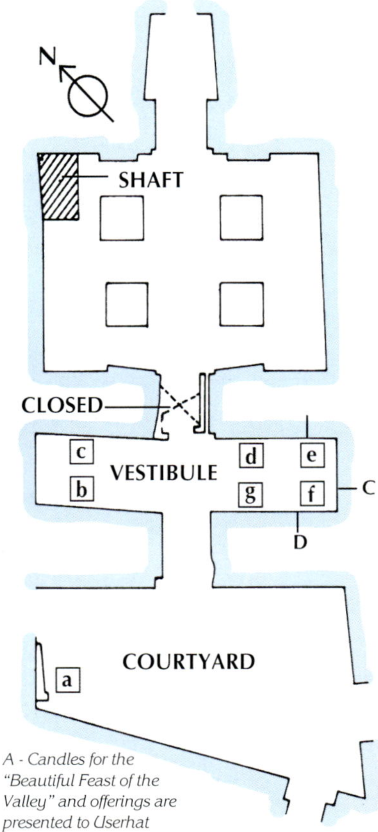

Description of the walls
a - *Steles with fragments of the funeral ceremony prior to the mummification. Lower down, text of the offering*
b - *Weighing of the soul; representation of Osiris and Hathor; the deceased worships falcon-headed Re-Harakhty; funeral ceremony before the mummy*
c - *Men bearing gifts; the deceased, leaving the temple, worships the royal boat; priests with flabellum and cartouche of Tuthmosis I*
d - *The deceased with two women and a son makes an offering to Osiris and to two gods*
e - *Priests with grieving women drink and make an offering to the deceased and his wife*
f - *The deceased with two women receives figs and fruit from the goddess of the Sycamore; over the two women, the representation of the two* ba*; representation of birds; pilgrimage to Abydos; the deceased and his wife before Osiris and Anubis*
g - *Scene of worship; in the kiosk, Anubis, Osiris and Thoth; purification of 8 priests for work; the deceased before the offerings*

Tomb no. 51 was constructed for Userhat, called Neferhabef, "First Prophet of the royal *ka* of Tuthmosis I" (not to be confused with the homonymous proprietor of tomb No. 56 who carried the title of "Royal scribe"), in the period of Sethos I. This is one of the most beautiful Theban tombs and is characterised by a series of representations of the owner, his bride and his mother in vivid colors. The eastern wall is decorated with very graceful scenes: the deceased, his wife Hatshepsut (also called Shepset) and his mother, are seated under a fig tree with three small birds perching on its branches, while overhead fly three spirits in the form of birds with human heads. The tree goddess pours water for drinking, and serves bread, apples and figs for eating. A double subscene represents the ritual pilgrimage to Abydos and the deceased and his wife in front of Anubis and Osiris, principal deities of the underworld. On the southern wall are displayed scenes of adoration and purification while the god Thoth, the divine scribe, presents to Osiris and Anubis his report on the life of the deceased, who in turn is represented in an act of worship to Montu and the goddess Meretseger. The southern wall on the left displays Userhat brought to justice by Anubis; the scene of weighing of the soul with the deceased on his knees before Osiris and the Western Divinities, and the funeral procession. On the northern wall a group of crying women draws the attention of the visitor while the deceased, with two wives and a son pours out a salve as a gift to Osiris, accompanied by two goddesses and on a brazier presents an offering to Tuthmosis I and Amosis Nefertari. The northern wall on the right displays the procession for the feast of Tuthmosis I and Userhat, which, on the way out from the temple, adores the boat and the royal statue in black representing Osiris, accompanied by fan carriers and crying women. The second room with four pillars and no decorations leads to the funeral shaft.

A - Candles for the "Beautiful Feast of the Valley" and offerings are presented to Userhat and his wife Hatshepsut.

B - Two sem*-priests dressed in the distinctive leopard skins carry out a purification rite and fumigations before the deceased, while a group of women lament his death.*

C - On the eastern wall of the vestibule, the deceased is depicted with his wife Hatshepsut, called Shepset, and his mother Tausert, before the goddess of the Sycamore, a tree that was considered to be one of the manifestations of Hathor and of Nut.

D - Userhat, "First Prophet of the Royal Ka *of Tuthmosis I" in an act of worship before the table of the offerings.*

B

C

D

BENIA
TT no. 343

"Overseer of Works, Child of the Nursery"
Eighteenth Dynasty

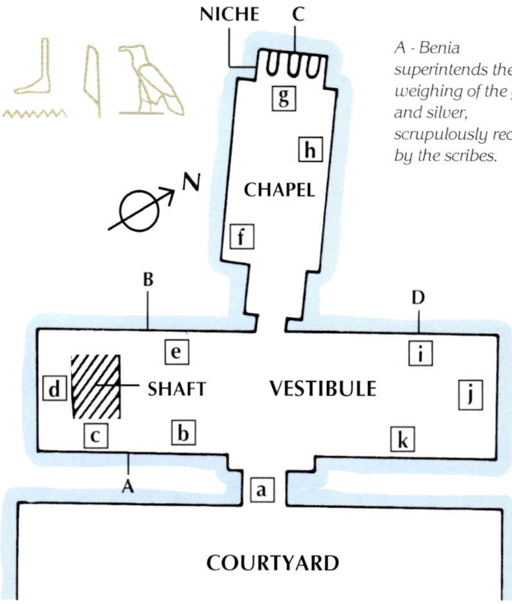

This tomb, TT no. 343, belonged to Benia, called Pahekmen, an official who lived during the Eighteenth Dynasty and carried the title of "Overseer of Workers, Child of the Nursery".
In the first room a number of scenes are shown: The deceased, with various types of food in front of him, offers two roast ducks on a brazier; the deceased seated on a chair in front of nine people, arranged in three rows, who bring offerings; a rich table of offerings. On the other wall the deceased, seated, wields a stick and inspects three rows of bringers of offerings: livestock, fish, birds, lotus flowers, food and vegetables. Entering from the left, the owner of the tomb is shown checking three ledgers regarding the number of ebony, ivory, silver and gold rings and the treasure, all of which are then weighed on a scale, with a counterweight shaped as a small calf, while two scribes write down the weights. On the opposite wall, there is a graceful scene with the deceased seated in front of a rich table carrying the offerings presented by a priest.
In the second part of the same scene a banquet is shown with musicians, a harpist and a lute player, followed by three applauding men.
The mother and the father of the deceased tower over this scene.
The mother affectionately embraces her husband; under her seat is a mirror. The western wall is composed of a false door, painted in red to simulate granite.
The eastern wall has a stele on the edges of which the deceased is displayed on his knees, giving offerings and performing a ritual ceremony. The hallway is decorated with the funeral procession in the presence of the goddess of the West, with the pilgrimage to Abydos and with scenes of offerings and the "Opening of the Mouth" ceremony, by which life was traditionally restored to the deceased.
The niche contains the statues of the deceased, placed between his mother Tirukak, on his right, and his father Irtonena, on his left.

A

A - Benia superintends the weighing of the gold and silver, scrupulously recorded by the scribes.

B

B - The musicians enliven the funeral banquet, playing before the deceased's parents, seated in front of the table of offerings, and their guests.

C

C - The three painted limestone statues arranged in the niche of the chapel, represent the deceased (in the centre) with his mother Tirurak and his father Irtonena.

D

D - Benia, "Overseer of Works", seated before a table of offerings, inspects the bearers of offerings (cattle, birds, fish, lotus flowers and a variety of food), distributed over three registers.

Description of the walls
a *- Fragments of conferring of title; the deceased in act of worship*
b *- The deceased worshipping before offerings*
c *- Weighing and storing of the gold and the turquoises*
d *- Steles with texts; alongside, the deceased kneeling in an act of offering*
e *- The deceased's parents before the table of offerings with musicians and male guests; the deceased before the table of offerings with a man making an offering to him*
f *- Funeral procession and offerings to the goddess Hathor Imentit with* was-*sceptre; the deceased before the table of offerings*
g *- Niche with statues of the deceased, his wife and son*
h *- The deceased before the table of offerings; offerings, purification; ceremony of opening of the mouth*
i *- The deceased, seated, inspects the herds and various country products*
j *- Steles surmounted by two* udjat*-eyes, alongside, the deceased kneeling in an act of offering*
k *- The deceased, before the table of the offerings, receives gifts*

ROUTES AND TRAILS OF THE THEBHAN MOUNTAIN

ITINERARY NO. 1
From Deir el-Medina to the Valley of the Queens
Duration: approximately one hour

160 A group of tourists follow the age-old path which leads from Deir el-Medina to the Valley of the Kings and the temple of Deir el-Bahri. Donkeys are still a great help, as they were to nineteenth-century travellers too.

The route: Leaving the craftsmen's village of Deir el-Medina on the left, you take a very well outlined uphill path, which runs to the west. After a few minutes' walk you arrive at the summit of a small hill. At this point the path forks in two directions: the right path runs north and rises at a considerable slope (see itinerary no. 2); the left path, instead, gently descends following the bottom of a small valley, known as Valley of the Dolmen because in a hollow which opens on its northern side there is a pile of rocks which resembles a dolmen. Continuing down into the Valley of the Dolmen, after a few minutes you will note on the left two steles carved in the stone and a votive niche from the period of Ramesses III followed by an ample shelter used by hermits during the Coptic period. It is a rocky sanctuary dedicated to the god Ptah and the cobra-goddess Meretseger, personification of the Theban Peak: a place of worship and prayer which the workers of the pharaoh erected along their path. Continuing, the Valley of the Dolmen opens up and joins the main wadi of the Valley of the Queens, where you arrive a little further on and continue on the main path.

If, instead, you take a secondary path which starts from the northern side of the Valley of the Dolmen, a few hundred meters before the opening to the Valley of the Queens, you arrive after a few minutes at the ruins of an ancient Coptic monastery called Deir Rumi, crossing a clay bank in which can be found numerous marine fossils, evidence of the presence of a prehistoric ocean. The monastery was built around the fourth century AD on a small rocky spur by the hermits who inhabited the area. After the visit to the monument, go down, following a path which again leads to the bottom of the main wadi of the Valley of the Queens. From this point it is possible to visit the Valley of the Queens and then return by taxi to the point of departure.

161 top The mountain of Thebes is made of limestone dating back to the Tertiary Era. It is not uncommon to find marine fossiles in the rock, like this lamellibranch, attesting to the time when the region was covered by the sea, some 40 million years ago.

161 bottom This curious rock formation is know as "the dolmen".

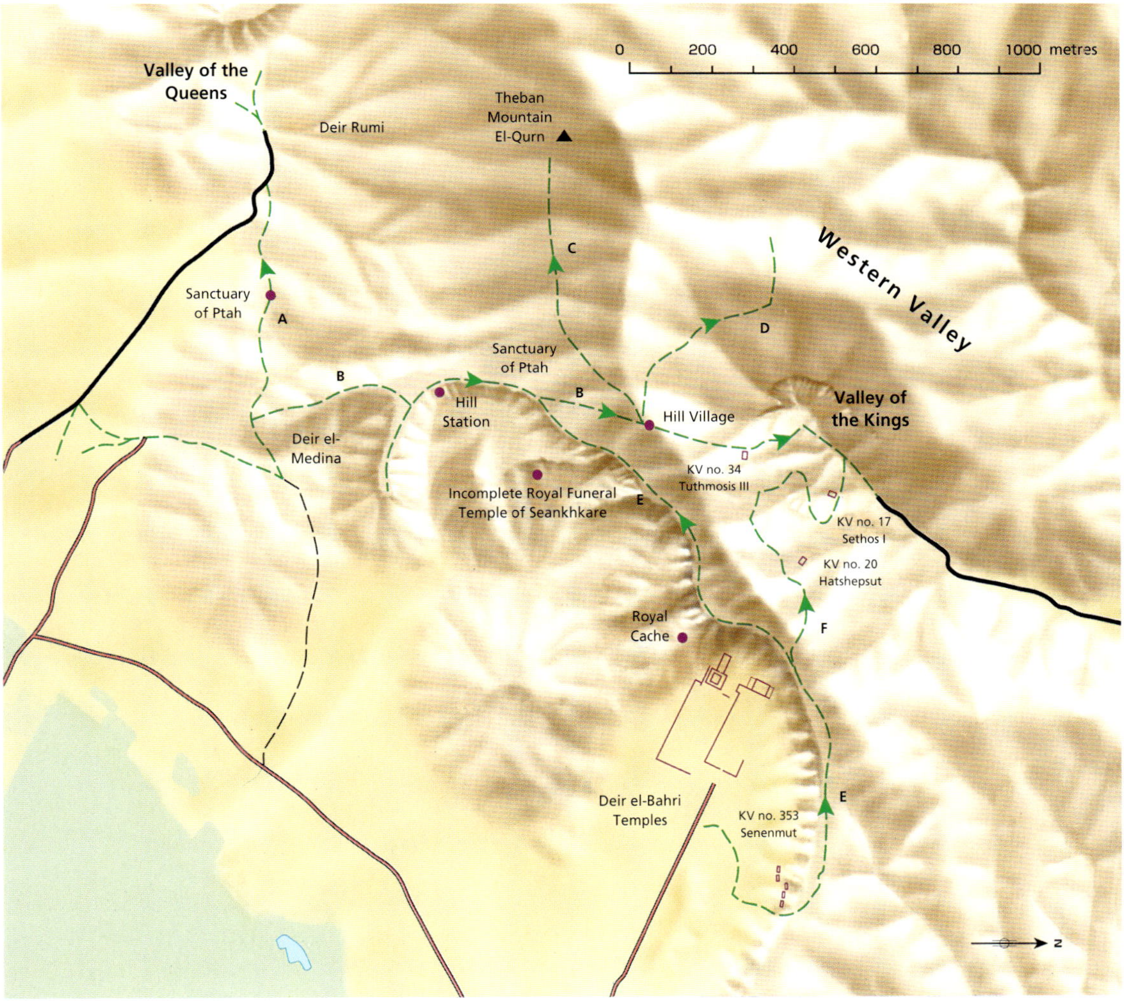

MAP OF THE PATHS OF THE THEBAN MOUNTAINS

- A Ancient path of the workers from the village to the Valley of the Queens
- B Ancient path of the workers from the village to the Valley of the Kings
- C Path to the Theban Peak
- D Path of the Western Valley
- E Path of Deir el-Bahri
- F Connection from Deir el-Bahri to the Valley of the Kings

ITINERARY NO. 2
From Deir el-Medina to the Theban Peak and the Valley of the Kings
Duration: approximately three hours

162 top A view of the ruins of the Coptic monastery of Deir Rumi, built at the entrance to the Valley of the Kings around the 6th century AD.

162 bottom In ancient times lobourers made their way every day along the path linking Deir el-Medina with the Valley of the Kings.

Along the path stands a small sanctuary dedicated to Ptah and to the goddes Mertseger, to whom the labourers were particularly devoted

The route:
Starting from the summit of the small hill above Deir el-Medina (see itinerary no. 1), follow a path which climbs steeply northward. After about ten minutes you pass a fork from which a small path leads to a rocky spur with a splendid view of the whole area of Deir el-Medina.
A few hundred meters on you arrive at level ground, from which can be seen the surrounding countryside all the way to the Valley of the Queens. If you look carefully, you can see crumbling stone walls; this is the Hill station with the remains of the barracks of an ancient guard post which controled access to the royal necropolises. After about 500 meters, on the right, at the bottom of a rocky outcrop, another level path starts which leads to the complex of temples of Deir el-Bahri. However, in order to continue our itinerary, we must follow the uphill path to the crest of the mountain chain. Here in a space which dominates the Nile plain and the Valley of the Kings can be seen the remains of many houses. This is the hill village, a sort of dependency of the main village of Deir el-Medina, which permitted the workers involved in the construction of the tombs in the Valley of the Kings, at times when the weather was extremely hot, or when the work was particularly arduous, to make use of houses closer and more rapidly accessible than those in Deir el-Medina. Three paths leave the Hill Village: the first descends toward the Valley of the Kings, the second leads to the western branch of the Valley of the Kings, also known as the Western Valley, and the third climbs to the summit of the Theban Peak. The ascent from this crossing to the Peak takes around half an hour.
At the point of departure, on the right, there is a small rocky sanctuary

dedicated by the workers to the god Ptah, while on the surrounding stone walls can be observed various graffiti, one of which mentions "the water fallen from the sky", perhaps a rain of exceptional importance. The path climbs and at a few points becomes very steep, but after a couple of tight spots you arrive

163 top At a certain point along the path from Deir el-Medina to Deir el-Bahri and the Valley of the Kings, travellers walk along the edge of a spectacular cliff, over one hundred meters high.

163 centre From the top of the cliff there is a wonderful view of the Deir el-Bahri site below: to the right is the temple of Nebhepetre Mentuhotep, in the centre the temple of Thutmose III and to the left the great temple of Hatshepsut, flanked by the shrine of Hator.

without further difficulties at the Theban Peak, crossing a clay bank very rich in fossils since in ancient times it was part of a coral reef. The countryside is magnificent and the view embraces the Valley of the Kings which extends further down, as well as the entire Theban necropolises. On the way back, walk down the same path to the Hill Village. From there, continue along the path which descends, leading north and, after passing the tomb of Tuthmosis III, cut in a narrow crack in the rock to the left of the path, you arrive at the heart of the Valley of the Kings, at the tomb of Sethos I and the area occupied until 1991 by the rest-house, now moved outside the archaeological site.

163 bottom This photo shows the path which climbs to the top of the pyramid-shaped mountain of Thebes, overlooking the Valley of the Kings. In the foreground is the village perched on the ridge which separates Deir el-Medina from the Valley of the Kings. The labourers who worked in the royal tombs often lived here during the working week, rather than walk huge distances every day.

AMUN
Divinity, "king of the gods", depicted as a human being with two tall plumes overhanging his headdress and sometimes as a ram, his sacred animal. Together with the goddess Mut and the god Khonsu, he formed the "Theban triad". He had also been assimilated to the god Re and worshipped as Amun-Re. Thebes was the main seat of his worship.

ANKH
Handled cross, symbol of life and of vital strength.

ANUBIS
Jackal-headed deity, presides over the embalming and accompanies the dead to the Afterlife.

ATUM
Divinity representing the sun as Atum-Re (the demiurge of Heliopolitan cosmology) and above all indicating the star at its setting.

BA
One of man's souls, figured as a bird with human head.

BOOK OF THE DEAD
A series of 190 "chapters" with magic-ritual wordings, illustrated with sketches, intended to assure the deceased of his survival in Underworld. The wording was inscribed on papyruses and placed beside the deceased: in the Late Period, spells and drawings were traced on the linen bandages wrapping the mumies.

BOOK OF GATES
Collection of magical/religious texts thanks to which the dead could pass through the portals of the Kingdom of Osiris.

CANOPIC JARS
Four vessels aimed at holding the lungs, the stomach, the intestine and the liver removed from the body of the deceased. The entrails were placed under the protection of Horus' four sons (Imsety, Hapy, Duamutef, Qebhsenuef) and the canopies were sealed by covers in the shape of these divinities.

CARTOUCHE
An ellipsoidal line originally representing a rope ring with a knot at the base, inside which the name of the Pharaoh is written. The use of the cartouche, symbolizing the universal power of the sun god, hence of the pharaoh, is reserved to the two most important names out of the five the pharaoh possessed, the nomen (preceded by the title "Son of Re") and the praenomen given at the time of coronation (preceded by the title "King of Upper and Lower Egypt").

DJED
Pillar, symbol of stability and duration. Very ancient amulet related to Osiris, was also used for the protection of the mummies, to whose neck it was suspended.

ENNEAD
The nine deities of the cosmogony of Heliopolis: Atum, Shu, Tefnet, Geb, Nut, Osiris, Isis, Seth and Nephthys.

FIELDS OF IARU
Fields of Osiris' kingdom, transposition into the Underworld of the green agricultural areas of the Nile Delta, where the souls of the deceased worked.

GEB
Personification of the earth and husband of Nut.

GESTATION
Period preceding the rebirth of the soul.

HELIOPOLIS
City in Lower Egypt, whose ancient Egyptian name was On (the pillar), seat of the sun's worship.

HATHOR
Goddess depicted a cow's head (or only ears): the Lady of the heavens was protectress of women, of music and of the deceased.

HEDJET
White-colored crown, symbol of rule over Upper Egypt.

HEQA (SCEPTRE)
Symbol of royalty characteristic of the god Osiris.

HORUS
Divinity with a hawks' head, or figured as a hawk, god of the sky and pharaoh's protector. As a son of Osiris and Isis, he is often figured as a child (Harpocrates) sucking his finger.

IBIS
Holy bird of the god Thoth, whose incarnation it was believed to be in the Late Period.

IMENTIT
Goddess of the Occident who welcomes the dead.

ISIS
Goddess, wife and sister of god Osiris, mother of god Horus. On her head is figured a throne, transcribing her name.

JUSTIFIED
The epithet "justified" (makheru) is attributed to the dead who have received favourable judgement from Osiris.

KA
One of man's souls, representing the vital force. Also defined as "double", it is created at the same time as man himself, but is immortal and ensures him the strength needed for extra-terrestrial life.

KHEPER OR KHEPRI
Divinity representing the rising sun, figured in the shape of a scarab beetle.

KHEPERESH
Blue-colored ceremonial crown with circular discs, used by the Pharaoh.

KHONSU
Moon god in the shape of a lad; at Thebes he was considered a son of Amun and Mut. He is often figured with a hawk's head, adorned with a crescent moon surmounted by a lunar disc.

MAAT
Goddess of truth and justice, she is the representation of the cosmic order. Her symbol is the ostrich plume.

MERETSEGER
Female deity, often represented in the shape of a woman-headed cobra and identified with the Theban Peak.

MIN
Mummy-shaped god, figured ithyphallic, with his raised right arm holding a scourge and with a headgear adorned with two plumes. He was considered a protector of fertility and of the eastern desert's tracks; the seats of his worship are at Coptos and at Akhmim.

MUMMY
Dessicated dead body of the deceased wrapped up in tight bandages of fabric. The word derives from the Arabic *mumiyah*, meaning bitumen: as a matter of fact the bitumen is found in the Egyptian mummies only in the Roman period.

MUT
Goddess originally figured as a vulture, later represented in human shape. Amun's wife, her worship took place at Thebes.

NAOS
Stone or wooden tabernacle where the god's statue was kept, inside the shrine.

NEBRIDE
Animal skin suspended to a stick, it was one of the symbols of Osiris and Anubis.

NEITH
Goddess originating from Sais in the Delta, linked to war and also to hunting; she had a protective function and, as such, played a role in the funerary cult together with Isis, Nephthys and Selket. Later on, in the New Kingdom, she was considered a creating divinity, mother of the sun. She is figured with the red crown of Lower Egypt; sometime she wears on her head a shield with two crossed arrows.

NEKHAKHA
Flail, symbol af authority, characteristic of god Osiris.

NEKHBET
Goddess figured as a vulture, worshipped at El-Kab and protectress of Upper Egypt.

NEMES
Woven cap used by the rulers: it covers the head and falls back on both sides of the face.

NEPHTHYS
Sister of the goddess Isis and Seth's wife.

NOME
Word of Greek origin indicating the different administrative districts (between 38 and 42, according to the periods) of ancient Egypt. This system of administrative arrangement of the country dates back all the way to the protodynastic age and reached its supreme development in the Ptolemaic era.

NUBIA
Territory extending between the first and the fourth cataract. It is divided into Lower Nubia, located between the first and the second cataract (called Wawat by the Egyptians) and Upper Nubia, known by the name of Kush.

NUT
Personification of the celestial vault, wife of Geb, god of the Earth and sister of Shu and Tefnut. She is represented as a woman with an arched body crossed by the stars. She is often figured, as protectrix, on the royal tombs or on the covers of coffins.

OCCIDENT, OR WEST
Represents the kingdom of the dead (the souls of the deceased go where the sun sets).

OSIRIS
Mummy-shaped divinity, Lord of the Afterlife, Isis' husband, has generated his son Horus, after his own death caused by his brother Seth. He is figured with an *Atef* crown, sceptre and scourge. Abydos is the seat of his cult.

OSTRACON
Terracotta potshard or stone splinter used for writing on, instead of papyrus.

PYLON
Monumental entrance of the temples formed by two massive trapezoid-shaped towers flanking the doorway.

PYRAMIDION
Monolithic block forming the apex of the pyramid.

PSYCHOSTASY
Weighing of the soul: after death, the soul of the deceased, that is his heart, was weighed on a two-scale balance and if it turned out to be as light as a feather (symbol of truth and justice) on the other scale it was admitted into the eternal beatitude of the Kingdom of Osiris, otherwise it was devoured by a monster.

PSCHENT
Double crown symbolizing the rule over Upper and Lower Egypt, formed by the white crown inserted in the red crown (see White Crown and Red Crown).

PTAH
Creator god from Memphis, husband of the lioness goddess Sakhmet and figured as a mummy-shaped man with the sceptre *was*. Successively he superimposed himself on Sokaris, the original god from Memphis and was worshipped in the syncretic form of Ptah-Sokaris.

RE
Ancient solar divinity originally worshipped mainly at Heliopolis. Re is represented with a hakw's head surmounted by the solar disc and with a ram's head during his nightly sailing. Starting with the Fourth Dynasty, the kings of Egypt took up the name of "son of Re".

RE-HARAKHTY
Sun god - Horus of the Horizons. He is represented as a hawk aspect and a solar disc and combines the chracteristics of Re and of Horus.

REGISTER
Horizontal subdivision of the decoration of the walls of tombs and temples and of objects such as the funerary stelae.

SEKHMET
Feminine divinity, represented with the head of a lioness, sometimes surmounted by a solar disc; protectrix of pharaoh's royal power.

SELKIS
Goddess exercising a protective function in the funerary cult. A scorpion transcribing her name is figured on her head.

SETH
God of chaotic forces, brother and murdered of Osiris, figured with a human body and an unidentifiable animal's head (greyhound? ant-eater?).

SCHAWABTI
Small statues working in the fields instead of the deceased in Underworld. The name derives from the verb *shwbty* (to respond), since they daily answered the call to work.

SOLAR BOAT
Boat on which the Sun god sailed in the sky: by day he moves from east to west and by night from west to east. During his night sail (mesektet) the divinity was represented with a ram's head.

SONS OF HORUS
Four mummy-shaped tutelary spirits respectively with heads of a human being (Imsety), a baboon (Hapy), a jackal (Duamutef) and a hawk (Qebhsenuef) who protect the viscera of the deceased, contained in the four canopy jars placed in the tomb.

SHU
Male divinity, embodiment of the dry air, Tefnet's husband.

SISTRUM
Musical instrument (a kind of rattle) sacred to the goddesses Hathor and Bastet. It can either be a box in the shape of *naos* with the rattle inside, or with small, transversal metallic handle-bars.

STELA
Slab of stone or wood, of various shapes bearing decorations and inscriptions having funerary. Of great importance are the historic stelae erected by the pharaoh for informative or propaganda purposes (large "royal stelae" or boundary stelae).

SYCAMORE
Tree sacred to the goddess Hathor and to the goddess Nut. Its very hard wood was used for the manufacturing of sarcophagi and for the funerary accessories.

THEBAN PEAK
One of the designations of Mount el-Qurn, with its characteristic pyramidal shape, topping the Theban necropolises.

THOTH
Divinity figured as ibis, or with a human body and an ibis' head, or also represented as a baboon. As inventor of writing and of sciences, he was protector of the scribes; seat of his worship was at Hermopolis.

TUTELARY SPIRIT
Demon. Often mummy-shaped, could be kindly or harmful.

TOWER
See Pylon

UDJAT
The eye of the celestial hawk god Horus; was used as a protecting amulet.

URAEUS
Royal cobra symbol of the light and of royalty, it is found on the forehead of the greater part of the divinities and of the pharaohs. in the act of rising. It was sacred to the goddess Wadjet and to the sun god, whose eye it was believed to be.

VIZIER
Title by which the head of the executive power is indicated in ancient Egypt, he replaced the pharaoh in all the aspects of the country's administration.

WADJET
Goddess figured as an *uraeus*, worshipped at Buto in the Delta and protectress of Lower Egypt.

WAS
Sceptre characteristic of male divinities.

BIBLIOGRAPHY

Baines J., Malek J., *Atlas of Ancient Egypt*, Oxford - New York, 1980.

Belzoni G.B., *Viaggi in Egitto e in Nubia*, edizione critica a cura di A. Siliotti, Firenze 1988.

Carter H., Mace A.C., *The Tomb of Tut.Ank.Amen*, London, 1922-1933.

Cenival De J.L., *Architecture universelle: Egypte, époque pharaonique*, Fribourg 1964.

Curto S., *L'Antico Egitto*, Torino 1981.

Donadoni S., *La civiltà egiziana*, Milano 1940.

Farina G., *La pittura egiziana*, Milano 1929.

Gardiner A.H., *Egypt of the Pharahos*, Oxford 1974.

Goyon J.C., *Rituels funéraires de l'ancienne Égypte*, 1972.

Grimal N., *Histoire de l'Égypte ancienne*, Paris 1988.

Kitchen K.A., *Pharaoh Triumphant - The Life and Times of Ramesses II*, Warminster, 1982.

Leclant J. e altri, *Le monde Egyptien - Les Pharaons* 3 voll., Paris 1980.

Mekhitarian A., *La peinture egyptienne*, Genève 1954.

Montet P., *Géographie de l'Egypte ancienne*, I-II, Paris 1957-1961.

Posener G., Sauneron S., Yoyotte J., *Dictionnaire de la civilisation égyptienne*, Paris 1959.

Reeves N. *The complete Tutankhamun*, London 1990.

Schiapparelli E., *Relazione dei lavori della Missione archeologica italiana in Egitto*: I, *la tomba intatta dell'architetto Kha*, Torino 1922; II, *L'esplorazione della Valle delle Regine*, Torino 1927.

Siliotti A. (a cura di), *Padova e l'Egitto*, Firenze 1987.

Siliotti A. (a cura di), *Viaggiatori Veneti alla scoperta dell'Egitto*, Venezia 1985.

Siliotti A., *Egitto - Uomini, templi e dei*, Vercelli 1994.
Vandier J., *Manuel d'archéologie égyptienne*, Paris, 1952-58.

TEBE
AA.VV., *Reconstitution du caveau de Sennefer dit "Tombe aux Vignes"*, Paris, 1985.

Aufrere, S., Golvin J.C., Goyon J.C., *L'Egypte restituée*, Paris, 1991.

Barguet P., *Le Temple d'Amon-Rê à Karnak. Essai d'exégèse*, Cairo 1962.

Bruyère B., *Rapport sur les fouilles de Deir el Médineh*, Cairo 1924-1953.

Cerny J., *A Community of Workmen at Thebes in the Rameside Period*, Cairo 1973.

Cerny J, *The Valley of the Kings, (grafments d'un manuscrit inachevé)*, Cairo 1973.
Golvin J.C., Goyon J.C., *Les bâtisseur de Karnak*, Paris 1988.

Hornung E., *Tal der Könige*, Zurich/Munich 1982.

Leblanc C., *Ta Set Neferou*, Cairo 1989.

Murnane W.J., *United with Eternity - A concise Guide to the Monuments of Medinet Habu*, Chicago - Cairo 1980.

Naville E., *The Temples of Deir el Bahari*, I-VI, London 1894-1908.

Porter B., Moss R.L.B., *Topographical Bibliography of Ancient Egyptian Hieroglyphic Texts, Reliefs and Paintings* I, Oxford 1960.

Reeves N., *Valley of the Kings*, London 1990.

Shedid A.G., Seidel M., *Das Grab des Nacht*, Mainz am Rhein 1991.

Siliotti A., Leblanc C., *La Tomba di Nefertari e la Valle delle Regine*, Firenze 1993.

Steindorff G., Wolf W., *Die Thebaniscne Gräberwelt*, Hamburg 1936.

Werbrouck M., *Le temple d'Hatshepsout à Deir el Bahari*, Bruxelles 1948.

Wilkinson C.K., Hill M., *Egyptian Wall Paintings*, New York 1983.

Wreszinski W., *Atlas zur altägyptischen Kulturgeschichte*, 1915.

LEGEND

KV = King Valley
WV = Western Valley
QV = Queen Valley
TT = Teban Tombs

ILLUSTRATIONS CREDITS

All the photographs published in this volume are by Archivio Image Service except for the following:

Antonio Attini / Archivio White Star: pages 2-3, 35 top, 123 top.

Marcello Bertinetti / Archivio White Star: pages 7 bottom right, 24-25, 32, 37 N, 46-47, 51 H, 59 top, 94-95, 95, 96-97, 109, 110 top, 110 centre bottom, 116-117, 118-119, 118 bottom right, 122, 122-123, 123 bottom, 124 top, 124-125.

Giulio Veggi / Archivio White Star: pages 24-25, 102 top, 102-103, 104, 105, 106, 107 bottom, 108 left, 114 top and centre, 126 top right, 127 top, 129 centre and bottom.

Archivio White Star: pages 8 left, 16 top and bottom, 52-53.

British Museum: page 120 centre bottom.

Giovanni Dagli Orti: page 108 right.

Fitzwilliam Museum Cambridge: page 62 E.

Griffith Institute / Ashmolean Museum: pages 20, 21, 22, 23, 23 top.

Archivio IGDA: page 38 bottom.

Library of Congress - New York: pages 16-17.

Jurgen Liepe: pages 1, 36, 37 bottom, 41 bottom, 42 bottom right, 43 bottom right, 119 bottom, 128 bottom, 131, 134 top, 135 bottom left.

Henri Stierlin: pages 4, 6, 34, 35 centre, 37 top, 38 left, 38 top right, 39, 40, 41 top and centre right, 42 top, centre and bottom left, 43 top and centre.

NASA: page 11 centre and bottom.

168 One of the splendid paintings decorating the tomb of Inherkhau (TT no. 359), in the necropolis of the craftsmen's village of Deir el-Medina, the dwelling place of the craftmen and the artists who worked on the preparation of the tombs of the Theban necropolis. The deceased, who lived in the time of Ramesses III and Ramesses IV, bore the title of "Team-leader of the Lord of the Two Lands in the Seat of Truth" and is figured in the act of worshipping the ash-colored heron, incarnation of the soul of the sun god Re.

Front Cover:
The gold mask of Tutankhamun, Cairo Museum
© Araldo De Luca/ Archivio White Star

Back cover top
The recunstructed sarcophagus in Ay's burial chamber.
© Araldo De Luca / Archivio White Star

Back cover center
One's of the Nefertari's splendid portraits.
© Archivio Image Service.

Back cover bottom
The tomb of Nefertari
Drawing by Elisabetta Ferrero / Archivio White Star

The publisher wishes to thank Yvonne Marzoni Fecia di Cossato for her valuable help and collaboration in the preparation of this book.

The tombs described in this book were selected by the author following criteria of scientific interest, artistic value, accessibility to the public, and the space constraints of the publication.